Gardening

4—

1/2

A PASSION
for DAYLILIES

Also by Sydney Eddison

A Patchwork Garden

A PASSION for DAYLILIES

The Flowers and the People

SYDNEY EDDISON

Henry Holt and Company   New York

Henry Holt and Company, Inc.
Publishers since 1866
115 West 18th Street
New York, New York 10011

Henry Holt® is a registered trademark
of Henry Holt and Company, Inc.

Library of Congress Cataloging-in-Publication Data
Eddison, Sydney.
A passion for daylilies : the flowers and the people /
Sydney Eddison.
p.   cm.
Originally published: New York : HarperCollins, 1992.
"An Owl book."
Includes index.
1. Daylilies.   I. Title.
[SB413.D3E33   1993]   92-39985
635.9'34324—dc20   CIP

ISBN 0-8050-2611-8 (alk. paper)

First published in hardcover by HarperCollins in 1992.

First Owl Book Edition—1993

Designed by Cassandra Pappas
Illustrations by Steve Buchanan

Printed in the United States of America
All first editions are printed on acid-free paper. ∞

10   9   8   7   6   5   4   3   2   1

This book is for my daylily friends, especially Greg.

It is not growing like a tree

In bulk, doth make man better be;

Or standing long an oak, three hundred year,

To fall a log at last, dry, bald, and sere;

A lily of a day

Is fairer far in May,

Although it fall and die that night,

It was the plant and flower of light.

In small proportions we just beauty see,

And in short measures life may perfect be.

> —Ben Johnson, "To the Immortal Memory and
> Friendship of that Noble Pair, Sir Lucius Cary and
> Sir Henry Morison"

Contents

Acknowledgments

Many people have made significant contributions to this book. First and foremost, Gregory Piotrowski of the New York Botanical Garden who read the manuscript, checked plant terminology, and put at my disposal his wealth of horticultural expertise. Other members of the New York Botanical Garden staff to whom I am indebted include Bernadette G. Callery, Lothian Lynas (retired Head Research Librarian), and Murial Weinerman.

From England, I received welcome assistance in obtaining information about George Yeld and Amos Perry from Roger Bowden of the British Hosta & Hemerocallis Society; C. D. Brickell, Director General of The Royal Horticultural Society, London; Neil Grant, author; John V. Mitchell, Archivist of St. Peter's School, York; Frances Perry, M.B.E., F.L.S, V.M.H., author and horticulturist, and her son, Roger Perry; and from Edna Squires of Feebers Hardy Plants, Exeter. I am also grateful for the unstinting generosity of Dr. Elizabeth Stout Rausch with family photographs and with reminiscences that provided insight into her father's life and work.

Keith Lapour, Catalog Production Coordinator for Henry Field's Seed & Nursery Co. of Shenandoah, Iowa, furnished me with a treasure trove of material about Helen Field Fischer and the Field family.

Boundless thanks go to the American Hemerocallis Society. In addition to those members mentioned in the text, I received generous encouragement and valuable information from many others, including Ruth Allen, Dorothea Boldt, John Benz, Ray and Jeanne Doyle, Frances Gatlin, Ra Hansen, the Herrington family, Carol Hull, Richard M. Kitchingman, Dr. John Lambert, Stewart Oakes, David A. Riseman, and Oscie B. Whatley, Jr.

Finally, Beverly Setz and other loyal friends gave me practical help and moral support, while my long-suffering husband displayed his usual tact, patience, and fortitude throughout the writing of this book. My heartfelt thanks to one and all.

Introduction:
Getting There from Here

Hemerocallis fulva

This book is about daylily people. It is also about journeys. One began in Armonk, New York, on a beautiful summer day in 1987. In the suburban garden of Mr. and Mrs. Paul Watts, I encountered for the first time a new race of daylilies. After twenty-five years of growing numerous old-fashioned hybrids and several species of *Hemerocallis*, I stumbled on to the fact that something had happened to daylilies, something wonderful and something about which I knew nothing. Having always considered myself a daylily person, I set out to remedy the situation. The following pages chronicle discoveries about the brave new world that has such flowers in it. My journey has taken me many miles, literally and figuratively. But it has been nothing to the journey of the daylily, which began in the Far East thousands of years ago.

Daylilies are native to China, Japan, Korea, and Eastern Siberia. Long before the birth of Christ, they were mentioned as an anodyne for grief in the religious writings of Confucius, China's greatest philosopher. By the fourth century A.D., they were being used to relieve physical as well as mental pain. A Chinese herbal of the period makes extravagant claims for juice extracted from their roots: "It quiets the five viscera [the heart, lung, liver, kidney, and stomach], benefits the mind and strengthens the will power, gives happiness, reduces worry, lightens the body weight and brightens the eye.... Now people often collect the young shoots and serve as a pot green. It gives a pleasant feeling in the chest." In addition, the thick roots were boiled and eaten like potatoes.

It wasn't until the seventeenth century that daylilies became cherished ornamentals for the pleasure garden. In a Chinese gardening treatise published in 1688, author Chên Hao-tzu describes a plant with leafless flower stalks (*scapes* in daylily parlance) and arching foliage: "The flower when it first appears, resembles the beak of a crane, then it opens with six radiant segments, yellow dusted red, opening in the morning and withering by night." This description still fits some of the old-fashioned daylilies.

No one knows by what circuitous path these plants came to Europe in time to be recorded and described in medieval herbals. Caravans with as many as four thousand heavily laden camels regularly plied the legendary trade arteries between East and West. Perhaps the plump, sturdy daylily roots which bear a token resemblance to the roots of ginger were included with the fragrant spices imported from the Orient by Arab traders. Alternatively, daylilies may have made the awe-inspiring trip by sea to Venice, where horses took them over the Alps to France and Germany. Or they might have entered through Hungary among the effects of Mongol settlers.

However they traveled, the ubiquitous orange daylily (*Hemerocallis fulva*) and its yellow companion, the lemon lily (*H. Lilioasphodelus*) had arrived in Europe by the sixteenth century. A hundred years later, this same pair crossed the Atlantic with pilgrims and took root in American soil. From the eastern seaboard, the tougher, more adaptable tawny orange daylily moved west with the settlers, earning itself the name of homestead lily. And during the late nineteenth century, a root or two of this hardy species wound up alongside the porch of a midwestern farmhouse. Here, it became an object of interest to young Arlow Burdette Stout, whose mother had planted it.

"Bert," as he was called by members of the family, was a country boy. Raised in then rural Wisconsin, he had spent every spare hour from earliest childhood exploring the woods and fields surrounding his home. By the age of twenty, he had become an able and observant naturalist. He noticed things, and what he noticed about his mother's orange daylily was that it produced no seed capsules. Having recently been exposed to Asa Gray's book *How Plants Grow*, his curiosity was piqued by the abnormal behavior of the daylily.

Solving the reproductory riddle of *Hemerocallis fulva* led Stout into the scientific life. At the age of thirty-five, he joined the staff of the New York Botanical Garden and spent the next forty-seven years pursuing related research. Fortunately for the gardening public, he did more than study daylilies. A gardener himself, he undertook an extensive breeding program to improve the plant and increase its garden value. Thus began another journey—the daylily's fairy-tale progress from stalwart immigrant to belle of the ball and darling of American gardeners.

At the beginning of the twentieth century, a handful of breeders using half a dozen wild species were producing yellow and orange hybrids. Today, hundreds of hybridizers working with an enormous gene pool are producing a thousand new cultivars a year. (*Cultivar* combines the words *cultivated* and *variety* to distinguish garden plants from naturally occurring species.) Previously unknown colors and designs are now emerging from nurseries and backyards all around the country, thanks to Dr. Stout and *Hemerocallis fulva*.

By whatever name it is known locally—tawny daylily, roadside lily, even outhouse lily—few plants in the United States are more widely recognized than *H. fulva*. In 1988, its cheerful orange flowers made it a strong contender for the nation's floral emblem, and many were chagrined when it was narrowly defeated by the rose. The argument in favor of a Far Eastern native as the National Flower ran that America has always been adept at assimilating the best from many different cultures and making it truly American. In the case of the daylily, this is not chauvinistic hyperbole; it is fact. America has taken the genus

Hemerocallis to its collective heart. This close bond was cemented in 1955 when the International Horticultural Congress selected the American Hemerocallis Society as the International Registry for all daylily cultivars. What this means is that wherever hybrids are created, whether in Britain, continental Europe, or Australia, or even in the daylily's homelands in the Far East, breeders must record the fruits of their labors with the American Society. This honor is heady stuff!

While the modern daylily is a direct descendant of *H. fulva* and other species, the flowers have changed dramatically since Dr. Stout began his work. Instead of the classic trumpet formed by six widely spaced, flaring tepals of roughly equal width, each tapering to a point, the new shape is flat in profile with overlapping, broadly oval tepals carried at right angles to the scape. (Generally, the outer three segments of a daylily flower are referred to as sepals and the inner three as petals. Botanically, all six are tepals.) The striking new form combined with a color range expanded from shades of orange, yellow, and arguably pink, to almost every hue and tint you can name—and a great many that you can't—constitute an all-American success story.

Today, the best and most beautiful daylily cultivars in the world are being hybridized in this country, and our commercial growers are the acknowledged leaders in their propagation and distribution. One of our foremost growers, Roy Klehm, who is also an avid hybridizer, told me gleefully, "We've beaten the British in hostas and peonies. But we've *really* got 'em licked in daylilies!" Here is one flower that has *not* been shipped off to England for an Oxford education and reintroduced to an admiring, respectful American audience. If we have failed in our loyalty to native New England asters, our handsome joe-pye weed and the rudbeckias, we have made up for it in appreciation of the immigrant daylily.

Britons are less enthusiastic about daylilies. One member of the British Hosta and Hemerocallis Society wrote, "Here, we find much less interest in 'Hems' compared to hostas, mainly I suspect because so often our summers are insufficiently hot to encourage prolific flowering." Others just don't know what they are missing. In a recent issue of *Country Life*, Christopher Lloyd, the gifted, curmudgeonly British horticulturist who created the gardens at Great Dixter, grumbles that Americans "have gone berserk in breeding and naming new varieties." But he is forced to concede that too few modern cultivars are represented in the hemerocallis trial beds at Wisley (the Royal Horticultural Society's display and experimental garden in Surrey). Indeed, he only mentions golden oldies from the fifties and sixties.

Elsewhere in Europe, new American introductions are causing a sensation. In Germany, crowds flock to the Frankfurt Palmengarten to hear Roswitha Waterman of Long Island, New York, describe the latest offerings by American hybridizers. For the past eight years, Mrs. Waterman, a war bride from the city of Bremen, has returned annually to her native land armed with slides solicited from American hybridizers. Amateur breeders and daylily fanciers from all over Germany and middle Europe come to hear her lectures and hang on every word. Half a world away, exuberant Australians nearly ran afoul of the American Hemerocallis Society in their enthusiasm. They wanted to form a branch of their own with an independent system of registering cultivars. Fortunately, the misunderstanding was cleared up and hybridizers from down under amiably agreed to follow the rules established by the International Horticultural Congress.

At home in North America, forebears of the modern daylily flourish along roadsides from Canada south to Virginia. *H. fulva* grows in almost every state of the Union. It is a familiar sight in Mississippi, where Elly Launius, executive secretary of the American Hemerocallis Society, tells me it rejoices in the common name of ditch lily.

A friend of hers learned the significance of the daylily's botanical name the hard way. Derived from two Greek words, *hemera*, meaning "day," and *kallos*, "beauty," the combined form has given rise to the translation "Beauty for a day." "My friend," recounted Elly, "taught English at a high school in northeastern Mississippi. It was a county school where teachers have to assume outside duties. At this time, Marion was in charge of the graduation. One day just before the end of spring term, she passed an old house surrounded by fields of orange daylilies. Well, the school colors happened to be orange and green, so Marion hit upon the idea of asking the lady of the house if she could pick some to put up on the stage for graduation. The reply was, 'Oh, Lord, yes. They have been there since my grandparents' time. Help yourself.' So Marion got to school, gathered up a few of her students, and went back to the field, where they started cutting daylilies. Early that afternoon, they decorated the stage. The county superintendent and the principal just oohed and aahed about how pretty it looked. Then, everyone went home. Graduation ceremonies weren't until seven-thirty. That evening, Marion walked into the auditorium and couldn't believe her eyes! She was devastated. Every last one of those daylilies had closed up!"

The unfortunate habit of closing at sundown has long since been overcome in modern cultivars, but individual blossoms still last only a day. In fact, it is part of their poignant charm. Not for the daylily a long, weary decline. Each blossom achieves perfection during the hours between dawn and dusk, casting its spell for one shining day. "Although it fall and die that night / It was the flower and plant of light." When you consider that a prolific cultivar may produce as many as fifty flower buds on a single scape and that an established clump boasts ten or more scapes, that makes five hundred flowers. That's a lot of light!

In addition to remaining open in the evenings, you may wonder what else sets the modern daylily apart from its wild ancestors. Quite simply, everything. First and foremost, the flowers. Today, no cultivated flower offers more diversity in terms of size, shape, color, pattern, detail, and surface texture and decorative edging. The scapes, which in nature are often thin and whiplike, have been given substance, the better to carry flowers of increased size. In several of the wild species, the flower buds develop in a tight knot at the top of the scape, while modern cultivars boast a system of widespread branches. Today's well-branched cultivars present their extravagant, frilly blossoms like debutantes at a cotillion. Many of the newer daylilies also have foliage that is broader, lusher, more upright in habit, and a deeper green than the pale, lax leaves of *H. fulva*. These improvements and a myriad of other wonders have been wrought largely by amateur hybridizers. But even in the world of commercial horticulture, most daylily breeders are "amateurs" in the sense of loving what they do.

Hybridizer David Kirchhoff is a professional. His father was a nurseryman who grew gladioli in four different states. But when the elder Kirchhoff retired, he picked up daylilies as a hobby, and according to his son, "They became his passion until the day he died. It happens to people. It's just like a fever. There's something about working with daylilies that transcends the pulling of weeds out there in the field. You just have to keep going—every day looking for that very special bloom. It's what keeps you young."

This book is a paean—a song of thanksgiving—to young-at-heart daylily hybridizers and to the flower that has kept them that way. I hasten to add that I am writing it, not as an expert, but as an ordinary gardener with a soft spot for the genus *Hemerocallis*, a sense of history, and a keen desire to gather together stories of the people—past and present—who have made the daylily what it is today. For every story I have come across, there are, of course, dozens that have eluded me.

It is just as Patrick Stamile said recently: "There are a lot of people involved in daylilies, and everybody focuses on different hybridizers as the giants. But it depends on when *you* arrived on the scene. I know when I came along, there were already major hybridizers. But when *they* came on the scene, there were also major hybridizers. It's a thing that's constantly changing. I think it's wonderful that we've all been able to utilize the advances made by others—to be able to stand on the shoulders of giants, is the way I like to think about it." And it is a good way to think about the daylily world, because my giants may not be yours.

Admirers of the daylily, here and abroad, must number in the millions. A hard core of more than six thousand enthusiasts belong to the American Hemerocallis Society, and from the ranks of this dedicated band have come my guides in the daylily world. These are the real "daylily people." They follow the season from Florida to Maine. They recognize every round, ruffled, upturned blossom in the garden and know every hybridizer by his or her special touch. With difficulty, they drag themselves away from their own daylilies to gather at Regional Meetings and National Conventions—sometimes at great distances from their homes. Ill-prepared Southerners endure bone-chilling rain in the Delaware Valley while perspiring Yankees brave the semitropical sun to admire the handiwork of their friends and competitors.

My own travels have taken me from the gently undulating landscape of northern Florida to within sight of the Adirondack Mountains in upper New York State. I have gone from person to person and from garden to garden on tips from members of the Society. I have followed where they have led and glimpsed the gardening life as daylily people live it. I have been welcomed into a company of amazing, amusing, inspiring gardeners. I hope this account does them justice and paves the way for other travelers.

Epiphany

'Hyperion' (Mead)

'Alec Allen'
(Carpenter)

Until I joined the American Hemerocallis Society a few short years ago, I considered myself a full-fledged "daylily person." My garden, which is a big, rambling country affair, is full of daylilies. The site—a former cow pasture—was no place for fussy little plants. It demanded big, vigorous, carefree plants with stamina and staying power. Daylilies filled the bill admirably. They were the first perennials I planted and have proved to be among the most enduring.

From early July until mid-August, dozens of different cultivars in shades of red, bronze, copper, yellow, and orange light up the fifteen-foot-wide bed that follows the contours of a hillside. Behind the border, grass paths separate ribbons of shrubs, trees, rocks, and ground covers. Wherever there is enough light, there are more daylilies. High up on the hillside, tall 'Purity' and the very similar 'Statuesque' float their clear yellow blossoms against a background of rhododendrons. Later, 'Autumn Minaret' adds a cinnamon-eyed grace note to the display.

I have been growing daylilies for more than thirty years. There are close to 150 cultivars in the border which still have their identifying metal labels. Others I know by heart, and quite a few more remain beloved but anonymous. In most cases, the hybridizers—whose names I have only recently learned—have been dead these many years. The flowers which have outlived their creators exhibit classic trumpet shapes similar to the wild species. In other words, I still love and grow a great many venerable hybrids whose dates of introduction I blush to tell you.

'Hyperion', a staple of old-fashioned gardens like mine, is tall and sweetly scented, with light yellow flowers. It was produced by a Mr. Franklin B. Mead of Fort Wayne, Indiana, and made its commercial debut in 1925. I have been unable to learn anything about Mr. Mead, but in 'Hyperion' he has achieved at least a scrap of immortality. His flower is still a great favorite in gardens all over the country.

In 1938, Elizabeth Nesmith, a pioneer breeder from Massachusetts, created an exciting new "pink" daylily which she named 'Sweetbriar'. This early pink along with 'Hyperion' weaves a soft rosy orange and pale yellow theme among the Aurelian hybrid lilies, sunflowers, and exclamation marks of lythrum at the back of my border. In front of them, 'Linda', a 1937 Stout cultivar, throws a bastion of yellow and orange flowers around a huge clump of blue globe thistle, while 'Marionette'—a 1950 introduction and the first daylily I ever planted—pops up here and there throughout the garden. 'Marionette' is egg-yolk yellow, with a handsome dark red eye.

Over the years, these and other vigorous cultivars that once consisted of a modest fan of leaves and a single scape bearing only a few blossoms have developed into great clumps of graceful foliage surmounted by bushel basket loads of flowers. Most clumps have subsequently been divided innumerable times, with the result that I have more daylilies than I know what to do with. But no matter how crowded the perennial border becomes, I can never resist adding more. Nor do I discard the old ones. I could never bring myself to abandon 'Norwegian Lass', which has large, open blossoms the color of clotted cream, or give up 'Melody Lane', a vigorous yellow airbrushed with paprika—both products of the fifties.

The first named cultivars arrived in our garden in 1961. Newly wed and financially overextended, I didn't dare buy the most expensive, up-to-date hybrids. But even the moderately priced cultivars thrilled me with their beauty. I used to go mad every spring when half-price sales were advertised. At that time, I was intrigued by the idea of pinks. A pink daylily! How novel and exciting! Of course, those that I could afford usually had more than a hint of orange in their makeup, and sometimes I was disappointed. No doubt the newest of the new were a good deal pinker than the older, more reasonably priced varieties.

The advances toward white were another story. Even at that time, some lovely, very pale pastel flowers were being introduced. I was entranced with everything—from the creamy shades of yellow to the pearly tones of pink and lavender, and finally the near-whites, such as 'Ice Carnival' and small, rose-dusted 'Arctic Dawn'.

In the seventies, I discovered tetraploids. The growth habit of ordinary daylilies (and other plants) is governed by the genes carried in two identical sets of chromosomes found in the nucleus of each plant cell. In daylilies, the basic number of chromosomes in each cell is twenty-two—eleven in each set. Because there are two sets, such a plant is called a diploid. *Tetra*, on the other hand, signifies "four." By the use of a chemical derived from the autumn crocus (*Colchicum autumnale*), plant breeders have succeeded in doubling the number of chromosomes in treated daylilies and their offspring. The resulting tetraploids have bigger flowers, more vigorous foliage, and sturdier scapes. I lusted after the largest flowers, tetraploids like nine-inch 'Yellow Pinwheel'. Then, during the eighties, I came around to miniatures less than three inches across and even the unimproved wild species such as *Hemerocallis Dumortieri*.

In short, I had grown and loved daylilies for a quarter of a century and never dreamed that these simple, handsome plants had meanwhile been undergoing a metamorphosis. And so it was that one day in 1987, friends who knew my fondness for daylilies invited me to go with them to a Display Garden approved by the American Hemerocallis Society. At that time, daylily enthusiasts from all points of the compass were converging on the Westchester County garden of Mr. and Mrs. Paul

Watts to see the newest and the best. It was considered one of the most complete and immaculately maintained Display Gardens in the country.

The Watts have since moved away, giving untold numbers of plants to the New York Botanical Garden. But on that memorable July morning, our host and hostess had been up since dawn removing thousands of spent blossoms. By the time we arrived, yesterday's rainbow had already been trundled off to the compost pile, and we were greeted by a brand-new one. Louise Watts had been able to make her escape before our slightly premature appearance. Her husband, however, was caught red-handed and still wearing his old gardening clothes.

Trapped in his driveway, he patiently explained the nature and purpose of an official Display Garden. "The idea is to have a place where people who are interested in daylilies can come and see them growing in a garden setting. We buy a lot of new ones every year because that's what a great many of the visitors are interested in—that is, the people who are real aficionados." The Watts used to add as many as 60 to 75 cultivars annually, disposing of about the same number in an effort to hold the planting down to a manageable 650 to 700 cultivars. At the time of our visit, they were in the process of trying to cut back. "Now, we get maybe twenty-five or thirty new ones every year." Paul Watts grinned rather sheepishly and amended the number to 35. "I keep digging up the grass to make more space, but it's almost gotten to the point where it's the maximum we can take care of—just the two of us. My wife is a great worker, and we work together all the time."

As if on cue, Louise Watts came to her husband's rescue and took us on a tour of the garden. Protected from the outside world by a dense planting of conifers and deciduous shrubs and trees, thousands of daylilies flaunted their splendor against the green backdrop. As required in the guidelines for Display Gardens, every size, shape, and style was represented. Among the older cultivars, which had been relegated to the back of the borders, there were a few familiar faces. But up front and center, the latest additions made my jaw drop. I had never seen such daylilies:

the wide, wide petals and golden frills of 'Alec Allen'; the luscious shades of pink in cultivars such as 'Yesterday Memories';
the dazzling whiteness of 'Driven Snow' and 'Gentle Shepherd';
the rich purple coloring of 'Hamlet' and 'Catherine Neal'.

Although a contrasting eye zone is found even in the common *H. fulva*, the recent manifestations were dramatically different: everything from bold areas of dark pigment against pastel
petals to chalky pastels on dark segments. The light-on-dark
reversal is called a "watermark." Along with so much else,
watermarks were news to me. Eyed daylilies, on the other hand,
were old friends. But the new color schemes were so vivid and
varied! Spellbound by an enchanting orchid pink flower with a
sumptuous purple eye, I leaned across its neighbor, causing
Mrs. Watts to say kindly but firmly, "Back up! You're bumping
'Angel Blush'!" Guiltily, I withdrew, but not before falling hopelessly in love with 'Siloam Bo Peep'.

In the course of conversation with our hostess, I learned
that the prefix "Siloam" identifies the daylily introductions of
Pauline Henry of Siloam Springs, Arkansas. In addition to
being one of the country's leading hybridizers, she is a collector
of antique dolls and a fine needlewoman. In daylily circles, it is
rumored that the energetic Mrs. Henry hybridizes all day and
sews authentic period costumes for the dolls all night. Certainly
her appreciation of small proportions is reflected in both her
enthusiasms—the neat, perfectly formed segments of her
daylilies and the scaled-down porcelain features of her dolls.

Louise Watts knew something about every hybridizer represented in her garden. Bona fide "daylily people" always have
this information at their fingertips. It is a prerequisite for admission to the "daylily world." But until that moment, I had never
spared a thought to the breeders whose skill, patience, and talent had furnished my garden with so many beautiful flowers.
Suddenly I wanted to know these people, and to obtain a pass-
port into the "daylily world" I joined the American Hemerocallis
Society. Reading the quarterly publication *The Daylily Journal*, I
began to get an inkling of what daylily people and their flowers
were all about.

There are two ways to look at a daylily—as a gardener and as a daylily person. Being a gardener, I tend to look at the whole plant. No matter how ravishing the flowers may be, they are only part of the garden picture—and a temporary part, at that. Scale, height, foliage, and plant habit are equally important in terms of design. For instance, I might choose a tall daylily with pale yellow flowers and arching foliage to echo the creamy variegations of an ornamental grass and to act as a foil for the grass's vertical leaf blades. To me, it is immaterial whether the petal margins of the daylily flower are plain or fancy. From a distance, the blossoms register as colored shapes in a collage.

Believe me, daylily people do *not* look upon their beloved flowers as colored shapes! Collectors study the blossoms the way philatelists pore over stamps. They examine each feature in the most minute detail, from the petal edges—which may be scalloped, shirred, pleated, or fringed—to the surface texture of the segments. Some modern daylilies have petals and sepals as thick and smooth as expensive vellum. Other cultivars have a rippled, puckered surface like seersucker or raised ridges like corduroy. Hybridizers are the dreamers of dreams. They look upon these embellishments as mere points of departure.

Thanks to past generations of dreamers, we have a revolutionary flower form—round, ruffled, and shallow in profile. Now hybridizers are looking in new directions. "Spiders" with exceptionally narrow, elongated segments are currently gaining in popularity. Then there are the doubles, with as many as eighteen extra segments. These may be arranged in numerous configurations that have already occurred and others which have yet to be imagined. Nor has the size range yet been exploited to the full. Spiders may have already reached ten inches across, but why not more? Or less, much less. How about a daylily flower like a tiny starfish?

And colors—have we seen them all? Impossible! The whites can be whiter; the reds redder, the pinks more truly phlox-colored; the purples more velvety; and of course, there's the elusive blue. In addition, every color can be modified by translucent washes or overlaid with a nacreous luster or spangled with crushed diamonds. Modern daylilies are already displaying stunning multicolored patterns. These may be applied as lightly as mist from a spray bottle or layered on like impasto in rich, opaque bands. The eye zones vary from neat circles of contrasting color to bold lashings of pigment that sweep out from the center of the flower, leaving only a margin of the base color. These contrasts in color can be dreamy or dynamic—the permutations are infinite. There are ivory-white flowers with intense purple eyes; shell pinks splashed with red; blood red on orange; and red-orange on light flame. But who knows what new combinations may lurk in fattening green seed pods around the country?

Unquestionably, Dr. A. B. Stout is the "Father of the Modern Daylily." During his tenure at the New York Botanical Garden, he made some fifty thousand *Hemerocallis* crosses. And today's cultivars have emerged from this wealth of genetic material. However, the modern daylily also owes an incalculable debt to backyard breeders. It is as much the creation of daylily people as it is their reason for being. Even the collectors have had a hand in its development. Their love of novelty has constantly inspired hybridizers to reach beyond the realm of reality into science fiction. And the daylily itself has made all this possible, bless its fertile little heart. Easily manipulated, it fulfills every whim and makes even the most impossible dreams come true. In short, it is the quintessential hobby flower.

Dreamers of Dreams

There is nothing coy about a daylily flower. In fact, part of its beauty lies in the elegance of the reproductive apparatus which it parades before appreciative insects and eager hybridizers. The female parts unite in a slender, translucent tube that sweeps forth, often extending beyond the rim of the fully opened blossom. Called the pistil, this fine tube is actually made up of three sections terminating in a three-chambered ovary which, if fertilized, contains the future seeds. At this premature stage, the seeds are called ovules.

Surrounding the pistil and attached to the base of each flower segment are six stamens, each ending in a tiny, oblong anther sac full of pollen. The stamens joined to the sepals appear shorter than those associated with the petals, and all six recurve deferentially behind the elongated pistil. On a warm day, the flower bud of a daylily flings wide its sepals and petals, exposing this graceful arrangement of parts—the curving pistil with its entourage of anther-capped stamens. Almost at once, the anthers split in half lengthwise, the outside edges roll back, and fluffy yellow pollen grains containing the male cells are offered up to the first taker—be it human hand or passing bumblebee.

The daylily eschews that hard-to-get nonsense of plants like the lady's-slipper orchid with its hidden pollen sacs or the stand-offish members of the pea family which actually enclose their pistil and stamens so that bees can't get in at all. Their flowers have to pollinate themselves to survive. Daylilies, on the other hand, are up-front, beautiful, and sexy. And they are easy to hybridize. Pluck out a stamen with your fingers, transport it to another flower, and brush the pollen-bearing anther across the sticky tip (the stigma) of the pistil. That's all there is to it. Your work is made easier by the presence of minute projections on the stigma which trap the pollen grains, and by a drop of stigmatic fluid which promotes germination. In short, the ever-obliging daylily makes it hard for even a clumsy hybridizer or the most bumbling of bees to fail.

Having spread pollen from the anther of one daylily onto the pistil of another, the hybridizer can sit back and relax while the daylily begins a day of feverish activity. Within minutes of touching the stigmatic projections, the pollen grain sends out a tiny, clear tube that enters one of the pistil's own hollow tubes and makes for the waiting ovule. As it nears its target, the pollen tube explodes, ejecting the sperm cells—one of which unites with the egg to complete the miracle of fertilization. Working at top speed, the daylily accomplishes all that is necessary in one day. That evening, the exhausted flower collapses, and within a few more days, the withered blossom drops to the ground. By this time, however, the future is secure.

In two to three weeks, the three-chambered ovary begins to look like a little green barrel with bulging staves. Within the staves, six or seven pairs of seeds, stacked one on top of the other like peas in a pod, are fattening up. Over the next three weeks or so, they will turn from white to brown to glittering jet-black. When the seeds are ripe, cracks appear between staves at the top of the barrel. In the normal course of events, the barrel would dry out in a few days, the cracks would widen, and the seeds would spill out onto the ground. But in our scenario, the hybridizer rouses himself or herself, harvests the seeds, and plants them—immediately where winters are mild, or the following spring in colder parts of the country. Either way, within a maximum of three years and a minimum of one, the first scapes will arise from sprightly green fans, and flowers—for which the hybridizer alone is responsible—will greet the dawn. Even if those flowers bear a striking resemblance to many others, to their creator they will be in a class by themselves. As the Little Prince learned in Saint-Exupery's fable, the flower for which you are responsible is "unique in all the world."

Somewhat to my own surprise, hybridizing has never exerted its magnetic pull on me. The unfurling bud of any flower is so astonishing that I can absorb no more, but if you wonder how it feels to look down upon a flower of your own creation, let amateur hybridizer Philip Reilly of Chelmsford, Massachusetts, tell you. "It's a religious experience. You feel godlike. You can't help it. When you look at these things, you say, 'Wow!' You're walking a foot off the ground and nothing can penetrate the euphoria—not the threat of losing your job—nothing."

Debby Schmidt lives in Connecticut with her husband and three children. Her garden has recently been designated an official Display Garden, and as president of the Connecticut Daylily Society, she is deeply involved with the whole daylily world. But the excitement of hybridizing is a relatively new experience. "It gives you this incredible feeling of success," she says. "Suddenly it doesn't matter that you've just broken a bottle of ketchup all over the kitchen floor, or that your kid has flunked a test. You walk out into the garden and see three daylilies that have just popped out of their little black lobster-eye seeds. You can't help feeling you're a success. You've created something, and that does wonders for your self-esteem."

If you think this degree of pleasure is felt only by the neophyte, think again. R. W. (Bill) Munson, Jr., of Wimberlyway Gardens in Florida has been breeding daylilies for over forty years. He fell in love with them as a teenager, began hybridizing at once, and has been at it ever since. His home is surrounded by a thirteen-acre mosaic of his creations. Over the years, he has seen and contributed to stunning changes in flower form and color and might be forgiven for being blasé about these developments. But he is far from blasé. "You can't know," he says, "how it feels to have been part of the transformation of the rather plain scullery maid of the horticultural world into a princess. It has been just wonderful! And it's still happening, the flower is still improving so dramatically that we're almost making quantum leaps in ruffling, in the range of colors, and in the different heights. I mean, now down to twelve and fourteen inches and up to four feet or more—rivaling the bearded irises in variety. It's all coming together, and it's so exciting!"

Patrick and Grace Stamile agree. They have been hybridizing for twelve years and find it an ongoing adventure. I visited the Stamiles on Long Island in the summer of 1990. Taking in their huge daylily field with a wave of his hand, Pat said, "This is just a hobby that ran amok. It grew and grew and grew, and one thing led to another which led to another, and so forth. But we just love it. We really enjoy ourselves and that's the important thing. If you turned this field into a nursery, you could make a lot more money but you'd lose the creative aspect. And for Grace and me, that's where the love affair began. The same is true for a lot of people. Some people barely have a garden but they start to hybridize because they start to dream of the possibilities. It doesn't take much to make a cross and to make some seed.... It's the possibilities that open—all the challenges. You're constantly dreaming. You are never quite happy." He paused to rephrase this observation. "Well, you *are* happy with your creation but there's always the feeling, 'That's wonderful! Now, what can I do to make it better?'"

To make a better daylily—there's the rub. It may be easy to make crosses. It is not easy to improve on the best of the existing cultivars. "Some of the ones now are so good," says Debby Schmidt, "that I don't see how they could be any better. It's the mystery of what different combinations will bring that appeals to me. I did a cross this summer using 'Inner View', one of Mort Morss's cultivars. I really love 'Inner View'. The base color is a beige-lavender with a very clear design of yellow on the inside. It isn't a blur or a smear, it is a perfect cutout of yellow. It's just wonderful. And yet, I would like more variation. You know, I like my kids but I'd like more and a little different. Anyway, I crossed it with a red by the name of 'Red Tide', and I was really happy to get seeds. Now I'm thinking to myself, 'It's probably going to be ugly. But by the same token, it *could* be that velvety rose with a cutout yellow center. That would be distinctive!' I suppose that's why you do it. You're like a kid in a candy store. You just can't resist."

In 1991, 238 hybridizers were unable to resist registering 1,079 new cultivars with the American Hemerocallis Society. It was the sixth consecutive year that the annual tally had exceeded 1,000, bringing the grand total to 33,368. Some members of the daylily fraternity deplore the number, but Bill Munson is not among them. Fastidious himself about what he chooses to name and introduce, he sees the burgeoning of hybrids and hybridizers as a positive force in improving the genus. During the fifty or so years since Dr. Stout precipitated daylilies into the spotlight, hundreds of amateur breeders, aided by only a handful of scientists, have made these plants into stars. As one of the moguls of the daylily world, Bill has this to say: "A lot of people bitch because we've gotten so many named varieties, and they claim that too many people are hybridizing. But my feeling is, the more the merrier!"

The message is clear: Jump right in! Be advised, however, that there is a world of difference between dabbing a bit of pollen around and developing a well-organized breeding program with clearly defined objectives. It takes mental discipline to establish goals by analyzing what you hope to achieve. And it demands perseverance to keep your goals in sight—perhaps for years. First of all, you will need to acquire an encyclopedic knowledge of existing cultivars and their desirable traits. There is no point in reinventing the wheel. In addition, you had better have a passion for detail and a mind like a computer. Accurate record keeping is the sine qua non of hybridizing. Come to think of it, a computer wouldn't be a bad idea, either. On top of that, a modicum of patience is necessary because each cultivar has its own agenda. Some are reliable parents, others are capricious, and a few are downright irresponsible.

Finally, before you embark on a daylily hybridizing program, you would do well to have a physical. If you are in less than tip-top condition, you might consider a few weeks at your nearest health spa. Daylily people are a disparate lot, as I have discovered. But one thing they all have in common is *energy*. At this writing, Bill Munson's eighty-six-year-old mother, Ida, still works full-time collecting seeds, planting them, and lining out hundreds of seedlings. *Lining out* means planting small daylily seedlings in rows with enough space between them for optimum development. It also means a great deal of stooping or bending. In short, it means work.

Back to your breeding program. Having received a clean bill of health from your physician, you are ready to begin. First, you must choose daylily parents (their compatibility remains to be seen) to further your specific aims. The next step is the easiest, making your crosses. After that, you must trust to luck. In about six weeks, environmental factors permitting, you will have a number of plump pods brimming over with seeds, as many as forty-two to a pod. Your ears pricked up at the mention of environmental factors. I neglected to say earlier that extreme heat can inhibit fertilization. Even after viable sperm has reached the ovule and fertilization has been accomplished, misfortunes can befall an immature pod. But let's assume you have been lucky. The pods have not dropped off, and you manage to reap your first harvest of a thousand seeds. Every one of those cute little black lobster-eyes has to be planted. And this is only the beginning.

Daylilies—being the amenable plants they are—grow quickly. You may have had room in your backyard for a thousand wisps of foliage the first year. But what about the second year? Even in the Northeast, you'll have a thousand sturdy fans. And picture your yard the third year, with a thousand clumps of vigorous leaves sending up all those longed-for scapes. It makes you think, doesn't it? It should. This arbitrary thousand seeds represents the crop of about twenty-three pods. And you'd be a piker not to harvest at least that many every year! Just one more item of conventional daylily wisdom: Out of a thousand blooming-sized plants, the average hybridizer finds only one worth keeping!

Are you still with me? In an essay from a collection entitled *The Art of Hybridizing*, Oscie B. Whatley, Jr., sums up the spot in which beginners find themselves at the end of two years:

> A lot of labor goes into the growing of seedlings and only the anticipation of bloom drives us on. Apparently this drive is quite formidable and with some, an obsession. If the labor causes undue stress on you and your loved ones, there is no sin in trash-canning some less desirable crosses. All this work will seem worthwhile when one special seedling unfolds its segments and your dreams become reality.

Did you pick up that reference to your loved ones? In this day of marriage contracts, you might also want to check the fine print. Hybridizing is a time-consuming hobby, and it can become expensive. Before long, you may find that the newest cultivars—the ones that cost anywhere from $25 to $200 and more—are absolutely vital to the success of your program. Your spouse, however, may not see it that way. One hybridizer of my acquaintance kept his first $25 purchase a secret from his wife for ten years, and rumor has it that after he finally told her, she gave him a hard time about it for the next ten. I just thought I'd mention it. Now, if you still want to try your hand at hybridizing, more power to you!

The Pioneers

Mr. George Yeld

The first brave soul to seriously tackle daylily breeding was British schoolmaster George Yeld. He began hybridizing in Yorkshire, England, in 1877—the year after Dr. Stout's birth. A gentle, self-effacing "Mr. Chips," Yeld dedicated fifty-two years of his long life to St. Peter's School, York, and to his youthful charges—boys between the ages of thirteen and eighteen. According to his friend G. P. Barker, he "became so identified with the school in the minds of many pupils who passed through his hands, it might have been said that he *was* the school."

During his years of service to St. Peter's, he lived at Clifton Cottage, a charming Regency building on school property. One of its charms was the garden in back, where he made his iris and daylily crosses and grew some of his more promising seedlings. School archivist J. V. Mitchell writes that Clifton Cottage now houses the Music School, but "still retains its long walled garden, though unfortunately, the borders are somewhat bare." In Yeld's day, the same borders were filled with irises and daylilies. Elsewhere in the garden, there were beds of his beloved alpines.

As a young man, Yeld had discovered the thrill of mountain climbing, and thereafter, spent all the school vacations in the high country. G. P. Barker was his frequent climbing companion.

"Almost every year from the date of his joining the Alpine Club in 1877 to 1913, when the time came for him to give up climbing, Yeld either visited the Alps in Europe or else would be found among the hills of Wales or the Lake Country. No wonder these visits gave him a love of the flora of the hills." If mountaineering fostered George Yeld's love of alpine plants, proximity to the Backhouse Nursery in York facilitated the development of his daylily program. The Messrs. Backhouse kindly set aside a plot for him at their nursery, where, according to Barker, he grew seedlings with "labels written in Greek so that crosses he made might not be known to others." Obviously, scholarship has its advantages.

Success, however, whether it was academic or horticultural, appears to have surprised the diffident Yeld. As a student at Oxford University, he followed in the august footsteps of poet Matthew Arnold, winning the prestigious Newdigate Prize for English Verse. Years later, he was awarded the Victoria Medal of Honor—the highest honor bestowed on gardeners by the Royal Horticultural Society. Established in 1897 to celebrate Queen Victoria's diamond jubilee, the medal was limited to sixty holders at any one time. (That number increased in 1900 to sixty-three to correspond with the years of the queen's reign.) In between, countless lesser medals came Yeld's way, many of them for contributing to the advancement of the genus *Hemerocallis*. Bemused, he wrote, "They tell me that I am the first hybridist of this family, the flower being Apricot." This original cultivar, which Dr. A. B. Stout described as "a variety of charm and beauty," was exhibited in London in June 1892 and received a Certificate of Merit.

Yeld came on the scene at a period in British horticulture when tender plants from around the world had caught the public's imagination. For the time being, hardy perennials like daylilies were out, and beautiful mixed borders were actually destroyed to make way for subtropical bedding plants. Fuschias, begonias, verbenas, calceolarias, and South African geraniums had become the rage, and geometric patterns, the latest fad. In greenhouses all over the British Isles, gardeners were raising thousands of showy exotics to fill the paint-by-number designs laid out in public parks and private gardens.

While modest Victorian homeowners tended their so-called "carpet bedding" schemes, the landed gentry avidly cultivated the new trees and shrubs being brought home by nineteenth century plant hunters. The Veitch family, the most famous British nurserymen of the time, introduced more than a thousand new plants from abroad, but apparently not one root of *Hemerocallis*. Nevertheless, a few species had slipped into Britain during the years following the arrival of the tawny daylily (*Hemerocallis fulva*) and the lemon lily (*H. Lilioasphodelus*). But the new additions might have gone unnoticed had it not been for George Yeld.

The first newcomers he was able to acquire were two semi-dwarf species, *H. Dumortieri*, originally from Japan, and *H. Middendorffii*, discovered in the vicinity of the Amur River, which forms the boundary between Manchuria and the former Soviet Union. Similar to one another in habit, they both bloom in the spring—late May in my Connecticut garden. *H. Dumortieri* has a compact form, upright foliage, and unbranched, two-foot scapes ending in bouquets of cinnamon-colored buds. These open a deep golden yellow. *H. Middendorffii* produces terminal clusters of yellow-orange buds, lighter-colored flowers, and taller scapes which carry the blossoms six inches above the arching foliage.

Next, George Yeld obtained the more refined species, *H. minor*, and added it to his collection. At the time, several different low-growing daylilies were cultivated under the names *H. minor, H. graminea,* and *H. graminifolia*. Be that as it may, an early spring bloomer with narrow, graceful leaves and lemon-yellow flowers was one parent of Yeld's selection 'Francis' which won the Royal Horticultural Society's Award of Merit in 1895.

That same year, he acquired a much more significant addition to his hybridizing program, the plant Dr. Stout knew as *H. aurantiaca* var. *major*. Writing about this plant some forty years later, Yeld's excitement was still palpable. He described it as "a glorious flower" and attributed to it great improvements in the genus. Dr. Stout was more restrained, possibly because the performance of this plant was disappointing at the New York Botanical Garden, flowering sparsely and frequently suffering winter damage.

Nevertheless, daylily growers who live below the Mason-Dixon line owe a debt to the species *H. aurantiaca.* Dr. Stout discovered that in warm climates *H. aurantiaca* and its hybrids remained evergreen and continue growing throughout the year. The significance of this characteristic was not lost on Stout. By incorporating evergreen species into his breeding program, new daylilies could be created that would survive in a wide range of climatic situations. Giant strides have been made along these lines in the last ten years. Of course, not all daylilies will grow in the tropics, any more than all daylilies will grow in the far north. But there are cultivars adapted to the different extremes, and progress is being made in the direction of widely adaptable cultivars. *H. aurantiaca* was the first step along the way.

In the relatively mild English climate, Yeld had no difficulty growing *H. aurantiaca* var. *major.* Indeed, many of his best hybrids were offspring of this variety. It would be hard for hybridizers today to understand George Yeld's delight in his uniformly yellow and orange seedlings. But the gene pool at his disposal was extremely limited, and other daylily hybridizers were few and far between. Moreover, they were all in the same boat. In Italy, Karl Ludwig Sprenger of Naples and his nephew, Willy Müller, head gardener at the University of Strasbourg, were making some crosses. But they, too, were restricted by their basic material—the few species available.

Then, in 1893, the year after Yeld was awarded a Certificate of Merit for 'Apricot', Sprenger was pleased to ship a collection of *Hemerocallis* to another Englishman. Upon receipt of this order, twenty-two-year-old Amos Perry joined the small band of daylily hybridizers. Full of energy and youthful ardor, he came rightly by his love of horticulture. His father, also called Amos Perry, was the founder of a well-known nursery (and also of a horticultural dynasty whose surviving member, Frances Perry, received the Victoria Medal of Honor in 1971). The elder Perry had started off in education, but on the unconvincing excuse of ill health switched to the nursery business. The change must have agreed with him, because he soon established the firm that his sons and later his grandsons carried on until after World War II.

Having inherited a green thumb, the younger Amos Perry undertook an apprenticeship at Ware's Nurseries in Tottenham. Here he discovered daylilies and, years later, recalled a bold clump of *H. fulva* which had impressed him as "being one of the most beautiful plants in their famous nursery." On the strength of that impression, he threw himself into hybridizing with missionary zeal. The going, however, was rough, and in seven years he produced only one hybrid he thought worth naming. Still, he persevered and toward the end of his life was acknowledged as Britain's answer to Dr. Stout.

In a foreword to Amos Perry's *Hemerocallis* manual, George Yeld summarized his colleague's achievements and foreshadowed events to come:

> Mr. Amos Perry was much attracted by the Day Lilies, and devoted himself with skill, perseverance, and patience to the production of such fine flowers as E. A. Bowles, Flavia, Margaret Perry, Winnie Nightingale, and George Yeld, and with the arrival of *fulva rosea*, a wild Chinese variety, I've no doubt we shall see many new forms of a lighter or deeper red, and red is a colour which advertises itself.
>
> Some idea of the advance of the genus in numbers may be gained from the fact that I began in 1877 with less than half-a-dozen varieties [of *Hemerocallis*], and now I have upwards of 30 varieties of my own raising, while Mr. Perry, in his most interesting and informative catalogue, offers upwards of 100.
>
> To those who begin to cultivate the *Hemerocallis* with the help of this catalogue (what would it not have been to me in 1877!) I will venture to suggest the following plants as a first selection. . . .

He went on to list ten desirable plants in order of their price. The species *H. flava* (nowadays known as *H. Lilioasphodelus*), *H. aurantiaca* var. *major,* and Amos Perry's 1920 cultivar 'Margaret Perry' were regarded as inexpensive. A trio of English hybrids, including one of his own, and three of Dr. Stout's creations were "somewhat more expensive," and the Chinese species which he called *fulva rosea* was described as "naturally costly, since the plants are so few." "But," he continued, "the enthusiast, if I may speak for him, is glad to get it at any price." So reckless a statement from a mild-mannered—and no doubt ill-paid—schoolmaster suggests that the daylily "enthusiast" has changed little over the years. It also suggests that Yeld was a man of vision. He predicted that the plant he knew as *fulva rosea* would "revolutionize the genus," and it did.

Unfortunately, taxonomic confusion surrounds this important plant. In addition to *H. fulva rosea*, it is variously known as *H. fulva* var. *rosea*, 'Rosea', and by a number of other epithets. Today there are botanists who would like to see it given the status of a species, in which case its name would be *H. rosea*. All of which makes it impossible to resist the pun: A *rosea* by any other name would still have made daylily history. As Dr. Stout's views on the subject remain the most highly respected, my choice for the purposes of this book is the name he used, *H. fulva* var. *rosea*.

In Stout's book, which is still the definitive scientific work about the genus, he includes this plant among reddish orange types under the heading *"Fulvous Daylilies of Wild Origin."* While some dictionaries define the word *fulvous* as "dull yellow" or "tawny," he uses it to indicate the presence of reddish brown pigment. Fulvous plants shipped to him from Japan exhibited variations of this color. But some of the plants that came to him from China boasted "bright shades of pink and red." This departure in terms of color paved the way for exciting changes. Thanks to the Chinese connection, we now have wonderful shades of pink and melon. If such records had been kept, we would also find *H. fulva* var. *rosea* in the pedigree of nearly every red, purple, and white cultivar of the present day. Surprisingly, pink rather than yellow has given us white in daylilies.

Color was one obvious difference between the Japanese varieties of *H. fulva* and the beautiful pink and red newcomers from China. Less obvious but equally important was a biological difference. The pink form of *H. fulva* was a diploid. All plants have a specific number of chromosomes located in the nucleus of each cell, and most plants are diploids. That is, they have the full or unreduced number of chromosomes characteristic of the species. In daylilies the magic number is twenty-two. The union of two plants requires that each reduce the chromosomes in its reproductive cells so that the new individual will inherit half from one parent and half from the other. The reduction results in a haploid number of chromosomes, which in normal daylilies would be eleven. A compatible match of pollen grain and ovule would then restore the number to twenty-two.

All well and good. But *H. fulva* harbors a genetic peculiarity. It happens to have three sets of chromosomes instead of two. Plants with three sets are called triploids, and triploids are notoriously hard to breed. Occasionally, their thirty-three chromosomes divide in such a way that a few cells containing eleven occur. In the unlikely event that a triploid pollen grain containing eleven chromosomes came in contact with the ovule of a diploid daylily, fertilization could take place. But happy accidents of this kind are rare. Dr. Stout is reported to have made 7,137 crosses using *H. fulva* in order to get twenty-three mature seed pods containing a total of seventy seeds. The significance of *H. fulva* var. *rosea* was that, being a diploid, it was easy to use in breeding programs. For this reason, along with its lovely color, it seems safe to say that no single plant, before or since, has had such a profound effect on the modern daylily.

Sadly, George Yeld did not live to see his own seedlings of *H. fulva* var. *rosea* in bloom. However, Amos Perry carried on where Yeld left off. Like his predecessor, Perry began with a limited palette: *H. fulva*, which—not surprisingly—proved "hopeless" as a parent; *H. Lilioasphodelus*, the early-blooming lemon lily whose scented yellow flowers open one day and remain fresh well into the next; and *H. Thunbergii*, the summer-blooming yellow with abundant three-inch flowers and tall, well-branched scapes. *H. citrina* was a later addition. In this species, wandlike scapes hold aloft numerous pale yellow blossoms with long, narrow tepals fused to a two-inch tube. The total flower length can reach as much as seven inches. Fully opened, the spread of the segments is about equal to the length of the whole flower. A midsummer bloomer of unique form and unusual habit,

H. citrina unfurls its elongated buds late in the afternoon. The blossoms shed their subtle perfume on the night air, and then begin to fade, closing by noon the following day. Modern cultivars always remain open during the daylight hours and beyond sundown. They owe this longer day of beauty to the nocturnal *H. citrina* and to the extended-blooming *H. Lilioasphodelus*.

These species and a few others were the raw material from which Sprenger, Yeld, and Perry wrested such improvements as were then possible. By 1930, Perry cultivars were displaying much larger, more attractive flowers than their ancestors, but the colors were still confined to shades of yellow and orange. It was the arrival of *H. fulva* var. *rosea* at the New York Botanical Garden that brought a real breakthrough. Amos Perry was one of the fortunate breeders chosen by Dr. Stout to receive a division of this much sought-after plant. Perry describes its importance to his program in the diary which he compiled during World War II:

> Then came the wonderful discovery of *H. fulva rosea,* found by Dr. Albert N. Steward at Kuling in the province of Kiangsi, China. Crosses and hybrids of this new introduction have given some outstanding results, rendering nearly all my previous work negligible; it has produced so many fine varieties which are still under trial and several thousands to flower in 1943 and 1944. I have to face the most difficult period since I started in 1893—what to keep and what to destroy.

Amos Perry's Diary, from which this excerpt is taken, was far more than a nostalgic trip down memory lane. Privately published in 1946, it contains a detailed record of plants that he raised and introduced, with their origins and dates of introduction. It covers everything from ferns, alpines, and aquatics (he wrote a respected book on aquatic plants) to perennials suitable for herbaceous borders, and it includes extended sections on *Iris* and *Hemerocallis*. I was fortunate to receive photocopies of the portion on *Hemerocallis* from Mr. Perry's great-niece and even more fortunate to catch a glimpse of the man himself in a letter from his daughter-in-law.

Frances Everett Perry is an eminent horticulturist in her

own right. She trained at Swanley Horticultural College in Kent during the twenties, at a time when women gardeners were rare. In those days, most nurseries simply did not want women. But Amos Perry took a chance on Ms. Everett. And he was not sorry. Nor was his son, Gerald, who married her in 1930. She remembers her father-in-law with warmth. "He was," she wrote, "the lively humorous man you imagined."

Much as "hem" fans might want to claim Amos Perry as their own, he belongs to everyone who loves perennials. He founded the most famous British nursery of its day, the Hardy Plant Farm of Enfield, where he grew and hybridized an enormous range of plants. Many American gardeners still know and grow Siberian irises with names like 'Perry's Blue'. This plant was introduced in 1916 and has been a favorite in my perennial border for years. Perry was also a champion of native American plants and appreciated their virtues before most American gardeners. His catalog offered our woodland phlox (*Phlox divaricata* subsp. *laphamii*), white gayfeather (*Liatris scariosa* 'Alba'), and many different color forms of beebalm (*Monarda didyma*).

If Perry's achievements in the field of daylily hybridization pale beside those of Dr. A. B. Stout, it must be remembered that Perry was not a research botanist with an institution behind him. He was a hardworking nurseryman with a wife and seven children to feed. He had a business to run and numerous other plant enthusiasms. But for that period his daylily cultivars were impressive in quality and number. In all, he introduced more than two hundred, and in recognition for his work on the genus *Hemerocallis*, he was awarded the Veitch Memorial Medal in 1950. But like George Yeld before him, Amos Perry cared less for the glittering prizes than for the excitement of seeing a new seedling in bloom. In the introduction to his diary he wrote:

> To those who succeed me — and indeed all young and ambitious horticulturists — I commend this Diary as an encouragement, for they will find cross-breeding, raising of the subsequent seed, resulting in flowers totally distinct from either of its parents, a delight

which has no equal. Not that commercial profit always results; the interest and pleasure far transcends financial gain.

Amos Perry and George Yeld were the original daylily people and deserve to be remembered. Let us leave these kindred spirits together on a warm summer afternoon in 1935. Late in life, Yeld had moved from York to the outskirts of London where Perry paid him a long-deferred visit. Perry's son Reginald recalled the meeting for a British publication called *The Gardeners' Chronicle:*

> The Hemerocallis were a wonderful sight when my father and I visited Mr. Yeld's garden at Gerrards' Cross toward the end of July. Our journey would have been worthwhile just to have spent an hour or two with this wonderful old gentleman ... but there was the added interest of beautiful flowers.
>
> Over 40 years ago at the York Flower Show, my father promised Mr. Yeld to pay a visit to his garden, and until lately that promise was unfulfilled. Mr. Yeld, at 93, is still as keen, especially with regard to Hemerocallis and irises, as he was 40 years ago. He was impatiently waiting to receive us, for we were a little late arriving. The greetings were warm but brief, for the two enthusiasts were anxious to compare and discuss the results of many years work with the Hemerocallis family. I, the youngest of the trio by many years, found it difficult to keep pace with them in their excited dashes from one group of plants to another.

The two pioneer breeders of daylilies left behind many traces of their personal lives. Beloved by generations of students, Yeld was greatly mourned at his death in 1938. His friend G. P. Barker eulogized him in ornate prose: "A man of a nature entirely unselfish, pure and lofty, I have never known him to say an intentionally unkind word about a single human being." Another friend pronounced him "an altogether charming man, modest, generous, humorous and well-read." From these descriptions and other contemporary accounts, the portrait emerges of a kindly, agreeable man who loved sports, history, and travel, adored gardening, and occasionally indulged in a round of golf.

When Amos Perry died in 1953, tributes filled British newspapers and gardening publications. One of the most heartfelt

and endearing appeared in the *Iris Yearbook* (the quarterly publication of the British Iris Society, of which he was a member). It
described him as "a man of small stature" with unbounded vitality and energy. "No one could talk to him for five minutes on
any subject connected with gardens and plants without being
infected with his enthusiasm, as well as being impressed with his
profound knowledge and experience in every branch of horticulture. Some of the giants have been forgotten or are remembered by a very few, but Amos Perry had claims to be remembered by many for his achievements."

Perry was survived by a large extended family and by his
second wife, whom he married in 1945. His first wife, the mother of his two sons and five daughters, died before World War II.
His legacy included the record of his horticultural life in *Amos
Perry's Diary* and a host of admirers, among them the colleague
who wrote: "Affectionately known as 'the Guv'nor' by all who
worked at the nursery, he was never too busy to enlighten those
who showed an interest in any plant, and was happy to give a
few relevant facts about the history and requirements of his
treasures which he knew and loved so well."

Dr. Stout

Dr. A. B. Stout

The year before his death, Dr. A. B. Stout wrote his own obituary. It was brisk in tone and factual in content. "His main technical research," it stated, "was concerned with experimental studies on the nature and genetics of intraspecific self and cross-incompatibilities in the sexual reproduction of flowering plants." It enumerated his horticultural and scientific awards and recalled the two research projects for which he was best known—the hybridization of daylilies and the development of hardy seedless grapes. The chronicle of his life was reduced to a mere skeleton, concluding with the mention of surviving family members, "his widow, Zelda, a daughter, Dr. Elizabeth B. Rausch, a granddaughter, Jane Elizabeth Rausch, and a brother, C. D. Stout." Had I not been fortunate enough to locate Elizabeth Rausch, I might never have discovered that a nine-year-old son, A. B. Stout, Jr., had died of polio in 1925. Indeed, without the insights of Dr. Rausch and access to family photographs, my impression of her father would have been quite different.

By all accounts, Dr. Stout was a dedicated scientist but not a gregarious man. William J. Robbins of the New York Botanical Garden praised his single-mindedness. "Hours meant nothing to him. He asked only for the opportunity to devote his energies to those important unsolved problems which had aroused his curiosity." His colleagues found him reserved and businesslike, and one acquaintance described him later in life as "a starchy old gentleman." While his daughter remembers him with fondness and respect, he could not be described as a demonstrative father, and after the death of his only son, he retreated further into his work. At home, he sought refuge in his garden. Here lay the key to this reticent man.

Elizabeth Rausch sent me a photograph of their backyard taken in the thirties. Laboring in his shirtsleeves, Dr. Stout had prepared the unwilling clay soil, laying out beds around the perimeter of the long, narrow lot, ingeniously incorporating the existing trees into the design. An oak, even then a large specimen, stood at the head of one of the center beds. At the far end, another shaded a stretch of perennial border running along the northern edge of the property. Judging from the photograph, it must have been late May or early June because the peonies have fat round buds and the early daylilies are in their full glory. There are Siberian irises, bearded irises, alliums, and the promise of summer phlox. Shrubs—evergreen and deciduous—give the beds authority, and the formal layout provides a framework for the burgeoning plant material. It was a beautiful garden.

Whatever else Dr. Stout may have been, he was a superlative gardener. He even wrote a book about gardening to introduce schoolchildren to its pleasures. All of which—for me, at least—explains his devotion to a daylily breeding program that did little to advance his scientific career. There is even evidence that he had his detractors at the New York Botanical Garden, and that some people felt the daylilies occupied too much of his time. But that is all water under the bridge, and no one living can say for sure. While he planned and directed extensive projects on other genera and made substantial contributions to agriculture, his work with *Hemerocallis* has earned him a place in horticultural history. And in the daylily world, his name will always be revered.

In *Arlow Burdette Stout: An Autobiography,* the author reveals himself sparingly. If only he had been as forthcoming as his brother! Claude D. Stout provides us with a possibly unreliable but far more colorful picture of their shared youth, each incident fattened up with anecdote and personal detail. In his own version, A. B. Stout recounts an event which exacerbated the struggle to finance his education. "I saved $300.00 which were on deposit in a bank and I planned to enter the State Normal School at Whitewater, Wisconsin in the autumn of 1898. But before that time arrived, the bank failed due to the defalcation of the cashier who fled to Canada and there lived in immunity."

Now, Claude had much more to say about this treachery. We learn that the cashier, one Burnham, by name, kept two sets of books. A falsified set was regularly produced for the auditor, while the incriminating set remained hidden. But one day, unbeknownst to Burnham, who had taken the afternoon off, the auditor missed his train. "Obliged to remain in town until the evening, he casually dropped in at the bank. On inspecting the vault, the books showing the true condition of the affairs of the bank were discovered cleverly tucked away in an obscure corner. Burnham fled to Canada and brother Bert's money was gone."

In 1971, Claude, then a retired attorney, prepared his own version of Dr. Stout's early life for the Albion, Wisconsin, Academy Historical Society. He also sent a copy to William C. Steere, who was then President of the New York Botanical Garden. Besides discursive footnotes to *An Autobiography*, Claude contributed recollections of his own. Five years Bert's junior and touchingly proud of his older brother, he depicts scenes from their childhood in which "Brother Bert" invariably plays a stellar role.

On one occasion, the boys were investigating a large oval hornet's nest suspended in an oak tree a few feet from the ground. Anxious to determine its method of construction, Bert crept up to the nest and plugged the entrance hole, instructing his younger brother to cut through the branch above the nest. But while Claude was manfully sawing away with his jackknife, a group of hornets that had left home earlier returned:

In the excitement, fearing that I would be stung and he blamed, Bert dropped the plug and more angry hornets poured out. He cried to me to get away and he started to run. I dropped to the ground, rolled over and over away from danger and crouched safely behind the body of the tree. The angry hornets pursued the fleeing culprit, striking his back protected only by a thin shirt with the impact of a bullet. A few rods away was a five-foot rail fence which he cleared at one bound and rolled over and over in the adjoining hay field in intense agony. But he never was willing to give up what he undertook. A few days later during a continued spell of heavy rain, we went with a saw and step ladder, smoked the naughty insects into submission and carried away the nest.

Once the hard-earned trophy was in hand, the budding naturalist cut it apart in order to study the behavior and life-style of the former inhabitants.

Recalled when Claude was over eighty, his memories have the appeal of old sepia-tone snapshots. My favorite shows Brother Bert with an uncanny understanding of wildlife capturing and bringing home pet squirrels for the younger boy. "So familiar was he with the habits of such wild creatures that he knew just when to take the baby squirrels from their nest so that they could be fed with a medicine dropper." While vignettes like this have a glow of nostalgia, they also have the ring of truth. And Dr. Stout did not underestimate their importance in his life.

I cherish many memories of home, school and social life in the humble and wholesome setting of the rural community of Albion, Wisconsin. At an early age there were chores for me; then came light labor in the care of a vegetable garden, and my mother was one of the best of gardeners; and later there were long days of hard work on the farm. But in that community honest labor was dignified; it brought not only the necessities but the pleasures of life; it was the privilege of everyone except unfortunates.

At that time at least three-fourths of the region about our home was uncultivated. There was a mosaic of virgin areas of prairie, lowland meadows, swamps and woodlands of several types. There were meandering creeks, larger streams to the size of Rock River and ponds and lakes, the largest of which was Lake Koshkonong. Plants and animals were diverse and abundant. To me it was a fairyland and almost every spare hour and day in all seasons throughout the years from the age of 10, I spent afield. I hunted, fished and

trapped; I spent much time learning by direct observation as much
as possible about the plants, animals (especially birds), rocks, fossils
and Indian mounds of the area.

There is an old saying that the life of a writer makes dull
reading; the same might be said about the life of a scientist. But
if we are looking for the real Dr. Stout, he is present in this
glimpse of an otherwise self-contained youth who harbored a
passion for the natural world. In his own words and in those of
his brother, the qualities that served Arlow Burdette Stout so
well for the rest of his life were demonstrated at an early age:
the scientist's keen powers of observation and intense need to
know—tempered with patience and perserverance. Fortunately
for lovers of the modern daylily, Stout brought these qualities to
the New York Botanical Garden in 1911 and put them at the
disposal of the genus *Hemerocallis*. As Claude would later
observe, "Brother Bert was most certainly the right man in the
right place for the thirty-six years he worked at the Garden."

In order to understand what Stout accomplished during
those years, we need to look back at daylily history through a
wide-angle lens. At the time young Bert began pondering the
mysterious behavior of the tawny daylily, George Yeld was at
last seeing results from nearly twenty years of hybridizing.
'Apricot' had recently burst upon the scene, winning the Award
of Merit in 1892 and launching the hybrid daylily as a desirable
garden plant. Meanwhile, Amos Perry—only five years older
than Stout—was hard at work on his first crosses, finally intro-
ducing a named cultivar in 1900.

Nine years after that milestone, Stout received a bachelor of
arts degree from the University of Wisconsin, having the day
before married a wife sympathetic to his scientific ambitions.
Two years later, the couple moved to New York. Dr. Stout—as
he was known to colleagues and even to friends—took up the
post of Director of Laboratories at the New York Botanical
Garden and forthwith embarked on his investigations into the
guilty genetic secret of *Hemerocallis fulva*. He began by assem-
bling the most complete collection of plants then available, and
from that day forward, the daylily was on its way to horticultur-

al success. During his tenure at the New York Botanical Garden, he methodically laid the groundwork upon which the breeding program of every modern hybridizer rests.

His first cultivars were the result of experiments. As a scientist, his chief field of interest centered on problems of sterility and the processes of reproduction. But at the same time he was cracking the code of *H. fulva* and laying bare its wily, triploid soul, he was producing seedlings with distinct garden merit. He also discovered during the course of his investigations that the limited flower colors of the species could "be broken up, recombined, and even intensified through hybridization, thus producing an increased diversity and yielding new forms of special interest and value to the flower-grower."

The next logical step was overall improvement of the genus. The collection of species and hybrids he had established provided a gene bank upon which to draw for breeding purposes. Preliminary work had, of course, been done by Yeld and Perry. *H. aurantiaca*, with its characteristically evergreen foliage, was already conferring this trait on some of Yeld's hybrids—which Dr. Stout quickly acquired for the collection. *H. citrina* and *H. Lilioasphodelus* had bestowed upon Perry's first cultivar their genetic capacity to lengthen the hours of bloom. But so far, improvements had been modest indeed.

Nothing before or since has equaled the range and magnitude of the Stout program. In fact, no other major scientific investigation of the genus *Hemerocallis* has been undertaken. As for its horticultural implications, they boggle the mind. In 1925, he wrote: "When compared with such groups of plants as the dahlias, the roses, and the irises the flowers of the available day lilies taken collectively are lacking in diversity of color and form. Their improvement along these lines has been the chief aim of the breeding work undertaken at the New York Botanical Garden." Think of today's hybrids with their glorious colors; their edges of silver and gold; their range of sizes, shapes, and styles; their frills and furbelows. Then recall a swath of orange daylilies growing along some country road and marvel at the phenomenon that literally had it roots in a midwestern dooryard.

Dr. Stout did not, of course, accomplish this transformation single-handedly. He had a labor force at his command and the scientific resources of an institution behind him. He also had an invaluable associate in Dr. Albert Newton Steward. In the early twenties, Steward, a graduate of Oregon State College with advanced degrees in botany from Harvard, was invited to teach at the University of Nanking in China. At that time, the gates of the Chinese empire had long since been pried open, but few Westerners were made to feel welcome. Dr. Steward, however, won the friendship and confidence of the Chinese people. Taking up his post in August 1921, he immediately immersed himself, and later his family, in the social and intellectual life of the country. The acceptance of the Stewards by their Chinese hosts was explained by botanist Dr. Shiu-ying Hu. As a very young woman, Dr. Hu studied with Dr. Steward and knew the family well.

> While in Nanking the Stewards' home was the meeting ground of people of all ages and backgrounds. During that period, half of China's botanists were Dr. Steward's students. Those who did not study with him were his friends. The Stewards respected the Chinese people and in return they received love and trust. By cultivating the friendship of the people Steward was able to reach the gardens of the rich as well as approaching the farms of the poor. He was able to obtain what the botanical explorers did not even have a chance to see. The establishment of the Steward-Stout connection was just ideal for the development of the knowledge of *Hemerocallis*.

It is interesting to speculate on the course of daylily history had the partners in the Chinese connection been reversed. Could the diffident Dr. Stout have won the affection of the Chinese and overcome their suspicion of foreigners? It seems doubtful. But fortunately, Dr. Steward succeeded. He was allowed to travel freely and was invited to collect plants and seed in places that were out of bounds to other Western plant hunters. In addition to exploring the countryside outside of Nanking, he made collecting trips to Shantung, a mountainous region bordering the Yellow Sea, and to the inland provinces of Honan and Kiangsi. Three plants of history-making *Hemerocallis fulva* var. *rosea* were gathered near Kuling in Kiangsi and arrived at the New York Botanical Garden in 1924.

A year later, an elated Dr. Stout received from Steward ten plants of an entirely new species, *H. multiflora*—the many-flowered daylily. "One outstanding character of this species is the rather large number of flowers which a scape may bear. The scapes are, as a rule, abundantly branched above and thus a single scape may produce as many as one hundred flowers during the entire season of bloom." For a large, well-established plant, Stout calculated there might be several scapes, each boasting from thirty to a hundred flowers which would open over a period of up to ten weeks.

This new species possessed another appealing trait—a succession of flowers beginning late in August and continuing until severe frost. Stout was quick to appreciate the horticultural possibilities of the new addition. "It is the hope that the desirable characteristics of *H. multiflora,* such as long period of blooming, numerous flowers to a scape, and late blooming, will appear among the offspring in combinations that give somewhat new types of daylilies for garden culture."

In 1930, nine plants of yet another new species passed through the hands of Dr. Steward on their way to the New York Botanical Garden and into the open arms of Dr. Stout. Allegedly collected in Kiangsi from the romantic-sounding "Purple-Enshrouded Mountain," *H. altissima* proved to be another late bloomer—August and September—and the tallest of all species of *Hemerocallis.* Its branched scapes soar to six feet or more and bear many slender, pale yellow trumpets which grace the night. This nocturnal giant was welcomed into the fold and was immediately crossed with the day-blooming *H. multiflora.*

Apparently the results of this cross stunned even the unflappable Dr. Stout. First-generation offspring towered over his head, and Stout, who was not a small man, was forced to look up at his creations. However, he had succeeded in creating a new race of tall, late-flowering daylilies which remained open during the day. "Thus far," he admitted, "none of these seedlings can be considered good enough for distribution for cultivation in gardens, but they give promise of worthy hybrids for the future."

Shipments of daylilies from Dr. Steward were forthcoming until 1940. In 1942, Dr. Stout assessed the value of the twenty-year China connection in the *Journal of The New York Botanical Garden:*

> The native flora of China has supplied several of the most distinctive of the earlier known species of the genus *Hemerocallis*.
> Recent introductions of living plants from China have continued to provide new species and botanical varieties which greatly increase the diversity of this relatively small genus and provide noteworthy characters of value in the development of new classes and clones of horticultural daylilies.

By this time, every horticulturally important species of *Hemerocallis* and every available cultivar of garden merit had been brought together by Dr. Stout. The stage was set for the emergence of an entirely new race of daylilies—forerunners of today's cultivars. But it would be unjust to measure Stout's contributions to the genus *Hemerocallis* solely in terms of horticulture. He was, after all, a scientist, and as such was responsible for the botanical debut of at least two new species. Had it not been for Dr. Steward on the spot and Dr. Stout at the New York Botanical Garden, *H. multiflora* and *H. altissima* might have continued to languish namelessly in the wild.

A plant without a botanical name, no matter how familiar to the local citizenry, has no scientific standing. For purposes of science, a species does not exist until specimens have been studied and a clear, concise botanical description has been set down in writing. Then, to clinch the plants botanical acceptance, the description must be validly published in a recognized botanical journal. Dr. Stout conferred this favor upon the two species mentioned and upon *H. exaltata* (which may, according to later scientists, be a form of *H. fulva*).

There are, of course, divergent opinions on the subject of naturally occurring species. Modern botanists are still wrangling about taxonomy, and there may easily be wild daylily populations distinct enough to be considered new species growing in remote areas of the Far East. In addition, there are natives of Japan and Korea which never found their way to the New York Botanical Garden in Dr. Stout's day, and therefore escaped his penetrating eye and powers of scientific analysis. For this reason, *H. hakunensis* and others have had no impact on the modern daylily. Nor did Stout use in his breeding program every species that he received. He singled out the few that would contribute something of value to horticulture. And indeed, he wrought such enormous improvements that by the time he retired in 1948, hybridizers no longer gave the wild species so much as a backward glance.

Incontestably, Dr. Arlow Burdette Stout is the Father of the Modern Daylily, but Dr. Albert Steward must be considered a close relation, and Bertrand H. Farr of the Farr Nursery Company, a generous, indulgent courtesy uncle. Mr. Farr came to horticulture relatively late in life. A pianist of considerable gifts, he was sent as a young man to the New England Conservatory of Music in Boston. While there, he appears to have spent a good deal of his time at the local arboretum. From this exposure, he developed an affection for plants which he eventually parlayed into a flourishing business—the famous Pennsylvania nursery that bore his name.

At a crucial period in daylily history, Dr. Stout was driven into the arms of the Farr Nursery Company. The New York Botanical Garden had adopted the position that as a scientific and educational institution, it could not justify the propagation of new daylilies for sale or general distribution. Fortunately, Bertrand Farr was interested in Stout's program and agreed to grow and propagate his seedlings with a view to eventually selling named Stout cultivars. Under the terms of the agreement, Stout cultivars would not be released until enough stock was on hand to keep the price down to $3 a division.

Accepting this arrangement was altruistic of Mr. Farr. Hundreds of the seedlings in his care would never qualify for introduction, but they would still require attention and occupy space at the nursery for several years during the trial period. A year after reaching the understanding with Stout, Farr died. But the nursery honored the agreement, and for more than thirty years continued to assist with the evaluation and the ultimate distribution of Dr. Stout's named hybrids.

At the time of Stout's death in 1957, the Farr Nursery Company had introduced eighty-three of his cultivars. (One, 'Jubilee', named in 1926, was withdrawn as being insufficiently winter hardy.) According to a letter from the nursery's treasurer to the New York Botanical Garden, Stout had transferred his collection and his latest crosses to the nursery on his retirement, but until 1955 he came during the summers to evaluate his seedlings. Twelve of his selections "from a new race of doubles which he developed from mutations during 30 years of assembly" were introduced after his death. Half the proceeds from the sale of these doubles went to Stout's widow. A note in the Farr Catalog of 1957 read: "Therefore, please supply two checks or money orders in equal amounts when remitting. One to Farr Nursery Company. One to Mrs. Zelda Stout."

Stout himself never accepted any money for the sale of his cultivars. His royalties went into a fund at the New York Botanical Garden to finance his research and to establish the Stout Medal, which was awarded for the first time in 1950. This medal is the highest honor a daylily cultivar can receive. Votes are cast by accredited Garden Judges of the American Hemerocallis Society and in order to win, a cultivar must gain the largest number of all votes cast. Lest modern daylily hybridizers forget the contribution of Bertrand Farr, a silver medal perpetuates his memory. It is awarded annually to an individual who has achieved distinguished results in the field of daylily hybridizing. Dr. A. B. Stout was the first recipient.

Stout died at his Pleasantville, New York, home on October 12, 1957. For a dozen years, his widow continued to live in the house on Grove Street, but in 1969 it became apparent that she could no longer do so. Over ninety and in frail health, she came to Florida to be near her daughter. Soon afterward, Elizabeth Rausch sold the house and donated her father's books, manuscripts, and papers to the New York Botanical Garden.

She has never been back. "Since then, I've been in Pleasantville a couple of times," she says. "But I've always made sure not to go by the house because I'm sure I would be very unhappy."

Pleasantville is an aptly named commuter town twenty miles north of New York City with maple-shaded residential streets, two prosperous commercial streets, and a landscaped railway station. In years past, the railroad was the raison d'être of the town. Seventy-three-year-old Salvador Moreno, who lives in the Stouts' old neighborhood, remembers those days. "When I was a little kid, there were a lot more commuters because companies hadn't started moving out to Westchester County. Back then, practically everybody from Pleasantville commuted." I could easily imagine Dr. Stout briskly walking the short distance from his home to the station to catch the 8:20 A.M. train.

Edgewood Avenue, where Mr. Moreno lives, is lined with large, rambling, turn-of-the-century houses with ample porches and small front yards. Overhead, the huge street trees meet to form a dense canopy of leaves in the summer and a network of bare branches in the winter; underfoot, the tree roots are beginning to crack the sidewalks. When the Moreno family moved here in 1923, the population was five thousand. "And it's only about six thousand now. The area is small, one-point-seven square miles, and it was fully developed by the mid-twenties. It hasn't changed that much. It has always been a very cohesive community: The merchants are fine; the neighbors are fine." He remembers the Stouts well. "There was a very bright daughter, Elizabeth. In fact, she went on and got a Ph.D. [Actually, she graduated from Cornell University Medical College and became a physician.] Her mother did a lot with the Girl Scouts, and Dr. Stout served on one of the volunteer committees in the community. I think it was the planning commission. I was working for the village at one time, and I knew him then. Just to say hello in passing. He was such a pleasant man, a real nice guy. In fact, all the dogwood trees here in Pleasantville were planted by him many, many years ago. He did a lot."

Grove Street intersects with Edgewood Avenue and is very similar in character, only the houses are smaller. Number four is the corner house at the opposite end, where Grove meets busy Manville Road. The railway station is two blocks away. On a recent visit, I parked my car opposite the Stouts' former home, having recognized it at once from an old snapshot—a modest frame house with a pair of oversized dormer windows and a front porch running the width of the facade. It bore an eerie resemblance to another faded snapshot of the Stout homestead in Albion, Wisconsin. The faithful Claude had furnished copies of both to the New York Botanical Garden for their files.

Mr. Moreno had told me the place was a shambles, and it was. The rotting front porch was cluttered with plastic toys and battered outdoor furniture, and the roof was in need of repair. In the front yard, an aggressive euonymus had taken over the remains of the yew hedge. But an attempt had been made at a little garden, and a few daylilies competed valiantly with the weeds. Suddenly a car drew into the driveway—two parallel cement tracks down to a dilapidated one-car garage. I was embarrassed suddenly to be confronted by the present owner.

Once I had explained the purpose of my visit, the young woman was cordial. She said she did know that a Dr. Stout had once lived there, but she couldn't seem to think what he had done. I mentioned daylilies, but she misunderstood. "I planted those," she said quickly, gesturing toward the patch of garden. The place had been a wreck when she and her husband had bought the property four years ago. Before that it had been rented to a group of young people who had "torn it apart." I asked if she would mind my looking at the backyard before I left. She shrugged. "We haven't been able to do anything outside yet," she said. "But go ahead, if you want to. Grass won't grow. It's too dark, but my husband bought a secondhand tractor, and we're going to start clearing the brush. You can still see where there used to be flower beds."

The oak, enormous now and supporting a climbing hydrangea that reached high up into the crown, shaded one end of the deep, narrow lot, and large maples shaded the other. In between, a little jungle of saplings had grown up in what remained of the beds. But I sensed the presence of noble ghosts in this overgrown backyard: 'Theron', the first red daylily with the blood of recalcitrant *H. fulva* in its veins; tall 'Chancellor' and 'Statuesque' from *H. altissima;* late-bloomers 'August Glow' and 'August Orange' from *H. multiflora;* coral pink 'Charmine Queen' from prized *H. fulva* var. *rosea;* and dozens more. The original plants are gone. But Dr. Stout's legacy endures in the genetic heritage of today's cultivars.

Birthplace of the Modern Daylily

The New York Botanical Garden is a 250-acre oasis of rolling lawns and trees in the heart of the Bronx, New York City's northernmost borough. Overhead, sleek jets bear down on La Guardia and Kennedy airports, and an endless stream of traffic roars along the main thoroughfares that encircle the grounds. Kazimiroff Boulevard wraps around from the west and joins Southern Boulevard. Beyond Southern Boulevard lies a teeming Little Italy. This is one neighborhood that Dr. Stout would still recognize. In the warren of residential streets, small single-family homes stand companionably cheek by jowl; commercial buildings are no more than two or three stories high; and church festivals here are celebrated with colorful parades. In the summer, shops spill their wares out onto the sidewalk, and the air is redolent of vegetables, fruit, and flowers.

Opposite the Botanical Garden's Mosholu Gate is the railway station at which Stout arrived each morning. While the station is probably much the same—except for new graffiti—nearby Mosholu Parkway has suffered many changes. What must once have been a gracious boulevard is now a strip of worn, tree-studded grass dividing six lanes of speeding cars. More struggling grass and barriers of trees check the tide of urban development that threatens to engulf the Parkway on either side. At certain times of day, crowds of high school students jaywalk nonchalantly across the traffic to the tune of squealing brakes. Serene in the midst of all the hurly-burly, the great rotunda of the New York Botanical Garden's museum building rises in the distance. Before the new library was built, Dr. Stout had an office beneath the Italian Renaissance–style dome. From this vantage point, he could look down on the most important collection of daylilies ever assembled.

Installed in 1933 on a gently sloping bank northwest of the museum building, the planting was laid out in six tiers facing the entrance to the Mosholu Parkway. The beds were designed to repeat the slightly curving line of the highway—Kazimiroff Boulevard—lying at the foot of the slope. In an article for *The Journal of the New York Botanical Garden,* Stout described the plan of the new daylily garden with more than characteristic enthusiasm:

> This arrangement gives a compact grouping and allows definite arrangements for ready comparison, which are desired features in a display which is primarily educational. But the variations in the size of the beds and the alignments combine to give a more pleasing effect than when the same number of square or rectangular beds are evenly spaced. Also the plan conforms to the contours of the site, which slopes gently from rear to the front and from the sides to the line of the central row, which forms the axis of the garden.

The garden was spread out against the hillside in the shape of a fan, with six horizontal bands of daylilies divided by narrow paths—the paths representing the ribs of the fan. The central axis was made up of six relatively small beds which contained representatives of all the known species of *Hemerocallis.* Named hybrids occupied long beds on either side, arching away from the center. Planted in bold clumps and already one hundred strong, these early named cultivars must have made a traffic-stopping sight viewed head-on from the Mosholu Parkway. Amos Perry was well represented by members of his family: orange-yellow 'Marcus Perry'; cadmium yellow 'Margaret Perry'; 'Iris Perry', reputedly the color of "a tawny fox," and rose-bronze 'Gladys Perry'.

From George Yeld, there was 'Apricot' and empire-yellow 'Winsome'. The still popular lemon yellow 'Hyperion' by Franklin Mead of Fort Wayne, Indiana, shared pride of place with Stout's own cultivars, among them the ground-breaking red 'Theron' and pink 'Charmaine', forerunner of 'Charmine Queen'.

Other beds in this hillside planting contained promising seedlings from experimental crosses made between two or more species, and plants raised from seed collected in the wild. Another bed was devoted entirely to *H. fulva* in all its cheerful guises, including the handsome double-flowered forms. While there is no record of their origins, tawny daylilies with extra segments were already popular in Japanese gardens during the eighteenth century and first appeared in European gardens a hundred years later. Two types arrived at the New York Botanical Garden during those early days: one with solid green leaves, the other with white-streaked foliage. The variegated form rejoiced in the name *H. fulva* 'Kwanso Flore-Pleno'; the solid form was known simply as 'Kwanso'. Taken all together, these novelties of garden origin, the species, and the greatly improved cultivars made up a remarkable display of daylilies. Even Dr. Stout, who was not given to exaggeration, concluded that the new daylily garden represented "without doubt the most complete collection of these plants thus far assembled."

As pageantry always has a purpose at a botanical institution, the daylily garden was intended to instruct as well as to impress. Stout already foresaw the day when enthusiastic hybridizers would begin producing a steady stream of new cultivars. And he felt that by acquiring as many as possible for comparison and putting them together in one place, the Garden was offering a public service.

It thus enables gardeners and nurserymen to become acquainted with the numerous daylilies and affords opportunity for the evaluation of the different kinds according to merit and class. This is a need which is strongly felt among growers today, because the horticultural group of daylilies is now in that stage of development which is characterized by a somewhat rapid and indiscriminate increase of clonal varieties, many of which have no distinctive merit.

In the four years between the time the Display Garden was first planted and 1937 when it was relocated along a nearby path, the number of named cultivars (in those days called clones) had increased by ninety-nine—a minuscule number by modern standards but enough to prompt the typically prescient Dr. Stout to note: "With so many new plants on the market some are bound to be much alike and the average gardener is not always able to recognize their distinctive characters."

The original Stout collection was maintained at least until 1950. Although he had retired by this time and had removed many of his best plants to the backyard of his Pleasantville home, he took an active interest in the display beds along the path west of the museum building. In a memo to Thomas H. Everett, who was Assistant Director of Horticulture at that time, Dr. Stout listed the contents of each bed. He drew special attention to one that contained several unnamed wild species "of much value in the further naming of species. I am still studying these and have full notes on the origins." What became of these plants, history does not, alas, relate. Eventually the collection was dispersed around the grounds and much of it was lost.

However, in 1958, during one of the Botanical Garden's periodic face-lifts, a new planting of daylilies was undertaken. For this display, a site adjacent to the Magnolia Grove was chosen. The year before he died, the retired Dr. Stout had personally chosen thirty of his best cultivars for this new daylily garden: 'Jennie Love', his most recent pink, introduced in 1956; the rose-red 'Allan-A-Dale', named for Robin Hood's dashing young henchman; and 'Penelope Stout', an unusual blend of colors including coral red and buff.

Penelope, I learned from Dr. Stout's daughter, was the matriarch of the large Stout clan. This stalwart woman came to the New World from Holland in 1640. Upon arrival, she was attacked by Indians and left for dead. But an Indian from a more hospitable tribe rescued her, nursed her back to health, and sent her on her way. Her destination was New York, where she married one Richard Stout and proceeded to raise an enormous brood of children. It is sad to relate that the flower bear-

ing her name disappeared when other projects eclipsed the
daylily plantings at the Botanical Garden. But Dr. Stout's cultivars were restored to a place of prominence a few years later,
thanks to Dr. Currier McEwen and the Long Island Daylily
Society.

If the name Currier McEwen, M.D., is familiar to you, it
may be that you are a physician who knows it from New York
University's School of Medicine, where Dr. McEwen was dean
for many years. If you are a gardener, you probably grow either
Siberian iris (*Iris sibirica*) or Japanese iris (*I. ensata*), in which
case you speak the name McEwen in tones of hushed awe. This
is the man who wrote definitive books on both species,
hybridized 'Raspberry Rimmed', the first tetraploid Japanese
iris, and established an international reputation as an expert on
these plants. Nor is he a stranger to the species *Hemerocallis*.

In 1954, he was, by his own account, very busy with absorb-
ing work and "no gardener." But a catalog from Schreiner's
Gardens, specializing in *Iris* and *Hemerocallis*, appeared by mistake at McEwen's Riverdale, New York, home. "I glanced
through it," he said, "and it was full of pretty pictures. The first
thing I knew, I'd ordered some irises and a few daylilies. That's
how I got into it—with no more planning or thought than that.
But when I do get into things, I jump in with both feet. So when
I noticed in the catalog that it suggested one should join the Iris
and Hemerocallis Societies, I did.

"In the first *Daylily Journal* that came to me, there was some
interesting material about hybridizing, and that's how I got
started. In the same *Journal*, there was an article by Dr. Stout,
and I discovered that he was at the Botanical Garden, so I just
picked up the phone that day and asked him if I could come up
and talk to him—get his advice. And he kindly said I could."

When Dr. McEwen got to the Botanical Garden, he learned
that Stout was out in his experimental garden. "There he was
with a big truck and an Italian helper, and he was going around
digging up plants and throwing them on the truck. It turned out
that I had come on his last day there—his very last day. He was
cleaning out the garden for his successor, whose research did

not involve daylilies. As we talked, Tony, the gardener, kept throwing things up on the truck. Then, all of a sudden, Dr. Stout said, 'Oh, Tony, let's give some of these to the doctor.' And I ended up at home that day with my car filled with one plant each of all the ones that he thought were his best."

The two men never met again. But after Stout's death, Dr. McEwen urged the Long Island Daylily Society to establish a memorial Display Garden on the grounds of the New York Botanical Garden. By October 1964, work on the site was well under way, and Dr. McEwen had inspected it. "Last Sunday," he wrote to Mr. Everett, "I drove over to the garden and saw the fine work which has already been done in getting the beds ready. I think the layout is excellent." The location and setting were perfect. In the eighteenth century, the Lorillard family of French Huguenot descent built a palatial stone mansion on this knoll overlooking the surrounding woods and fields. When Dr. Stout arrived at the Botanical Garden in 1911, the mansion was still intact, but in the early twenties, it suffered fire damage and was subsequently torn down, leaving a level grassy spot. Here in a semicircular garden with a trimmed hornbeam hedge (*Carpinus Betulus*) as a background, four beds approximately six feet by seventy feet had been readied for the daylilies — many of which were to be provided by the Long Island Daylily Society. Others were donated by Gilbert H. Wild & Son, Inc., of Sarcoxie, Missouri, with instructions that "the surplus of these daylilies in the distant future can be used in landscaping the New York Botanical Gardens or given to another park or something...."

Members of the Long Island Daylily Society helped plant their own contributions in the late spring of 1966. At that time, the collection included forty-seven Stout hybrids and cultivars from fifty-six other hybridizers. And plans were afoot for a bed "of special historical interest" which would contain examples of the species from which Stout had derived some of his introductions. Another bed was intended to contain Stout Medal winners down through the years arranged in chronological order. By midsummer, Dr. McEwen was able to note with pride that the plants were in place and a reasonably good display could be expected by the following year. "But the garden will not," he wrote, "reach its peak until 1968 when we hope it will attract many of the 185,000 people who visit the Botanical Garden at daylily season each year."

For a time after that, daylilies and the reputation of Dr. Stout flourished at the New York Botanical Garden. However, institutions have shifting priorities and short memories. In the mid-1970s, all available manpower was siphoned off outdoor projects and directed toward the renovation of the conservatory, a gigantic turn-of-the-century valentine of glass and wrought iron. Everything became secondary to restoring this Crystal Palace of the Bronx. The grounds were neglected, and the daylilies fell upon evil times. Meanwhile, artemisia overran the beds, but daylilies are survivors. Like the mythical phoenix, the Stout Memorial Garden was destined to rise, rejuvenated, from its own ashes.

Keepers of the Faith

The Stout Garden
NYBG

In 1978, the drills and hammers fell silent. The conservatory had been restored to its former splendor and renamed the Enid A. Haupt Conservatory, but the damage had been done in the Stout Memorial Garden. No one seemed interested in the daylilies anymore, and they would have been discarded had it not been for Michael A. Ruggiero, a twenty-one-year veteran of the New York Botanical Garden staff. Mike has recently acquired a glamorous title—Senior Curator of the Peggy Rockefeller Rose Garden and Special Gardens. However, this new eminence has changed his life very little. "Now I can afford to buy the dog food," he grumbles cheerfully. The dog food, incidentally, is for Cookie, the elderly German shepherd mascot of the horticultural department.

In the course of his career at the Botanical Garden, Mike has done almost everything there is to do there. "They even made me an orchid grower," he told me with an incredulous shake of his head. "Would you believe orchids? I hate 'em. These were all cultivars, and I couldn't tell one *Cattleya* from another even though I was watering them!" He chuckled and added that the same might be said for some of the recent daylilies.

After the orchids, he spent a year working out-of-doors, an assignment that suited him a great deal better. Next, he was put in charge of the Native Plant Garden for two or three years. But as Mike tells it, "the fellow died who was working in the plant records office, and I did that for five years. Then the foreman of the propagation range retired. The day his wife got hit by a car, he just left and never came back. So I was asked to do his job." The propagation range—complete with greenhouses—is the horticultural nerve center of the Botanical Garden, where all the annuals and perennials for the display beds are grown.

When a new Vice President of Horticulture, David Scheid, was appointed in the early eighties, Mike's reaction was highly favorable. Scheid was young, energetic, and knowledgeable. "He really had all the basic skills, and he was brilliant," said Mike with open admiration. "Moreover, what he wanted to do was bring back some of the areas that had gone downhill during the reconstruction of the conservatory. He said to me, 'I need you outside because you know where things were.'" This was music to Mike's ears. As a man who hates waste and never throws anything away—his cluttered office provides ample proof of this conservative tendency—he was appalled by the neglect he saw around him. "There are things that you should never, ever let get out of hand and die off. After all," he observed, "you only have one history."

Fortunately for the Stout Memorial Garden and several other historic plantings, David Scheid was in complete agreement. When I called him at his new post as Executive Director of the U.S. Botanic Garden in Washington, D.C., I learned that he was involved in another preservation effort. The U.S. Botanic Garden is the oldest in the country and as such is a landmark in the world of botany and horticulture. And Scheid is bent on assuring its permanence. "One of the things I'm interested in," he said on the phone, "is the history of institutions. I think it is important that we understand our past in order to move into our future. That's what brings a whole era alive." At the New York Botanical Garden, he realized there was an important story to be told about the development of the modern daylily. "I felt," he said, "that the work A. B. Stout did there was very important, and we still had the remnants of his collection. It would have been an absolute shame to let that information just disappear. So that's why we tried to resurrect that garden when I was there. But I couldn't have done it without the efforts of Mike Ruggiero from day one, and later, Gregory Piotrowski. Greg is extremely interested in daylilies — as well as in history."

When I first met Greg, he had already embarked on the quest for lost or strayed Stout daylilies. Along with other members of the American Hemerocallis Society, I had received a letter from him requesting information leading to the whereabouts of Dr. Stout's daylilies. He patiently followed up this letter with a phone call. In those days, I was cavalier about the hybridizers represented in my garden and couldn't tell him whether there were any Stout cultivars or not. (As it turned out, there was one, but Greg had already acquired 'Linda'.) In any case, we became friends despite my ignorance. I began to take an interest in the refurbished Stout Garden and discovered that Greg had been in on the ground floor of the project. But with characteristic modesty, he is quick to acknowledge David Schied's primary role.

"As you know," he told me, "David had started the ball rolling. We got our first shipment of daylilies in the summer of 1986. I had already graduated [from the New York Botanical Garden's School of Horticulture] and was working per diem when the daylilies started coming in. I kind of grabbed them." As a teenager back in Michigan, Greg had fallen under the spell of daylilies and joined the American Hemerocallis Society. Once at the Botanical Garden, his love of *Hemerocallis* became apparent to his superiors. Richard Schnall, who at that time was Grounds and Arboretum Manager, put him in charge of the daylilies. "I was only in charge," the unassuming Greg insists, "from the viewpoint that nobody else was in charge." We both laughed about that. It is so often the way things happen. "Anyway," he went on, "that's when we started looking furiously for as many Stout cultivars as we could find."

The garden was to be rebuilt on the site of the former Stout

Memorial Garden. By this time, the hornbeam hedge had grown so tall it had to be pruned from a ladder, but the bones of the original design were still there: two large curving beds at the back of the garden and two long rectangular beds parallel to the road. The addition of a fifth bed was planned to introduce present-day enthusiasts to the species Stout used in his breeding program. Greg envisioned a garden in the spirit of the earliest daylily display garden—an attractive presentation of an educational collection. To this end, he set about finding both Stout cultivars and winners of the Stout Medal, beginning with 'Hesperus', the first recipient. But fulfilling this goal turned out to be easier said than done.

Nevertheless, like Dr. Stout before him, Greg was the right man in the right place at the right time. With infinite patience, he began poring over nursery catalogs. He described his method of operation in an article for *The Green Scene*, the magazine published by the Pennsylvania Horticultural Society:

> We worked from a tentative master list of introduced Stout daylilies. However, the more research I did on Dr. Stout, the longer the list became; we are still adding new names to it. Once we exhausted the supply of recent catalogs, we began to look through old catalogs on the chance that some of these nurseries, if still in business, might be growing the older daylilies.

Slow and laborious as the process has been, Greg's perseverance has paid off. Today, of the ninety-seven Stout cultivars believed to exist, sixty-eight now flourish at the New York Botanical Garden. And it is to be hoped that these historic plants will never disappear from cultivation. Certainly, as long as Greg Piotrowski and Mike Ruggiero remain at the Botanical Garden, the daylilies are in safe hands.

Visiting the guardians of the Stout legacy at the propagation range is like going backstage in the theater. The glitter of the Enid A. Haupt Conservatory and the grandeur of the Italianate museum building are left behind. The real work of the Botanical Garden takes place in a discreetly hidden brick building adjoining the greenhouses. Offices at the propagation range are

cramped, shabby, and furnished with Salvation Army specials.
Mike shares his office with Bob Russo, foreman of the Arboretum crew. Both desks are buried under books, papers, catalogs,
piles of plant labels, and miscellaneous debris. An attempt has
been made to brighten the dingy walls with photographs held in
place by thumbtacks. There is a purple daylily enlarged to the
size of a bath mat; a picture of a handsome German shepherd,
Cookie's predecessor; and a few framed horticultural awards. I
came to this inner sanctum last fall to hear the story behind the
Stout Memorial Garden reconstruction.

Even before David Scheid arrived at the Botanical Garden
with his mission to preserve important old plantings, Mike had
been quietly disentangling the neglected daylilies from the invasive artemisia. He and his crew had lifted the plants and
stripped them to their bare roots. "That's what's great about
daylilies; you can do that. We planted some of them in the nursery and put the rest of them on the hillside in the perennial garden. There's a forty-five-degree slope, and it was a good place
for them, so we put everybody there in groups. Then we started
labeling. That's when we discovered that very few of them were
Stout cultivars. It was like we had lost a piece of our history."

Mike was doubly chagrined when a colleague showed him
an article about Stout daylilies at Winterthur Gardens in
Greenville, Delaware. The article claimed for Winterthur the
distinction of having the largest collection of Stout cultivars outside of the New York Botanical Garden. "It was a big embarrassment," Mike said sheepishly. "We really didn't even know
what we had, and we didn't know where they were, either."

Here Greg picked up the thread. "People were giving us
more credit than we deserved."

By this time, David Scheid had left, but his successor, Carl
Totemeier, was equally interested in seeing historic plantings
maintained and refurbished. "Projects that Dave had started,"
Greg continued, "such as the rose garden, were completed by
Carl. [The gloriously restored Peggy Rockefeller Rose Garden
is based on landscape architect Beatrix Farrand's original plan.]
As for the Stout Memorial Garden, we just went to Carl with

the article about Winterthur. He was great like that. If we had a good idea, we'd just present it, and he'd say, 'Yes, that's fine.'"

With Totemeier's blessing, Greg and Mike began combing the grounds for Stout cultivars. The only labeled Stout daylilies were in nursery beds near the propagation range. Among these, they found the double orange 'Arlow Stout', one of his last hybrids posthumously named and introduced by the Farr Nursery. Next, they tackled the hillside planting, crawling around on their hands and knees looking for labels. Some were broken; others were marking the wrong plants. But they found elegant, lovely 'Statuesque', one of the *altissima* hybrids with small, creamy yellow flowers borne on graceful four-foot scapes. 'Poinsettia', a wonderfully eye-catching orange-red, turned up here, too. Gradually others were found, identified, and assembled in the freshly prepared beds of the renamed Arlow B. Stout Daylily Garden.

Many of the plants for the bed of Stout Medal winners were found on Long Island. The Long Island Daylily Society, which at Dr. McEwen's behest had taken such an active part in establishing the original garden, again came forward. Roswitha Waterman, whose daylily presentations arouse interest in Germany every year, donated the stunning red 'Ed Murray' and other venerable medal winners. "She's the one," said Mike, "who ran around getting them for us. It was tough to find some of the old ones."

Today, thanks to generous gardeners like Roswitha, the collection is complete. A parade of champions—all forty-one of them.

In addition to the completely restored portions of the original garden, two new beds were planted in the spring of 1991 with all the cultivars presently under consideration for the Stout Medal. A complex procedural system governs the awarding of daylily honors. To guarantee that the Stout Medal is bestowed only on the best of the best, a cultivar must come up through the ranks, winning first an Honorable Mention (the initial stamp of approval), and then an Award of Merit (which signifies that a cultivar is not only distinctive and beautiful but a proven performer over a wide geographic area). The Stout Medal winner is chosen from this elite group.

"During some years," Greg explained, "there will be a maximum of thirty plants. Three years after a plant wins an American Hemerocallis Society Award of Merit, it is eligible for three years for the Stout Medal. What we've done is put in two beds that mimic the back curved beds, except that they're only about a third the size. I think Mike got the idea for this planting because of Carl Totemeier and the roses. Carl was an American Rose Society judge, and when he was here, the Botanical Garden was an All-American Rose Selection Garden. The AARS was established to test new varieties for a two-year trial period. We would get up to fifty roses which were under consideration for the award, and I think that's probably where Mike got the idea of doing something of the sort with the daylilies."

Neither Greg nor Mike is willing to claim responsibility for the spectacular new Daylily Walk. Greg thinks it was probably Mike's idea. Mike, whose interest in daylilies "snowballed" with Greg's arrival, thinks it was the other way around. Either way, it is a source of great satisfaction to them both. To date, 210 different daylilies in huge clumps fill long, curving six-foot-wide beds along both sides of a graceful walk that sweeps through the green lawns of the Botanical Garden. In midsummer, the two ribbons of graduated color stop visitors in their tracks. The view is particularly effective looking from the bottom of the slight incline toward the conservatory.

The perpetrators of this glorious sight are modest about their accomplishment but excited by the possibilities they foresee. "We want to show as many varieties as possible," says Mike, "so that people realize how wide the choice is—fifteen hundred wouldn't be out of hand. Of course, we could make a nice display, a real pretty wave of color, with fifteen hundred of a single cultivar, but you're not teaching people anything that way. When you show fifteen hundred different cultivars, you're saying, 'Look, you have a choice.'"

Greg took up the story. "People's eyes are opened; they say, 'Wow, that's a daylily?' They are really amazed. They're used to seeing the orange roadside daylily and now they see some wild, frilly, ruffled thing, and they can't get over it! You hear all kinds of things. 'That looks like an orchid' or they say it looks like a hibiscus—whatever idea they have of some frilly, lacy, fancy cultivated flower.... Visitors go wild when I take them on a tour down Daylily Walk."

Thematic weekends are a relatively new enterprise for the Botanical Garden, and not surprisingly, the inaugural Daylily Weekend in 1989 was a howling success. Greg and Mike delivered an antiphon of enthusiasm. "We gave tours; we answered questions; we distributed American Hemerocallis Society literature; we gave out plant sources and sold divisions from named cultivars in our own collection. People just snapped them up!" Looking ahead to next year, they are propagating more plants to sell. Greg explained the rationale of the plant sale. "For any of these collections, like the daylilies, to go anywhere or to improve, you need money—you need money not only for adequate staff to maintain the collection, but you need money to write up and print brochures, to put up signs and labels. Those metal stake labels with two-by-five-inch plaques cost about ten dollars apiece to make. Most important of all, money talks. As long as there is money coming in, the daylilies will keep going.

"Hopefully, now that we've brought the Stout Garden back to life, people will realize that it is something that should stay here. It is important to the Botanical Garden. Little by little, we are hoping to become known as the place to come if you are interested in daylilies. Put that together with our history, the interpretive material we are developing, and the sheer number of cultivars we are growing, I don't think there's a public or private garden where you can get a better education about daylilies than we offer here. I really believe that."

Mike nodded agreement. But daylilies at the New York Botanical Garden are by no means all work and no play. "Mike and I both say the same thing. If we don't have fun, we don't do it, and that's how we look at our jobs—it has to be fun for us. That's why becoming involved with the daylilies has sparked us on a little bit. We're really enjoying it. That's one of the great things about gardening and horticulture—it's fun—it's a hobby."

Again, Mike grinned and nodded. "The thing is that Greg and I and a few other people are willing to stay a little extra to play with the daylilies, as long as we can do some hybridizing on the side. That's one of our first loves. So we don't mind weeding a bit more on our own time. Greg often comes in on Saturday, not on paid time or anything, but just to do it. And once you get that sort of thing, and the garden is looking good, you get more people and more support." For daylilies, these two men will go to any lengths.

Sitting on a battered wooden chair in the office of the Senior Curator of the Peggy Rockefeller Rose Garden and Special Gardens, I marveled again at the people who have been drawn together by this one plant: Mike, the Bronx boy whose first job at the New York Botanical Garden was weeding the brick paths with a penknife. Another of his early jobs was planting portulaca. Now in his forties—big, disheveled in appearance, with a drooping mustache and rather long gray-streaked hair, it is hard to imagine his thick fingers sowing the tiny seeds.

"It was one of the first things that I did that wasn't weed pulling. My friend Joe and I were supposed to sow the seeds; when they came up, we were supposed to water and weed the planting and keep it edged—that was one of our first assignments as sixteen-year-olds. Well, Louis Politi, the horticulturist, got us good! He told us how expensive the seed was and that it was rare and all this. We didn't know. But every day at lunchtime and after work, we'd collect seeds." Mike threw back his shaggy head and laughed. "You know how portulaca has those little seed caps with pop-off lids? We were picking those things off.... We must have had close to half a pound of seeds before we were through—probably worth a dollar eighty-five! Lou really got us ... he set us right up!" Mike holds no grudge against his former boss. In fact, one of his goals in hybridizing is to produce a daylily worthy of Politi's name.

Opposite Mike, tilting a wooden chair similar to mine against the office wall, Greg looked as if he had stepped out of a catalog featuring casual clothing: white fisherman's sweater, the collar of a button-down shirt showing at the neck, and neat slacks. But even in his green work clothes, he is always well groomed and immaculate. Only in his twenties, he has somehow acquired the patience of a saint already. My endless questions about daylilies, about botany and botanical nomenclature, and even about himself have all been met with equanimity and unfailing good humor. I doubt that I could have written this book without him. Born and brought up in Michigan, Greg came by his love of plants from a gardening grandmother who grew beautiful roses. There was never any question about his true love—first roses and then daylilies. But he arrived at his career in horticulture by a roundabout route that included a detour in a machine shop. Upon discovering that he was not cut out to be a machinist, he quickly switched to horticulture and has enjoyed life ever since. Today, he is in his element.

It is indeed a brave new world that has such daylily people in it. And I do believe that Dr. Stout himself would approve of the present keepers of the faith. In the final paragraph of his autobiography, he admitted that his life's work had been as much a pleasure and a pastime as it had been a profession:

> During a recent visit with relatives in the village of my boy-hood days, a young cousin of a later generation asked me to explain what my work is. My attempt to answer in non-technical terms brought the comment "Well that seems more like the pursuit of a hobby than real work." I confess that my efforts in botany through-out a half century as first hobby and then vocation have never seemed to me to be work that is toil or labor. And I am certain that this may also be said for the botanists and horticulturists whom I have known most intimately.

Significant Others

'Nevermore' (Wheeler)

'Salmon Sheen'
(Taylor)

'Purple Finch' (Nesmith)

As history never runs in one convenient, sequential line, events in the unfolding story of the daylily often occurred simultaneously, and careers coincided. The towering figure of Dr. Stout dominated the scene from the twenties until his retirement from the New York Botanical Garden in 1948. But he was by no means the only American attracted to the stalwart, striking *Hemerocallis*, with its warm colors and equable disposition.

The year before Dr. Stout left Wisconsin for the Bronx, the remarkable Bertrand H. Farr laid aside his musical career to concentrate on growing, selling, and hybridizing flowers. "Blessed is he," proclaimed the former musical prodigy, "who has a hobby and can make it his business." In 1909, he sold his music enterprise and established a nursery, first on the grounds of his home in Wyomissing, Pennsylvania, and later in nearby Womelsdorf. Here, he hybridized some of the first named daylily cultivars in America. Tall, floriferous 'Ophir', descended from *Hemerocallis citrina* and named for a biblical land rich in gold, bears witness to his skill. 'Ophir' is still beloved in many old-fashioned gardens. But with the dawn of the Stout era, Farr discontinued many of his own introductions in favor of propagating the superior Stout cultivars—which is perhaps even more to his credit. Thirty years after Farr's death, his nursery was still selling daylilies. Indeed, they were the only plants the Farr Nursery Company continued to market nationally—"mainly," according to H. G. Seyler, who was then treasurer, "because they withstand the rigors of shipping and of widely varying conditions in weather and soil." And because compared to other plants, they required "a minimum of 'trouble correspondence.'"

Possibly it was their rugged constitutions that endeared daylilies to Hans P. Sass, who, with his brother Jacob, ran a nursery near Omaha, Nebraska, prior to World War I. The climate of eastern Nebraska is about as tough as it comes. Summers are hot, winters are severe, and rainfall is light and unpredictable. But daylilies can take it. They grow like weeds there in the fertile prairie soil. Maple Road Gardens consisted of the Sass home sheltered by big old trees, several outbuildings, and ten acres of rich farmland. Color came early to the growing fields with lilacs, poppies, and iris. However, nothing rivaled the glow of the yellow and gold daylilies basking in the summer sun.

Sometime before 1915, Mr. Hans Sass ordered a few *H. citrina* hybrids from the Farr Nursery Company. At the same time, he came by a plant of *H. aurantiaca* var. *major* and began crossing them back and forth. By the mid-twenties, this line had produced some lovely yellows and golds. Nephew Henry E. Sass was a lad of sixteen when his uncle introduced 'Sunny West', 'Golden West', and 'Midwest Star'; later came 'Hesperus', winner of the first Stout Medal. Two years after that, 'Revolute' repeated the triumph.

In 1933, a Chicago attorney named David Hall visited the Sass garden and was charmed by what he saw. He purchased eight yellow seedlings which gave rise to some of the great daylilies of the fifties. That same year, eight hundred miles away in Dover, Ohio, one Ray Cheetham stopped by the garden of Carl Betscher to buy gladioli and came home with daylilies instead. Betscher had insisted upon showing him the new *Hemerocallis* he had produced. Of these, no fewer than sixteen are listed in Dr. Stout's 1934 book—proud names like 'Bay State',

'Cressida', 'The Gem', 'Golden Dream', and 'Gypsy'. The latter became one of the most heavily used cultivars in the early history of daylily hybridization.

Meanwhile, back in Nebraska, young Henry E. Sass, building on the foundations laid by his late uncle Hans, started his own breeding program. He carried on the family tradition until another giant in the daylily world purchased the whole Sass collection. After the 1956 National Convention of the American Hemerocallis Society, Hugh M. Russell decided to purchase the entire inventory of Maple Road Gardens and move it—lock, stock, and barrel—to his nursery in Spring, Texas. Russell did everything in a big way. He was the first daylily grower to advertise nationwide, and his nursery was in keeping with the tradition of his adopted state—big. The daylilies covered thirty acres!

Described by one admiring colleague as "flamboyant, pithy, entertaining, and enduring," Hugh Russell didn't scale the heights of the daylily world by being shy and retiring. Like the flowers he loved, he was rugged, determined, and a born survivor. The Russell family had homesteaded in the Oklahoma Territory where he was born shortly before the turn of the century. The youngest of ten children, Hugh barely knew his father, who died young. The senior Russell had been a plant breeder of considerable note, having developed an improved strain of cotton, and his youngest son inherited the taste and talent for hybridizing. Hugh, however, was more interested in horticulture than agriculture and became a nurseryman. He took an early interest in the landscaping potential of daylilies and began to collect, test, and hybridize those best suited for mass plantings on large estates. The bigger the job, the better Russell liked it. He thought nothing of using a thousand plants at a clip.

Engaged for years in a celebrated feud with another prominent member of the American Hemerocallis Society, he was obviously not everybody's cup of tea, but Hugh Russell was nothing if not colorful and courageous. Diagnosed in 1952 as suffering from a rare and incurable form of lupus, he confounded physicians by continuing to work and hybridize for another eight years. In 1958, he swept up every major award bestowed by the American Hemerocallis Society, including the Bertrand Farr Award. But his greatest service to daylilies and to ordinary gardeners like myself was that he popularized this wonderful garden plant through his informative catalogs.

I had never heard of red and pink daylilies until I received a catalog from Russell Gardens. On the spot, I ordered 'Crimson Glory' and deep pink 'Marianne Russell'. Both have bloomed faithfully in my garden for thirty years. I am grateful to Hugh Russell for his 1951 Stout Medal winner 'Painted Lady', a big, handsome daylily with flowers the color of orange marmalade. It may be old-fashioned, but it is still a striking plant. Nor am I ashamed to admit that many other early hybridizers are still represented in my garden.

The year that 'Painted Lady' was honored, the name Elizabeth Nesmith appeared repeatedly among the award winners. Two of the five runners-up for the Stout Medal were her cultivars 'Royal Ruby' and 'Pink Charm'. Perhaps I am intrigued by Mrs. Nesmith because of a sentimental attachment to 'Sweetbriar', one of her first pinks, and 'Morocco Red', which I still grow. Alternatively, I may find her interesting because she was the first woman to make an impression on the daylily world. A contemporary and friend of Dr. Stout, she was among the few to receive from the master's hand a division of *Hemerocallis fulva* var. *rosea*. Indeed, if Henry Sass may be relied upon, she was responsible for making this coveted plant available to the general public, and for this service alone her name should be hallowed.

In the forties and fifties, Mrs. Nesmith's Lowell, Massachusetts, garden was a mecca to daylily enthusiasts. She grew not only her own cultivars but those of every important breeder in the United States. The most up-to-date introductions were artfully arranged in long beds down either side of the large city lot on which she lived. It was a big garden by city standards, extending perhaps 175 feet behind the house, with a tall fence dividing the display area from her seedling beds. Hugh Russell once came all the way from Texas just to spend a few hours at

Fairmount Gardens—named for the street on which the Nesmiths lived.

Every year, Mrs. Nesmith published an elaborate catalog that read like a Who's Who of iris and daylily breeders. She was famous for her apt descriptions and, according to one breeder whose iris she introduced, she would improve upon the text he provided. She would ask him for his version "and then reword the descriptions to make them sound irresistible!" Her own daylily cultivars bore evocative names, like 'Doeskin' and 'Starlight', 'Carved Ivory', and 'Fire-opal'. Today, Fairmount Gardens catalogs are collector's items.

Beginning in 1910, Elizabeth Nesmith started methodically collecting every species and hybrid on which she could lay her hands. Recalling her early work for the 1969 yearbook issue of *The Hemerocallis Journal*, Mrs. Nesmith described her correspondence with Carl Betscher in Ohio. He wrote to her in indecipherable longhand "going into great detail about what he had produced." Later, she visited Dr. Stout at the New York Botanical Garden and began acquiring his cultivars. "I obtained many of his new varieties from Farr Nurseries," she reported, "and naturally, I commenced to hybridize. Many of my deep reds and red-purples were crossed with 'Theron' and 'Vulcan'...." And her pink line traces directly back to *H. fulva* var. *rosea*.

In many respects, she was a woman ahead of her time. Nesmith is an old, distinguished name in the Massachusetts manufacturing town of Lowell, and it must have given local matrons pause to have such an ambitious young woman in their midst. In the days when "ladies" were not expected to work, Elizabeth Nesmith was an exception. She had a part-time secretary who helped with correspondence, and one regular gardener. Otherwise, Fairmount Gardens was a one-woman band. She not only made the crosses, shelled and planted the seed, lined out the seedlings, and kept accurate records, but she also prepared the catalog, attended to direct sales, and handled the lion's share of the packing and shipping.

Unlike other great women in the daylily world, her participation in the American Hemerocallis Society was limited chiefly to writing articles for *The Journal.* Nesmith articles, I might add, are models of clarity—and brevity. The subject matter was broad in scope. She had strong feelings about breeding for cold tolerance and was among the first hybridizers to consistently cross hardy dormant varieties with less hardy varieties from the South with a view to expanding the range of the daylily. Most of her introductions were what she termed "semi-deciduous." She explained, "By this I mean those that lose part of their leaves as winter comes on, but retain their center growth of green throughout the season. These seem to thrive both in the North and the South." Today, many breeders are preoccupied with adaptability, but Mrs. Nesmith was a trailblazer in this direction.

Her other hybridizing goals were "large flowers, firm substance, good branching, and many blooms on a scape." In addition, she contributed substantially to the development of the first real pinks. "I think I had my greatest thrill," she wrote with understandable pride, "when I first saw 'Pink Prelude' in bloom as a seedling and realized what an advancement it was in producing pinks, as was quite evident by its receiving awards both in England and America." She was also attracted to purples and lavenders and tantalized by the prospect of white.

Elizabeth Nesmith was an old lady when the man-made tetraploids burst upon the scene. While colchicine-treated daylilies with forty-four chromosomes instead of the normal twenty-two offered hybridizers exciting new possibilities, many diploid breeders felt threatened by these developments. Not the doughty Mrs. Nesmith. She welcomed them. "More power to those who have made such a successful adventure possible, for I have always been thoroughly interested in creating distinctive and better daylilies."

Currier McEwen, who knew Mrs. Nesmith well, summed up her long career: "She was a great old war horse, believe me, who did an enormous amount of work to popularize hemerocallis in her day. And for that time, she produced a lot of very, very good daylilies."

Another formidable woman breeder whose career overlapped Mrs. Nesmith's was handsome Ophelia Ann Taylor of Ocala, Florida. In 1927, Mrs. Taylor, young, recently wed, and with a new home to landscape, joined the local garden club to learn about suitable plants for the subtropical climate. As fate would have it, the club's first speaker that season was daylily buff Dr. H. Harold Hume, Dean of the Department of Agriculture of the University of Florida. Naturally, he talked about his favorite plant.

Mrs. Taylor promptly ordered a collection of daylilies and was hooked for life. A friend of hers, Mrs. Thomas, charted the course of Ophelia's affair with daylilies. "She went through the various stages all plant enthusiasts know of collecting and evaluating, but it wasn't until she made her first cross in 1940 — between *H. aurantiaca* var. *major* and *H. fulva rosea* — that she was completely overcome by the 'daylily fever.' From a series of crosses originating between these two varieties came the incomparable 'Prima Donna', winner of the Stout Medal for 1955." We further learn that the name for this famous pastel daylily was suggested by Ophelia's husband, an insurance man who shared his wife's interest in gardening.

In 1939, just as Mrs. Taylor had arrived at what she described as "that second stage of hemerocallis frenzy — collecting and aspiring to grow every daylily there was," she met Ralph W. Wheeler. "I saw a slight spare man with greying hair, keen grey eyes, the sensitive face of a scholar and the dedication of a true plantsman.... He had been crossing daylilies not too long but had just bloomed that season an exciting new red. It was open that day in his garden and he took me over to see it."

Mrs. Taylor was overwhelmed. What she saw was a large flower for those days with deep ruby red segments and petals embellished with a narrow gold line through the center. Christened 'Ruby Supreme', this cultivar, in her words, "did a great deal toward putting hemerocallis, Florida breeders, and Mr. Wheeler on the map." Appearing on the same Award of Merit list as Mrs. Nesmith's 'Royal Ruby' and 'Pink Charm', 'Ruby Supreme' never won a Stout Medal. But it founded a dynasty of splendid daylilies. Their parentage, which might have provided a clue to Ralph Wheeler's achievements, remains a mystery. He employed the peculiar practice of mixing pollen from several sources. Nevertheless, his magnificent mongrels were the envy of contemporary breeders. Surprising new forms and colors turned up in his "hem patch": a spider called 'Scorpio' with enormously long, narrow petals; amaryllis-shaped 'Cellini'; 'Amherst', a large, light purple with wide milk-white midribs; clear orange 'Playboy', which won the Stout Medal in 1961; and a host of other distinguished cultivars.

Like Wheeler, Ophelia Taylor eschewed the laborious record keeping of Mrs. Nesmith and other hybridizers, and no doubt luck played a part in her success story. But her genius for choosing good parents and selecting the best of their offspring carried her far. Dumb luck rarely strikes twice in the same place. She went on to become the "Queen of Pastels," turning out one beautiful flower after another.

Late in life, Mrs. Taylor gave heed to the earnest admonitions of youthful Bill Munson and began keeping track of her crosses. Her efforts were just beginning to pay off at the time of her death. But even if she fell short of her intention, it was of small consequence. In a letter written a year before she died, she expressed with touching eloquence what daylilies had meant to her:

> Geography began to have a meaning. Des Moines and Council Bluff[s] and Shenandoah were no longer black dots on the map, but places where this friend and that one lived. People had more meaning, too. My circle of friends increased. A shared interest is a wonderful catalyst—rich and poor, old and young, the wise and the foolish meet on common ground and find pleasure in association.
>
> Last but not least, is the satisfaction of accomplishment, of being part of the world about you, of working with Nature to make something a little better. There is the thrill that comes each spring in anticipation. Some morning, among the plants so carefully and prayerfully cultivated will be THAT ONE! Even though you never reach your goal—and you never do, for it is constantly changing and moving ahead just beyond you—there is great pleasure in the doing, great comfort just in being, even so small a part of the great world around you.

Thanks to the promising creations of early hybridizers like Taylor, Wheeler and Nesmith, the Sass family, swashbuckling Hugh Russell, and the rest, the popularity of the daylily soared. In California, iris breeder Carl Milliken was quick to see possibilities in the newly fashionable daylily and from 1940 to 1949 devoted himself to its improvement. From Colorado, LeMoine J. Bechtold, whose pale yellow spider 'Lydia Bechtold' once graced my garden, described this point in daylily history:

> Unquestionably there are greater advances to be made in the evolution of hemerocallis. Near-whites (possibly pure white), near-blues (perhaps true blue), better pinks, purples, finer bicolors, more ruffled and crinkled petaled and sepaled types, more blooms and branching to the stems, plus better remontant (re-blooming) qualities—all will come.
>
> May Providence preserve us older fans that we may live to see these and even more.

With one exception—there still is no true blue daylily—Mr. Bechtold's prophecy has been fulfilled beyond his wildest dreams.

Saxton Gardens

'Orchid Corsage'
(Saxton)

When I first began my journey through the daylily world, Gregory Piotrowski said, "You'll certainly want to talk to Stanley Saxton. He was a charter member of the American Hemerocallis Society, knew Dr. Stout, and worked with Stout's plants. He is still breeding daylilies himself and has seen fads come and go." Indeed, Saxton Gardens in Saratoga Springs, New York, is a repository of daylily history. The introduction dates of Mr. Saxton's plants span a century of breeding, from George Yeld's 1893 'Apricot', to Sarah Sikes's 1987 cultivar 'Second Thoughts', to his own introductions for next year. At eighty-six, Mr. Saxton is particularly excited about a cross he made in 1988 between one of his own miniatures and 'Super Stella', offspring of the fabled 'Stella De Oro'.

To digress briefly, 'Stella De Oro' is probably the best known daylily in this country. Named for a cookie and called into being by another elderly gentleman, the late Walter Jablonski, she won the Stout Medal in 1985. Only the second miniature ever to achieve this honor ('Bertie Ferris' won in 1980), Stella's small, cheery yellow face now beams from the pages of mail-order catalogs from coast to coast. But her claim to fame is not just a sunny countenance and exemplary garden manners; it

is for her remontant character that she is so greatly prized—
especially in the North. Other daylilies rebloom in warm climates, but in New England and other chilly parts of the United
States most daylilies produce only one flush of bloom, while
Stella sends up twelve-inch scapes all summer long. And guess
where she acquired this desirable habit? From Stanley Saxton's
forty-year-old 'Pinocchio'!

It pleases Mr. Saxton that his little old-fashioned daylily—a
cross between Dr. Stout's 'Mignon' and a seedling with species
parents—is not so old-fashioned after all. "'Pinocchio' was one
of the parents of 'Bitsy'. And 'Bitsy' is a parent of Stella. Practically all those little ones have 'Pinocchio' in their parentage," he
said, chortling. When pleased or amused, he laughs in short,
staccato bursts: "Heh, heh, heh!" But what pleases him most is
the cross he made two years ago using Stella's daughter 'Super
Stella'.

"One of the seedlings," he announced with pride, "has
turned out to be phenomenal! At two years of age, it's got something like twelve fans and eight flowering stalks—at two years
of age! I was amazed! I went out, and there was this clump in
my box just covered with flowers! [He grows his seedlings in
raised boxes to thwart the invasive goutweed.] I've named it
'Winning Starlet', and I'm going to introduce it next year. Just
think, it will only be three years old at that time!"

When Stanley Saxton began his hybridizing career, the
long, productive life of George Yeld had not yet ended, Dr.
Stout had only recently introduced 'Theron', and Mrs.
Nesmith's 'Sweetbriar' was the latest thing in pink daylilies.
There were just a few American breeders then, and Mr. Saxton
knew them all. "I used to squire Mrs. Nesmith to the Conventions," he told me. "She liked young people, and in those days I
was a young fellow getting interested in daylilies. She was a nice
old lady. I liked her very much. She was offering daylilies in the
1930s along with Stout, Hans Sass, Ralph Wheeler—whose cultivars I introduced from 1945 to 1952. Before the American
Hemerocallis Society was formed, daylily introductions were
recognized in *Herbertia*, the yearbook of the American Plant Life

Society. My early named ones were listed in *Herbertia,* too. I am possibly the only one still growing many of these early culti-vars."

At Saxton Gardens, you can enjoy Mrs. Nesmith's 'Pink Prelude' and recall how thrilled she was that day in the forties when she first saw it bloom. Remember, pink daylilies were a novelty then. Nearby, you will find other Nesmith cultivars: late-blooming 'Autumn Red'; 'Dresden China', appropriately named for its creamy yellow coloring and light pink halo; and 'Windsor Tan', which the hybridizer described in her own inim-itable style as having petals "of glowing golden brown with sepals of yellow lightly finished with warm sepia."

Elsewhere among the blocks of daylilies look for Dr. Stout's geranium-pink 'Jennie Love'. He considered it one of his choic-est cultivars. Thereby hung a tale which Mr. Saxton was eager to relate. "I cointroduced 'Jennie Love' with the Farr Nursery Company in 1956. It was a 'Rosalind' seedling—very pretty. I agreed to take a hundred plants because I knew Dr. Stout. I used to go down to the New York Botanical Garden to confer with him. He loved to talk about daylilies and would regale you with stories of things he had done in the field. Incidentally, my *Hemerocallis fulva* var. *rosea* came from him. Originally, there were three clones of that name, and he told me that he was going to pick out the one that he thought the best, give it a name, and distribute it. That was 'Rosalind'. There is an inter-esting story about the other two."

Apparently the two remaining plants of *rosea* were—by Dr. Stout's uncompromising standards—inferior to 'Rosalind'. However, he permitted a Connecticut daylily enthusiast to use one of these plants for breeding purposes, on the strict under-standing that he or she would not release it to the public. But somehow it turned up in the garden of a Boston hybridizer, who published it in his catalog as 'Pastelrose' and sold it for a steep price. Dr. Stout was very much upset by this perfidy and exer-cised more caution after that.

He confided in Stanley Saxton that even at the New York Botanical Garden, his daylilies and their progeny were not safe.

It is a matter of record that plants were surreptitiously removed from the selection beds and seed capsules pilfered. "He told me, 'You know, I raise these hybrids, then people come in here and steal the seeds off them. I have therefore made my new garden with a six-foot brick wall around it.' He escorted me to the garden, and sure enough, it had a wall with a locked gate. The only people he let in were those he accompanied himself. But he took me in and showed me his new hybrids."

The walled garden is now the Children's Garden, and the gate is no longer locked. On weekends and during the summer, youngsters from the Bronx and elsewhere congregate within to tend and till their plots in noisy, carefree ignorance of the garden's original purpose. Meanwhile, the refurbished Arlow B. Stout Daylily Garden across the road attracts admiring visitors with the products of Dr. Stout's arcane labors.

One Dr. Stout story led to another, and Mr. Saxton next recalled another memorable visit to the inner sanctum. "He had a bunch of small-flowered red hybrids—very, very pretty; medium tall stems, three-inch flowers—beautiful bright reds. He had a whole row of them and I said to him, 'You're going to introduce one of these, aren't you?' And he said, 'I don't know. I'm not especially enthralled with them. I might, but I don't know yet.' He never did, though. You see, he was very particular about what he introduced and just because I liked them, that wouldn't affect him at all. He was like that. Very particular."

Mr. Saxton is just as particular and just as independent. Not one to run with the pack, he has clear priorities, and they do not necessarily include the popular round, flat shapes of today. As his own garden lies at the foot of the Adirondack Mountain Range, his requirements are for cold tolerance, vigor, and dependability. In addition, he wants a high bud count and plenty of attractive flowers—which are perfectly welcome to be trumpet-shaped. In other words, he has some old-fashioned notions about what constitutes a good daylily, and he isn't loath to express them.

"You may think that I'm just a critical old codger," he remarked with a shrug. "But I'm interested in getting good daylilies to the public. I've been selling them since 1945—before the American Hemerocallis Society was founded. I have very good sales to ordinary gardeners because what I sell are plants that are mainly listed at five to ten dollars and have been grown for years—established, reliable varieties. I don't try to sell hundred-dollar varieties. I think it's foolish. If you buy some of these expensive new daylilies, the chances are they've only been grown for a couple of years. But when a daylily gets down to five or ten dollars, it has probably been tested all over the country and you know what you're getting."

Ordinary gardeners, of whom I am one, certainly can't go wrong at Saxton Gardens. The prices are reasonable; the daylilies, reliable and beautiful. Moreover, Mr. Saxton is always going forward—albeit in his own direction. He embraces the new if he likes it. He liked 'Second Thoughts', the frilly, broadpetaled, thoroughly modern diploid introduction from southern hybridizer Sarah Sikes. But he hangs on to the old. He had 'War Eagle', hybridized in the mid-fifties by Chicago lawyer David Hall, converted into a tetraploid. A magnificent red in its day, he is still using 'War Eagle' while other breeders have moved on. One parent of his glowing red 'Toreador's Cape' was tetraploid 'War Eagle'. 'Toreador's Cape' sells like hotcakes to gardeners—but not to daylily collectors, who would find its flaring lily shape passé.

However, Mr. Saxton greeted the dawn of the tetraploid era with more warmth than most of his contemporaries. And he has continued to produce both diploids and tetraploids. Last year he introduced an almost black tetraploid double which he described as "a beauty!" He has also worked on blues and whites. The whites have been successful, while the blues have proved "problematical."

"Getting lavenders is easy enough," he remarked. "I have lots of lavenders. I just introduced one this year called 'Lilac Spire'. That's a real lavender. We have good purples, but I don't call that blue. For comparison, I plant blue flowers like balloon flower and ageratum around my garden, and so far we haven't got anything that blue yet." Mr. Saxton's interest in the cool side of the color spectrum dates from his early experience with the innovative Ralph Wheeler, who had a penchant for lavenders and purples.

"In the early forties, my father lived in Florida, and I went down there every year. At that time, Ralph Wheeler lived in Winter Park and I used to visit him in his garden. He had seven or eight acres solid with seedlings. Oh, he had some beautiful things—you can imagine—all those thousands and thousands of seedlings! Anyway, he was quite an elderly man at the time and so busy hybridizing that he didn't have time to merchandise his daylilies. Well, we talked quite a lot, and he figured that since I was very much interested, I might take over the introduction of his daylilies. We agreed to do that."

The course of the Wheeler-Saxton connection did not run smoothly because the tender southern plants languished in Saxton's frigid northern garden. The first year, he lost about half the crop. But through a process of elimination, he discovered which of Wheeler's introductions could take the cold, and those that could did very well in Saratoga Springs. He still grows nearly a dozen Wheeler cultivars, among them deep wine purple 'Vega', orchid pink 'Show Girl', and 'Tiara', which has golden flowers dusted with bronze and is the strongest growing of the lot. Mr. Saxton learned one trick from California grower Carl Milliken about growing tender varieties in the North. Milliken shipped his daylilies with the roots clipped down to about an inch in length. The rationale for this drastic "pruning" was that the new roots would acclimatize more readily than those accustomed to the warm soil of California. The theory proved valid, and Mr. Saxton has successfully grown a number of Wheeler daylilies by treating them in this manner.

Nevertheless, ironclad hardy daylilies are what Saxton Gardens is all about and, I was soon to discover, the reason Stanley Saxton became interested in *Hemerocallis* in the first place. I had been wondering how a concert organist, composer, and professor of music arrived at daylily breeding and was pleased to be enlightened by this born storyteller.

At the time, we were sitting at his kitchen table, which was littered with catalogs, seed lists, and the remains of what may have been breakfast. The kitchen had the unmistakable signs of bachelor occupancy. Mr. Saxton's wife died years ago and he shares the house with his son Peter. It is a pleasant, restful arrangement for them both. Peter helps with the daylilies during the growing season and in the winter works as a draftsman for a company that designs special machinery. They get along very well. "He starts out early in the morning and I don't see him till night," said his father, "but we always have dinner together, which is nice."

Encouraged by an attentive listener, Mr. Saxton launched into his early adventures with daylilies. "You see," he began, "my field was teaching music at Skidmore College. But I had my summers off, and I owned a place up in the Adirondacks—up near Tupper Lake. There's also a little private lake and that's where I had my place. Well, I always liked gardening—even as a boy. I grew up in Port Plain, New York, in the Mohawk Valley, and I always enjoyed raising vegetables and flowers. So I thought, 'As long as I'm here with nothing to do, I might as well start a little garden and raise some flowers.'

"Well, across that same lake, there was a lady from New Jersey who had been very active in the garden club down there, and I went to her one day and said I'd be interested in raising some flowers. 'You can't raise perennials up here,' she said. 'It's too cold. Roses die; chrysanthemums die. But you could try a few annuals.' I thought that was interesting. But I had noticed the wild *Hemerocallis fulva* growing along the roads. And I thought, 'Now, there's a plant that apparently grows in the Adirondacks.' So I looked it up and discovered that there were these people who were hybridizing daylilies. Then I got in touch with Ralph Wheeler, Mr. Sass, and Mr. Betscher, and of course, Dr. Stout. And that's how it all began." Pausing to reflect a moment, he concluded, "Those early days were quite interesting, and some rather nice plants were produced back then."

Today, Stanley Saxton's garden bears witness to the talents of early hybridizers who took the scanty material available and coaxed a rainbow from the limited collection of species and hybrids. But Saxton Gardens is by no means a museum. It is very much a going concern. The day I was there, Peter was digging an order of forty plants of 'Toreador's Cape' from the backyard daylily plots. There is another garden containing thousands of plants over on Route 9 north. The mystery is how two men—one in his eighties—carry on a breeding program, provide pounds of daylily seed for the George W. Park Seed Company, produce a catalog every year, and sell daylilies to whomever stops by.

In addition, Stanley Saxton continues to compose organ music—dozens of his pieces are published every year. "Composition is just like a job," he says matter-of-factly. "If somebody says to me, 'Write me a song on these words,' I sit down and write the song in maybe an hour. I make up some of my pieces while I'm lying in bed at night. If I can't sleep, I make up a piece. The reason I wrote the piece I'm sending off today is that it was raining yesterday, and I couldn't go out in the garden. So I thought, 'What am I going to do?' Then I sat down and wrote a Finale in C Minor. Would you like me to play it for you?" I said that I would.

He made his way across the living room rather slowly. His gait is the only thing that belies the impression of a man years younger. He continued talking as he arranged the sheets of music on the electronic console organ. "It's a postlude, really, and publishers are glad to get them because not many people are writing church music these days." For some minutes, the room reverberated with alternatively plaintive and finally triumphal chords. "I wrote that in about two hours yesterday morning!" he announced with a grin as he stepped down from the organ.

The Society

Helen Field Fischer

Even before the founding of the American Hemerocallis Society, daylily people managed to find each other. Dr. Stout corresponded with Amos Perry and George Yeld in England and sought out Bertrand Farr in Pennsylvania. Elizabeth Nesmith made contact with Dr. Stout and purchased his cultivars from the Farr Nursery Company. She exchanged letters with Carl Betscher and H. P. Sass and, later, George Sass. From Saratoga Springs, Stanley Saxton journeyed to the Bronx to visit Dr. Stout, made excursions to Mrs. Nesmith's Fairmount Gardens in Massachusetts, and looked up Ralph Wheeler in Florida. Mr. Wheeler, in turn, inspired Ophelia Ann Taylor, whose enthusiasm rubbed off on still more people through her local garden club. Nor were lovers of the daylily confined to the East Coast. They were scattered far and wide throughout the United States.

In the twentieth-anniversary issue of *The Hemerocallis Journal* (a publication of the American Hemerocallis Society, later called *The Daylily Journal*), charter members of the Society reminisced about their earliest awareness of the plant that would eventually bind them together. "Daylilies are included in my earliest recollections of garden flowers, when old *fulva* was in nearly every Kansas garden," wrote Mrs. Olive M. Hindman, who loved them even then. Ruby Whitcomb's introduction to the genus *Hemerocallis* was effected when she acquired a ramet of *H. flava* from her great-grandmother's garden on the banks of Lake Superior. Mrs. Goldie Jutkins of Folsom, California, had discovered daylilies in the thirties: "I lost my heart to a clump of old *fulva* growing and blooming beautifully in a neglected spot, and that day my love for daylilies was born." New Englander Frederick Stuntz had a deep affection for the Lemon Lily (*H. flava*) that grew in his mother's Massachusetts garden. "Its sweet fragrance in spring was an annual joy." Mr. Stuntz was delighted, therefore, to see a 1930 advertisement for a new Lemon Lily imported from England. It was named 'Mrs. Perry'.

Wherever and however these and other daylily fanciers came by their initial enthusiasm, all were brought together by a single historic event—the first postwar flower show sponsored by the Henry Field Seed and Nursery Company of Shenandoah, Iowa. Before World War II, the shows had been an annual event attracting gardeners from far and near. But gasoline rationing brought to an end unnecessary travel, and the shows were discontinued. In the meantime, resourceful Midwest gardeners found other ways of keeping in touch with each other and with the rest of the horticultural world. Separated by miles of prairie, these brothers and sisters of the spade took up their pens and joined round-robins organized by *Flower Grower* magazine.

The other saving grace for garden-loving midwesterners was a radio program aired daily on station KFNF operated by the Henry Field Seed Company. Called "The Garden Club of the Air," the program was composed of informal thirty-minute segments devoted to a wide variety of garden subjects. The program's hostess was Field's sister Helen, who shared her horticultural expertise in a warm, folksy manner that won her an enormous following. Mind you, this was no cute little old lady in sneakers. A well-read and well—if unconventionally—educated woman, Helen Field Fischer was the second child and eldest daughter of intelligent, engaging, intrepid parents.

Her mother, Lettie (Celestia) Eastman, had been raised in

Illinois by a father who believed in the intellectual equality of men and women. Fortunately, she found in Solomon Field an enlightened young man who shared this belief and admired her brains as well as her shining braids. They were married in 1870 and soon afterward abandoned the civilized comforts of Illinois in favor of the Iowa prairie.

This adventurous young couple set up housekeeping in a fourteen-by-sixteen-foot shanty in the Nishnabotna Valley, where Henry, the first of their seven children and founder of the seed company, was born. Soon after Henry's birth, Lettie resumed her teaching in nearby Shenandoah, where Solomon also taught school. Years later, daughter Helen told the story of their journey on horseback to and from classes encumbered by the baby. In *The Memory Book* the seven Field children compiled for their parents, she wrote, "They took turns in carrying him, and in the winter had great sport keeping him right side up as they passed him bundled back and forth."

By the time Helen was growing up, Solomon and Lettie had moved to the brick house "Sunnyside" closer to town. Helen described her home in affectionate detail for *The Memory Book.*

> The square red brick house stood well back from the road with a wide, green lawn between. In front of the front door stood two tall evergreens and between them started the path that ran flower-bordered all the way to the front gate. It had roses — pinks, thousand leaved ones and Royal George and velvet and nameless early red and yellow ones.... The annual flowers were in a bed to the right side of the lawn as you went in, and quite at the right edge was a fringe of wild plum trees and a crab apple tree, planted for their blossoms which went so well with the blue bells (*Mertensia virginica*) at their feet. The blue bells started from a root which Mother brought in her trunk when she came as a bride from Illinois. (I think there must have been a bit of horticultural passion in Mother's blood, too!)

It was Helen's father, however, who imbued the children with his own love of gardening. Helen, the eldest daughter, and Susan, the youngest, were "papa's little boys." Despite the neighbors' raised eyebrows, they wore overalls and helped him in the berry patch and cherry orchard. Brother Henry knew at the age of five that horticulture was for him. The little boy became fascinated with a seed catalog published by the James Vick Company and begged his mother to read it to him. There and then, he resolved to become a seedman and asked his mother to write a letter informing Mr. Vick of this decision. When the kindly Mr. Vick replied, Henry was set for life.

By the 1920s, the Henry Field Seed and Nursery Company ranked among the largest seed businesses in the nation, and just as he was about to slow down and rest on his laurels, Henry discovered radio. The medium was still in its infancy and local stations were hard put to fill their hours on the air. In 1923, WOW, owned by the Omaha Grain Exchange, invited Henry to bring some of his "seedhouse folk" to the studio and provide an evening's broadcast. Inspired by the possibilities of this new medium, Henry applied for an operating license and, with the help of local radio enthusiasts, built a five-hundred-watt station. With no experience but a profound belief in the service radio could perform and sensible of its public relations value, he picked up the microphone to address the needs of the local farming community.

The success of station KFNF can be judged by the deluge of mail that arrived at the studio. Its appeal was explained in an article by Bob Birkby and Janice Nahra Friedel in *The Palimpsest*, a publication of the Iowa State Historical Society. "Out in the empty countryside people heard Henry's plain, friendly voice coming into their homes. It was as if a good neighbor had just dropped by for a visit, and they couldn't help but believe in him. They wrote letters by the thousands and bought whatever he offered, sight unseen." Most of the broadcasting on KFNF (affectionate listeners insisted that the call letters stood for "Kind Friends Never Fail") was done by employees of the Henry Field Seed Company, local talent, and, fortunately for lovers of the daylily, Henry's sister, Helen.

Frail as a teenager, Helen had been educated at home. While relatives looked askance at this indulgence, her parents had stuck to their guns. They encouraged her to study art, music, and anything else that took her fancy. She was allowed to paint murals on the living room walls and to learn about wild-flowers. She was a voracious reader and her parents provided her with books. When she was sixteen, they gave her a camera, which she soon mastered and used with skill. In vindication of her parents' unorthodox theories of education, she breezed through the examinations for her teacher's certificate and taught school for ten years before marrying a kind, supportive older husband. Together, they raised three daughters.

When Gretchen, their eldest, expressed the desire to study landscape architecture at Cornell University in Ithaca, New York, Mrs. Fischer gathered up the whole family and came East to look the place over. The Fischers rented an apartment for the summer, and when Gretchen brought home the prospectus, Helen Field Fischer "took one look, hung up her dishpan, and announced, 'I'm going, too!'" For the next two summers, she pursued courses in botany, landscaping, and horticulture, and from 1923 to 1950, shared the fruits of her knowledge over the airwaves and through dozens of articles for *Better Homes and Gardens*, *Successful Farming*, and *Flower Grower.*

Mrs. Fischer's reputation and influence extended far beyond her four-state listening area. When the "Flower Lady"—as she was called with affection and respect—said something, garden-ers listened. And in the early forties, Mrs. Fischer began to say a lot about daylilies. The story goes that, heretofore, she had been no admirer of the "Red Corn Lily" (yet another name for *Hemerocallis fulva*). She had, in fact, struggled to banish it from her flower beds. When listeners began writing to her in praise of the new hybrid daylilies, she turned a deaf ear. But she was instant-ly won over by a visit to an Iowa garden resplendent with tall golden 'Ophir' from Bertrand Farr; Dr. Stout's stunning papri-ka-sprinkled 'Wau-Bun'; and H. P. Sass's ethereal 'Moonbeam'. "They were as strange and new to me," she wrote, "as though imported from some distant country." As of that moment, daylilies had found a persuasive and articulate champion. By extolling daylilies at every opportunity, over station KFNF and in writing, Mrs. Fischer stimulated so much interest that she could no longer answer the flood of mail, and under her aegis, a hemerocallis round-robin evolved.

The first transcontinental daylily round-robin was formed in 1943 under the leadership of Mrs. Hindman—who remembered good old *fulva* from the Kansas gardens of her youth. Letters "flew" between distant members of the round-robin group. Each, in turn, received the precious package, added a letter of his or her own, and sent the "flight" on its way. During the war years, round-robins formed a horticultural lifeline among participants. With the return of peace, these birds of a feather began writing to each other about the possibility of resuming the well-loved flower shows previously sponsored by the Henry Field Seed Company. Mrs. Fischer was apprised of these sentiments and agreed to see what could be done. The rest is history.

Aided by the "Flower Lady," arrangements were made for a flower show to be held July 13 and 14, 1946. Years later, Mrs. Fischer's daughter, Gretchen Fischer Harshbarger, remembered the drama of that landmark event:

> Mother encouraged the meeting and helped to make it come true. Her sister, Jessie Field Shambaugh of nearby Clarinda, Iowa, took over as chairman. And what an affair it was! A real gala! The invitation went out over radio through Iowa, Nebraska, Kansas, Missouri, South Dakota and Minnesota. Everyone was to come, bring flowers for a Show, a well-filled picnic basket, and camp-out bedding for use in temporary dormitories.
>
> The Henry Field Seed Company offered its building for the displays, its auditorium for the meeting, and its basement for slide shows and dormitory beds. The congregational Church gave space for an additional "Robin Roost" of cots.
>
> No one knew who would come, how many people or whether there'd be any flowers for the Show! I get goose pimples now, after all these years, just thinking about the excitement and suspense. I lived 300 miles away, but got a telephone call from mother saying that I must drop everything and come. And I did!
>
> We needn't have worried. The day of the meeting, cars began arriving from everywhere. The trains and busses [sic] brought more. Flowers? Tons of them! Every kind, but especially Hemerocallis for this was to be their "coming out party."

On the second day of the flower show, a meeting was held in the auditorium. During the proceedings, Mrs. Fischer's sister wrote out a motion which Mrs. Viola M. Richards of Greencastle, Indiana, read to the assembled company. Twenty years later, Mrs. Richards still experienced a frisson of pleasure in recalling her part in this momentous occasion: "To this day, I have a vivid recollection of the thrill I had when the motion 'that we here today organize the Midwest Hemerocallis Society' was unanimously adopted. I felt it was the beginning of a national organization, as it truly was."

The horticultural grapevine carried the news and word spread like a prairie fire. Applications for membership poured in. East Coast daylily enthusiasts got wind of the newly formed Society and begged to join their midwestern counterparts. By the end of 1946, the fledgling Society was barely six months old and already had 757 members. When July 1947 rolled around, members flocked to a "big family reunion and flower show" in Shenandoah, where Gretchen Fischer Harshbarger was duly elected the second president of the Society. At the same meeting, the Midwest Hemerocallis Society was obliged to consider the writing on the wall. Within a year, they had become a national Society with members in forty-one states. They needed a name to reflect the broader base of their membership. Before the last visitors left the grounds of the Henry Field Seed Company, the group had become simply The Hemerocallis Society.

The first two meetings in Shenandoah had the ingenuous charm of a Norman Rockwell cover for the *Saturday Evening Post*. The atmosphere was part quilting bee, part hoedown, and reports of these gatherings exude warmth, camaraderie, and goodwill. Even the Hemerocallis Society publications during the early years had a familial ring. Through the flower shows and the round-robins, everybody knew everybody. This is not to say that the yearbooks and *Hemerocallis Journals* of the forties and fifties were naive. They often boasted scholarly articles by Dr. Stout and other scientists. But there was a quality of innocence that has been lost along the way. The hoedown has long since been replaced by the convention, and over the years the publications have developed a high degree of sophistication.

In 1950, the Convention moved east to Cleveland, Ohio, and at that time, a new constitution and bylaws were presented and adopted. A twelve-member Board of Directors was established to share the responsibilities of the President, and a program of awards and honors was established to encourage and reward those individuals who most effectively spread the gospel and furthered the purposes of the Society: the development and improvement of the genus *Hemerocallis*. With this added inducement, more and more breeders leapt into the field. From 1948 to 1957, an average of twenty-eight new hybridizers a year joined the ranks. And during the next decade, that number nearly doubled. Incorporated in 1955 as The American Hemerocallis Society and selected by the International Horticultural Congress as the International Registry for the genus *Hemerocallis*, the Society had come of age.

Ironically, Helen Field Fischer died at the time of year when daylilies are at their peak. Members of the Hemerocallis Society attending the National Convention in 1953 stood, heads bowed, to honor her memory with a moment of silence. But the most lasting tribute to Mrs. Fischer is the thriving American Hemerocallis Society of today. Her husband was not overestimating her impact on the daylily world when he wrote: "She influenced and guided the lives of countless people. Her life on earth is ended, but her spirit will go on forever."

The tenth anniversary meeting of the newly christened American Hemerocallis Society was held in Omaha, Nebraska, at the Hotel Fontenelle. But on Friday, July 20, 1956, busloads of daylily people made the pilgrimage to Shenandoah, Iowa, and the Henry Field Seed Company where it all began. The last stop of the day was at the garden of Judge Frederick Fischer and the late Mrs. Fischer. Advanced in years but determined, the judge had succeeded in maintaining the garden as his wife had left it. During their life together, he had been her prop and stay. She was so nervous at the time of her first radio broadcast that he had remained in the studio, keeping a protective arm around her until she gained confidence. He used to refer to himself as "the godfather" of the Hemerocallis Society and was the volunteer Secretary and Treasurer who advanced the necessary funds to get out the first yearbook.

In the history of the modern daylily, it is impossible to calculate the importance of the American Hemerocallis Society. On the occasion of the Society's twentieth anniversary, Mrs. Mary Lester, an eminent hybridizer from Atlanta, Georgia, paid homage to Dr. Stout and other pioneers "who showed the way." However, she added that "the forming of the Midwest Hemerocallis Society [forerunner of the American Hemerocallis Society] was the impetus which caused the greatest advance in developing the daylily." As Dr. Stout is the Father of the Modern Daylily, so this Society has been a combination of adoring, pushy stage mother and nurturing extended family.

Bertie Ferris: Networking

Bertie Ferris

Mrs. Royal A. Ferris became a member of the American Hemerocallis Society the year the articles of incorporation were drawn up. At this writing, thirty-seven years have passed, and for thirty-three of them Mrs. Ferris, known to all and sundry as Bertie, has worked tirelessly to advance the cause of daylilies through the Society. At first she confined her efforts to her immediate circle of gardening friends. At that time, there weren't many local daylily groups in the Lone Star State. Bertie set out to remedy the situation, and now there are a dozen, three of which were formed only recently. "In 1955," she recalled, "I was just beginning to get involved—I didn't go to my first National Convention until 1958. But I'd always been interested in daylilies, and I tried to get other people here going. Once we all got together, the local society took off with a bang!"

Bertie hadn't been working with the Dallas group very long when a fellow Texan became President of the national Society. Miss Annie T. Giles of Austin was a forceful character. A Daughter of the American Revolution, Daughter of the Republic of Texas, and former schoolteacher, she was accustomed to being obeyed. It came to Miss Annie's attention that Bertie Ferris was taking a lively interest in daylilies on a local level. Why wouldn't she be the person to serve on the national board of the American Hemerocallis Society? "You might just as well get in on the fun" was the way she put it. "Don't say no. Think about it for a few days and let me know."

So Bertie thought about it and said yes. Next, she was asked what she wanted to do. Somewhat at a loss, she replied that the only thing she knew and loved was flowers and flower shows. "Good!" said Miss Annie. "You can be exhibition chairman." It transpired that among the duties of the exhibition chairman was the task of revising the *Judges' Handbook,* an act tantamount to revising the Bible. (Bertie has been involved with every subsequent revision of the *Handbook.*) The new board member had no sooner negotiated this hurdle than Miss Annie had another idea. "I hear you're going over to Europe," said the incumbent President of the Society. "Well, you can go to Austria. They are going to have an international exhibition, and you can talk to them about getting a hundred daylilies over there."

Fortunately, Bertie knew Hubert A. Fischer (no known relation to Helen Field Fischer), a noted amateur horticulturist and daylily hybridizer with international connections. "Don't worry," he told her. "We'll see that you have a hundred daylilies representing ten different hybridizers." Fischer was as good as his word. However, the promised plants still hadn't arrived two days before Bertie was scheduled to leave for Europe. It was a cliff-hanger, but all's well that end's well. They came twenty-four hours before her flight; she packed them immediately and got to the airport in the nick of time. Working with the Director of the Display Garden for the 1964 World Exhibition, Bertie was largely responsible for the success of the daylily exhibit in which a number of the cultivars won medals for their creators.

Becoming President of the American Hemerocallis Society in 1969 and winner of the Helen Field Fischer Medal for "distinguished and meritorious service" in 1970, this indefatigable daylily evangelist still travels extensively, spreading the daylily gospel. "You can't do the job sitting at home," she says. "We're always working on getting more members and talking people into joining the Society." Among those she personally "talked into joining" were various Pittsburghers. Her particular affection for the Pittsburgh Daylily Club dates from the time she inveigled them into playing host to a Regional Meeting. If the Regional Meeting I attended in Charlotte, North Carolina, last year is anything to go by, the planning alone must take months. Sumptuous accommodations had been arranged at the Sheraton Hotel, complete with a flower show set up in the lobby. Slide programs, judging clinics, banquets, and garden visits were orchestrated smoothly and efficiently, and the tour gardens were impressive.

Persuading the innocent Pittsburghers to undertake a similar project was a tribute to Bertie's salesmanship and to the stamina of the local group. But that was only the thin end of the wedge. Just as the weary organizers were congratulating themselves on the success of their first Regional Meeting, she announced that they were ready to tackle a National Convention! Now the hapless members of the Pittsburgh Daylily Club are in the midst of preparations for the 1993 National Convention. Their mentor shows no signs of remorse. Instead, Bertie is jubilant. "Interest in daylilies has really ballooned during the time I've been working with the Society!" And no wonder! She has charmed, cajoled, or shamed *Hemerocallis* lovers into joining the American Hemerocallis Society and becoming involved in its activities. Through educational workshops and clinics, she has led the crusade to improve the genus by helping judges hone their powers of discrimination. In order to keep her own critical standards high, she has traveled countless miles to visit gardens and observe the performance of daylilies in different parts of the country.

I met Bertie for the first time at the Region 15 meeting in North Carolina. We were both boarding an airport van for the Sheraton Hotel, and it wasn't easy for her to mount the awkwardly high step. She is, by her own admission, "a senior citizen, after all." But she has an ageless face and distinguished features. During the course of the weekend, I would catch glimpses of her, hatless even at midday under the hot southern sun.

Oblivious of any discomfort, she was always absorbed in the daylilies.

A month later, I saw her at the National Convention in Pennsylvania. In between, she had been up to Michigan City, Indiana, and down to Indianapolis in the center of this long, rather narrow state. From there, she hit a few private gardens in Ohio en route to Pittsburgh—to check on her protégés there— arriving at the Convention rested and refreshed. "Before that," she told me airily, "I went to a meeting in east Texas and on a car trip to Florida, visiting three gardens in Louisiana on the way. There are about twelve Louisiana daylily gardens. You can't see them all, but you're in the doghouse down there if you don't try! Then we went over to Mississippi and on to Jack Temple in Pensacola, Florida. Jack is the one who has kept alive the spiders when everybody else was throwing them out. He has a wonderful collection of spiders." This puzzling state- ment indicates that Mr. Temple is interested in daylilies with narrow flower segments, not in arachnids.

Bertie knows or has known everyone in the daylily world, and her Florida trip last year was especially arranged to include a visit with Bill Munson (W. R. Munson, Jr.) and his mother, Ida, at Wimberlyway Gardens in Gainesville. "He's the tops," she told me. She also mentions prominent figures from the past whom she has admired: Hubert Fischer's Chicago colleagues, eminent men who made outstanding contributions to the genus *Hemerocallis* during the fifties and sixties, and from the same period, Miss Edna Spalding.

In those days, Bertie and two or three traveling companions would get in the car and drive to Louisiana once a year to see Miss Edna and her flowers. Unlettered and strapped for money, Edna Spalding was nevertheless one of the great daylily breed- ers of her day. She only grew four hundred or five hundred seedlings a year—selling for "pocket money" those that she didn't use for breeding. If she considered them unfit for either purpose, she ruthlessly gouged them out of the ground with a big butcher knife and chucked them over the garden fence.

Although writing was a chore for her, Miss Edna had sent

away to Fairmount Gardens for her first two daylilies, Dr. Stout's 'Rosalind' and Mrs. Nesmith's 'Killarny Lass'. The order was scrawled on cheap, lined paper, but Spalding had an unerring instinct for choosing the best daylilies then available. Once she began making crosses, she would spend from two to four hours daily studying the color, form, and plant habit of her seedlings. In her quest for a truer pink and a whiter white, she maintained the cool ability to discard any seedling that failed to measure up to her standards. Three years before her death, this insistence on quality was rewarded with the Bertrand Farr Medal for outstanding results in the field of hybridizing. The year was 1965, the same year her famous lavender-pink 'Luxury Lace' won the Stout Medal. By remaining extremely particular, Miss Edna succeeded in producing the forerunners of today's beautiful clear pinks and lavenders.

Bertie has warm memories of visits to Miss Edna Spalding's garden. "One time we got there at six o'clock in the morning. She came to the door and said, 'Come in and have breakfast.' There was plenty of homemade bread fresh out of the oven — you could smell it. But there was only a little bit of jelly, and there were four of us. 'That's all right,' said Edna Spalding, 'We'll just have to ration the jelly.'"

If Bertie responded to Miss Edna's spunk and simplicity, it may have been because her own life hasn't always been easy. She and her twin brother were the oldest of nine children growing up in a little town twenty-one miles east of Dallas. Most of the two hundred people in her hometown of Heath, Texas, were related to Bertie by blood or marriage, and she learned about plants from her mother and two grandmothers. "They all loved gardening and exchanging plants. And I helped them in their gardens. My mother taught me to do rose cuttings when I was eight years old."

Until she was in seventh grade, Bertie went to the tiny local school. Then her grandparents on her father's side moved to Dallas and invited the two oldest grandchildren to live with them and continue their education at the high school nearby. Her parents agreed, as long as the children came home at weekends—Bertie, to help with her younger siblings; her brother, to work on the farm. As soon as she finished high school, Bertie announced her intention to become a registered nurse. In those days young women didn't have careers and her parents were less than enthusiastic, but she was determined. "When I was nursing," she remembers, "I said I needed a car. They said, 'Single women don't drive cars.'" But an uncle promised that if she could get together $300, he would find her a car. The same uncle also said, "You don't want to live in a rooming house all your life. Why don't you buy a house?" Bertie recollects with amusement that some family members were scandalized. Only "kept women" had houses in those days.

Bertie went calmly ahead, purchased a house, and planted a few *Hemerocallis fulva* around it for a bit of color. No sooner had she settled in, perfectly content with her state of single blessedness, than one of her hospital patients proposed to her. Somewhat to her own surprise, she accepted, and they were married the next day. The following year, the newlyweds were separated for the duration of World War II. When her husband returned from England, where he had been stationed, he insisted on building her an English-style house. Upon its completion, Bertie moved the orange daylilies from her old house and set about making a garden.

It so happened that her new next-door neighbor had a yellow daylily. Bertie offered to swap a few roots. "Yours," her neighbor told her disdainfully, "is common. Mine is a hybrid." Although she had never heard of a hybrid daylily, Bertie eagerly accepted a division of the yellow cultivar and a pamphlet describing some of Dr. Stout's introductions. That was in 1947. She asked her husband if he thought they could afford $20 worth of Stout daylilies, and he said yes, as long as they were red. And that is how Bertie came by 'Red Knight' and 'Red Lady'. To this day, she grows some of the old cultivars. But like the flowers she has done so much to promote, Bertie is always looking ahead.

I asked her recently how the American Hemerocallis Society had been instrumental in the daylily's forward march, and she answered promptly, "The Awards and Honors Program and the rules and standards of excellence established by the Society." This year, to ensure the organization's ongoing success, she is hitting the road to plug for the William E. Monroe Endowment Fund. "Nonprofit groups like ours just have to have an endowment fund to meet their expenses," she says. I am not surprised to learn that so far, most regions have been "pretty responsive."

The Chicago Scene

Intimations of the need for a national organization were stirring in Chicago even before the Midwest Hemerocallis Society was founded in 1946. The Windy City was already a hotbed of horticulturists, many of them friends of Hubert Fischer's. From this group, there emerged a quartet of diploid daylily breeders whose achievements left a permanent mark on the daylily world. Fischer and Elmer A. Claar had been brought together by a local men's garden club. Mr. Claar, a Harvard-trained lawyer, discovered that he preferred flowers to briefs and eventually eschewed the bar for real estate and more time in his garden. Fischer was a dealer and importer of precious stones who readily conceded that business interfered with his horticultural pursuits.

The two men had come to gardening at about the same period in their lives. Hubert Fischer was born in 1896 and began planting flowers almost as soon as he could lift a hoe. His first garden was a plot of land behind his father's store on Chicago's northwest side. When young Fischer was called upon to serve in World War I, he found a girl to look after the plants. She did such a creditable job that upon his return he married her, and they began gardening together. Their first daylilies were the species *H. flava* and *H. fulva,* followed later by *H. Thunbergii* and *H. citrina.* Then a friend sent them Bertrand Farr's 'Ophir'. Hubert Fischer lost his heart to this stately golden beauty and soon was ordering plants from every known source. By the mid-thirties, he found himself hybridizing.

A similar fate befell Elmer Claar, who also had loved gardening from an early age and was attracted to daylilies as a young man. He acquired all Dr. Stout's introductions and those of the Sass brothers, Carl Betscher, and Mrs. Nesmith. It was in his nature to be a collector. His interests included antique silver, porcelains, and snuffboxes, but daylilies became his passion. Before long, he, too, caught the hybridizing bug. At the same time, he began visiting gardens and taking photographs of his favorite daylilies. Soon he was being asked to talk about daylilies and to show his slides. It was just such an invitation that brought him into Chicago one evening from his home in Northfield, Illinois. Hubert Fischer wrote about that night at the time of Claar's death in 1961:

> It was many years ago that I first met Elmer Claar at a meeting of the Chicago Men's Garden Club at which he gave an illustrated lecture on daylilies. As we had a kindred interest, a visit to his garden followed, and our friendship grew. I still have a Kodachrome slide of one of his first red daylily seedlings. Even at that early time, he was breeding for color in that direction. He was the first in the Chicago area to grow seedlings in quantity, and through the years his interest never diminished.

The blossoming of this classic daylily friendship attracted other local daylily growers. Again, Fischer was a source of information: "At that time, the interested growers in the Chicago area started what was to be a national society. We all contributed dues and a member was instructed to start the organization. This work, however, languished, and later when the Midwest Hemerocallis Society was organized, we became charter members of that."

Mrs. Viola Richards, who read out the actual motion proposing the Midwest Hemerocallis Society, remembered receiving a letter from the Chicago gentleman (who remains nameless). "He had written me that he was trying to organize a Hemerocallis Society and enclosed a printed prospectus. He asked me to send him the addresses of my round-robin members so he could contact them." That Mrs. Richards refused to do. The prospectus offered three-year memberships for $10 in advance. "As I did not approve of that, I agreed to merely present the idea of forming a society to the members." The heartfelt response led, of course, to the historic gathering in Shenandoah, Iowa, and the Chicagoans were welcomed with open arms.

Why, one might well ask, were gardeners in the Chicago area so susceptible to daylilies during the forties and fifties? What was in the air blowing off Lake Michigan that kindled such fervent interest? The answer lies not in the air but rooted in the earth on the campus of the University of Chicago. At Wychwood, an estate owned by the University, Dr. Ezra Jacob Kraus, chairman of the Department of Botany, had assembled the most extensive collection of named daylily cultivars in the Midwest.

Dr. Kraus, like Dr. Stout before him, was a serious-minded scientist and not at all the sort of person to arouse passions. But the daylilies produced by his meticulous, scientific methods caused a sensation. Once again, Hubert Fischer tells it how it was: "It is difficult to describe the thrill and excitement that we felt on first seeing row on row of daylilies, hundreds of selected seedlings in colors undreamed of, clear, clean colors, fine forms, and a variety of styles. Truly, here was a preview of things to come. Here, under numbers were many of the lovely varieties now named and introduced and growing in our gardens." (The term *under numbers* refers to the identification by number of the promising but as yet unnamed offspring of crosses.)

While Dr. Kraus had great success with daylilies in shades of red and pink, his unique contribution to the color range was the introduction of the cantaloupe hue commonly called "melon." At one time, his cultivar 'Ruth Lehman' was the only large-flowered, melon-colored daylily in existence. But within a few years, this shade became so popular that it was held in low esteem by the cognoscente. Even Dr. Kraus was beginning to have reservations: "Personally, I confess I am becoming somewhat alarmed because I am now obtaining too many seedlings whose flowers are the color of the flesh of a ripe cantaloupe, tinged with flesh pink." Be that as it may, when I look at daylilies in shades of melon-pink, my mouth begins to water, and I think kindly of Dr. Kraus.

As a bachelor, Kraus was able to devote himself full-time to his teaching, his students, and his consuming horticultural hobby. He liked to say that it was not his knowledge of plants that brought him success in hybridizing, but his determination. The observations of Edgar C. Lehman, who introduced the Kraus daylilies, give credence to this assertion. "It was not unusual for him to work for ten or twelve years on a certain cross to wait for a break he was certain would come—if enough crosses were made. Fifty seedlings were a minimum he considered necessary to be able to judge the characteristics of a given cross. I remember vividly in the summer of 1946 making over three thousand crosses of two parents which resulted in more than a quart of seed. Day after day, I worked making this same cross and tagging each flower. When we selected from these seedlings, we saved six plants and named one."

Although Dr. Kraus was wholly absorbed in his work and far from hail-fellow-well-met with his students, he nevertheless received more than respect from them. Paul Voth studied with him in the thirties and followed in his footsteps as a professor of botany at the University of Chicago. Professor Voth later paid his teacher this tribute: "Although 'E.J.' would have been the last to admit it, this great botanist, horticulturist, and benefactor probably possessed more friends of greater diversity and from a wider geographic range than any other plant scientist of his generation."

Another former student remembers him with appreciation. I spoke recently with Dr. Wendell R. Mullison, who had been a Ph.D. candidate in Dr. Kraus's department before World War II. Dr. Mullison, a charter member of the Midwest Hemerocallis Society, credits his love of daylilies to Dr. Kraus. "While I was working for my degree, I had a job during the summer on the estate which the University owned at Lake Geneva, Wisconsin. As part of my job, Dr. Kraus asked me to make some crosses on daylilies. So I did, and that was my introduction to hybridizing. Afterward, I thought it would be fun to grow some daylilies at home and try breeding them. And I've been breeding them ever since."

As a hybridizer, Dr. Mullison has exercised exceptional restraint, learned perhaps from Dr. Kraus. He has introduced only one daylily in all this time. However, his 1984 introduction 'White Stripe' is truly distinctive. The foliage is variegated with a longitudinal white band running from the base to the tip of the leaf. Normally the flowers are of a very light yellow, but occasionally a dead white one occurs. Of this anomaly, Mullison says, "While I describe it as white, it is, of course, albino—all color is absent, but it looks really white."

Ezra J. Kraus died in 1960, leaving behind not only exquisite flowers but precise records on which other hybridizers might build. And build they did. Elmer Claar worked closely with Dr. Kraus. Not a record keeper himself, he achieved quality by using only first-rate daylilies—many of them Kraus cultivars. To better evaluate his seedlings, Claar planted them by color—all the reds in one bed, all the pinks in another. Being particularly enamored of broad flower segments, he would take a petal from one of his best seedlings in a given color and hold it up to every flower in that bed. Even today, 'Annie Welch' looks positively modern with wide, rolled-back segments in a lovely shade of pink. Alas, it was not until after Claar's death that his gorgeous red 'Bess Ross' was awarded the Stout Medal.

Hubert Fischer also received help and encouragement from Dr. Kraus. A faithful chronicler of those days, Fischer wrote:

> The real desire to grow more seedlings was sparked by Dr. E. J. Kraus after a visit to his fields, where every available named daylily was growing, as well as thousands of seedlings. It was an inspiration, and to stop and admire a seedling meant to own it, together with its pedigree. He was most generous in offering plants, pollen and advice. The hours spent among his plants at the University of Chicago Garden, the lunches at the Quads Club, and later,

the visits to his office, checking pedigrees in his stud book are a cherished memory.

Armed with what he had learned from Dr. Kraus and sharing his mentor's enthusiasm for small flowers, Mr. Fischer went on to win honors for charming little flowers like 'Corky' and 'Cricket'. When the Fischer's only child, a talented stage designer named Donn, died tragically young, they established an award in his name—the Donn Fischer Memorial Award. The award recognizes outstanding achievement in the breeding of miniature-flowered daylilies. Ironically, the first winner was Fischer himself in 1962—for 'Golden Chimes'.

The indefatigable Hubert Fischer was both hybridizer and historian. In writing about his friends, he preserved several chapters of daylily history. On the occasion of David F. Hall's winning the Bertrand Farr Medal in 1956, Fischer furnished the text of the citation. I will let him introduce the fourth member of the Chicago quartet: "When asked to write about David Hall, I wondered what I could tell about so well known a horticulturist that is not already common knowledge. I have had the pleasure of knowing Dave for twenty-five years and feel that I am familiar with his work with daylilies and iris; but about his personal history, what could I tell?"

As the story unfolds, we learn that Hall was born in Blenheim, Ontario, in 1876, the same year that Alexander Graham Bell applied for a patent for the telephone. That instrument would dominate the rest of Hall's working life. His first job was logging timber for telephone poles in the Canadian wilderness. At twenty-one, he came to this country and got a job with the American Telephone & Telegraph Company. Toiling in the construction department of the company soon palled. He set about improving himself by studying law at night school and wound up as regional attorney for the company's long-lines division. Upon his retirement in 1940, his real life began.

Already an enormously successful hybridizer of iris—Hall had produced the first flamingo pink, which won him a Dykes Medal from the Iris Society of England—he now trained his clear, intelligent gaze exclusively on the daylily. The genus

Hemerocallis was not an entirely new enthusiasm. You may recall that he bought his very first daylilies from the Sass brothers on a trip to Nebraska in 1933. He was there in the summer, and the iris, which were his particular interest, had finished blooming. But it was the height of the season for daylilies. Years later, he wrote in a letter to one of his daylily friends: "I liked these hardy yellow flowers that kept the garden alive after the iris were through blooming, and decided to secure some and try my hand at breeding them as I had been doing for a few years with iris. I purchased eight unnumbered yellow seedlings and commenced crossing them."

From this modest beginning came a seedling with which he was quite pleased. It was introduced in 1945 as 'Mission Bells'. He described it as having "a good stout well-branched scape which carried up to 52 good sized yellow flowers with wider petals than any other daylily I had seen." Having recently heard about a pink species, *Hemerocallis fulva* var. *rosea*, he decided to add a pink hybrid daylily to his objectives. With the acquisition of *rosea*, he began at once, making crosses with 'Mission Bells'. From this line came all his lovely pinks, apricots, melons, and near whites. The smashing reds for which he was justly famous descended from a division given him by Dr. Kraus. He readily gave credit where it was due in an article for the 1954 *Hemerocallis Yearbook:* "First, I want to acknowledge my gratitude to the man who has been most helpful to me in achieving any small success I may have had in breeding daylilies. This man is Dr. E. J. Kraus, formerly Dean of Botany of the University of Chicago, now retired. To know this internationally famous breeder of many plants and shrubs is to admire and love him."

I cannot personally vouch for the lovable nature of Dr. Kraus, although every word I have read about him is filled with sincere regard. But I can testify to the beauty of his daylilies. I still grow 'Ringlets' and think that no perennial border should be without it for a seemingly endless supply of tidy, rounded golden flowers on moderately tall, well-branched scapes. Another of my favorite small-flowered cultivars is his well-named 'Sparks'. Burning orange gleams from the throats of the starry flame-red flowers.

If Saxton Gardens in Saratoga Springs, New York, is a repository of daylily history from Stout to the present, my Connecticut garden is a tribute to the Chicago hybridizers of the forties and fifties. In an alcove between rhododendrons, 'Golden Chimes' ring in the season, and I feel gratitude toward the remarkable Hubert Fischer, whose creation has given me pleasure every June for years. In July, David Hall's 'Shining Plumage' still stops me in my tracks with its incandescent red flowers. 'Bright Banner' is the perfect brick red and light orange foil for clumps of blue globe thistle (*Echinops ritro*). Although 'Lady Inara' has been superseded in my affections by other daylilies of a similar shade, she still offers up medium-sized goblets of translucent peach in an informal planting against the stone wall. Show me more prolific bloomers than Mr. Hall's yellow, cinnamon-dusted 'Melody Lane' and primrose-yellow 'Norwegian Lass'! Although Elmer Claar is not represented in my garden, I am prepared to take on faith Hubert Fischer's assessment of his friend's career: "He left a trail of beauty which will continue to enhance our gardens and provide a path for others to follow."

The Wonderful Wilds
of Missouri

Today, Shirley Gene Wild and her brother, Jim, are entirely responsible for the annual catalog of Gilbert H. Wild and Son, Inc., the largest daylily nursery in the world. Whether or not they alone can be blamed for my current daylily dilemma is a moot point. But having been involved with the family business ever since I placed my first order, they have a lot to answer for! I had already been buying daylilies for a couple of years when the fatal Gilbert H. Wild catalog came into my possession. *How* remains either a mystery or a Freudian lapse of memory. All I know is that in 1963, I began ordering daylilies from this source.

My first order that year included Ms. Wild's namesake, 'Shirley Wild', a dandelion yellow with narrow, spidery segments. There were two more spiders, 'Lydia Bechtold' and 'Kindly Light'. Apparently I was in my yellow phase, because everything I ordered that year was some shade of yellow. There were David Hall's pastels 'Sandalwood', 'Swansdown', and the lovely 'Norwegian Lass', which continues to delight me every season. At the darker end of the scale, I chose two more Hall creations, 'Evergold' and 'Gladys Kendall'. I now realize that the preponderance of Hall cultivars in my garden can be explained by the contract he signed with the Wilds in 1953 to handle his introductions.

Not three weeks after my original order had been acknowledged, I confessed to my garden notebook that I had gone "daylily mad" and announced that "today I am ordering more from the Wild's half-price sale." By this time, I had a rough plan for a flower bed seven feet wide and thirty-two feet long and needed twelve plants of 'Hyperion', twelve 'Sweetbriar', and three 'Pinafore' to fill it. How could I fail to take advantage of the sale? Think of the money I was saving. Thus began a long, ardent affair with the Wilds of Sarcoxie, Missouri.

Their 1965 catalog catered to my "pink period." I ordered seven different shades, and my notebook records the admission that "I don't know just where I'm going to put them, but I can't resist that sale!" The majority were Hall cultivars from four generations of line breeding using 'Mission Bells' and *Hemerocallis fulva* var. *rosea*: 'Coral Mist', 'Mary Anne', 'Betty Gerlash', 'Bright Spot', and 'Heart Throb'.

During the next ten years, cultivars hybridized by Ms. Wild's father, Allen, made up the bulk of my purchases. It was unfair of him to name a tall, handsome, yellow introduction 'Echo Valley'. I live on Echo Valley Road. How could I be without it? A color photograph of his 'Sweet Harmony' with dark-eyed, pale pink flowers guaranteed its entry into my garden, where it is still a great favorite. There is 'Winnie the Pooh', which I divided this fall for the umpteenth time, giving away dozens of plants of this buff cutie. 'Whir of Lace' from 1964 still provides a cool light yellow contrast to the meltingly warm apricot pink 'Lacey Queen'. Both occupy roughly the same spot in the border that they did twenty years ago. I still have Mr. Wild's 'Melon Balls', 'Bambi Doll', 'Golden Candles', and 'Channel Islands', and I love them all. Now, what I want to know from Gene and Jim Wild is, where am I going to put my new daylilies?

The Wild family has been wreaking havoc with the finances and self-control of flower lovers for five generations. In the nineteenth century, it was only peony fans who were at risk; in the twentieth, iris and daylily enthusiasts joined the ranks of the endangered. Today, iris lovers are being spared the temptations of the Wild catalog because the number of daylily devotees has risen so dramatically. "Now," Gene told me over the phone, "we're concentrating on daylilies and peonies. The daylily sales kept increasing so rapidly that we just couldn't dig iris and daylilies at the same time. We didn't have enough help or enough energy."

The Wilds have long been known for their collective energy. Both Gene's parents were dynamos. Her mother Haidee worked almost until her death in 1983. Gene talked about the division of labor. "Mother prepared the orders for the diggers, got the labels made, and processed the orders to get them ready for the packing room. Then, I've always done the book work, and of course, Daddy ran around overlooking everything: hot-footing it here and there, taking people out to the farm when they came in, and just being general overseer. After he began not to feel very good the last couple or three years of his life, Jim took over from him." Allen Wild died in February 1989. Gene and Jim are on their own, but they are carrying on the family tradition and forging ahead with the hybridizing program.

In the days before Allen Wild's health began to fail, an admiring observer described the family modus operandi: "During the season, Allen will be dabbling his pollen, walking up and down the rows of daylilies while at the same time giving orders to the workers for something he just thought about. Each night the whole family goes out to the new seedling bed several miles from home and office, where they view thousands and thousands of blooms each day, walking up and down the rows, marking what attracts attention."

Professional horticulture seems to run in families, and the Wilds are a prime example. The genetic predisposition for gardening surfaced first in Gene Wild's great-great-grandfather. In 1846, Herman Wild dropped out of a westward-bound wagon train to settle at the edge of the Ozark uplift. Here, the land was level and the fields filled with wildflowers. A lover of plants and flowers, he reasoned that if the soil would support luxuriant native vegetation, it would also support flourishing crops. Having emigrated from Germany and traveled halfway across a strange country, he was ready now to put down roots.

No doubt Herman's Germanic work ethic and sound management of the land accounted for his success. Inspired by his example, three sons followed him into the allied fields of horticulture and agriculture. One, James B. Wild, founded the nursery that bears the name of his own son, Gilbert Herman. The story goes that in 1885, eight-year-old Gilbert was given $45 worth of peony roots by his father. The lad lavished such tender, loving care on his peonies that three years later he had enough to send a crate of blooms to a wholesale dealer in Omaha, Nebraska. His reward for diligence was the princely sum of $3. He was eleven years old at the time, and from that day forward, he devoted his life to raising flowers.

In his turn, Gilbert's son Allen carried on the horticultural tradition, working closely with his father. Cooperation is another tradition with the Wilds. At the time Gene was awarded the Helen Field Fischer Gold Medal, tribute was paid to the Wild family's solidarity: "It is hard to dissociate any member of this family from another member. It is a credit to each one that they can work together so well. Theirs is a lesson in family relationships."

There is something infinitely reassuring to receive the Gilbert H. Wild and Son catalog every year. In this footloose, fragmented world with its scattered families and mobile population, it is a comfort to know that in a small town in Missouri there is a flower-loving family that has lived in the same place for over a hundred years. Gene Wild was born in the house her great-grandfather built. It is a handsome house, and the present owners are discovering beneath the old paint fine oak and cherry paneling. That wood was hauled up out of Arkansas by team and mule to embellish the living room, dining room, and parlor. Although the Wilds no longer own the house, it stands right next door to their cold storage and packing room. The back windows of the house overlook the field where Gilbert Herman Wild raised his first peonies.

The Wilds' front door is on the main street of Sarcoxie, but their back door is in the country. Pastures where Appaloosa horses graze roll away to the tree-fringed horizon. There are no streets or houses to obstruct the view of farmland and flowers. Thirty years ago, Allen Wild expressed the significance his family attached to flowers in one of the catalogs: "In this day of high speed, flying saucers and atomic and hydrogen bombs, flowers are needed as never before as a balance over hate and war."

Other horticultural dynasties have devoted their talents in part to daylilies. In South Barrington, Illinois, just outside Chicago, Roy Klehm and his brothers are heirs to a 136-year-old family nursery business. There are parallels with the Wilds' story. Roy's great-grandfather John came from Germany and settled in the town of Cunton, Illinois (now Arlington Heights), where he grew fruit trees, bramble fruits, and Colorado blue spruce for the Christmas trade. Then, at about the time young Gilbert Wild was planting the peony roots his father had given him, John Klehm also took a shine to these lush, stalwart perennials. In due course, John's son Charles displayed the family penchant for growing peonies, as did grandson Carl. Roy and his brothers honor their father Carl and their grandfather Charles by retaining the name Charles Klehm and Son Nursery.

It was Roy who introduced daylilies into their midst. "I think I brought the daylilies into our company. We first had a peony catalog. But not everyone in the world is interested in peonies, and we had to diversify in order to draw a bigger audience. It was the late sixties, and I just thought daylilies were such wonderful plants and had such wide-open opportunities." It would be hard not to be aware of daylilies in the Chicago area, and Roy knew all the local hybridizers. He has particularly fond memories of Hubert Fischer, who aroused his interest in both hosta and *Hemerocallis*. The Klehm nursery has added both to its categories of specialization, and Roy himself is an active daylily breeder.

In Fishersville, Virginia, a three-generation love affair with daylilies is being carried on by the Viette family. Andre Viette's father Martin, a well-known nurseryman on Long Island, began hybridizing daylilies in the 1920s. He continued without pause until his death in 1979. Andre and his own two sons have followed in the same well-trodden path. While the 210-acre Andre Viette Farm and Nursery is by no means devoted solely to the genus *Hemerocallis*—hundreds of genera share the property—daylilies have been on the family agenda for more than sixty years. Viette cultivars are favorites and have been honored with their share of awards. Andre's miniature 'Peach Fairy' won the Hubert Fischer Trophy in 1984.

I grow and enjoy both 'Peach Fairy' and the stunning little 'Bittersweet Honey'—perfectly named for its sharp red-orange coloring which is mellowed by gold. I yearn to have more of the Viettes' little ones. There are many from which to choose: double miniature 'Little Carnation', hybridized by son Scott; Andre's 'Little Heart'; and 'Little Bee'. It would be easy to compile a long wish list.

Dedicated, hardworking families like the Viettes and the Klehms who have provided gardeners with such a banquet of daylilies and other beautiful flowers deserve our gratitude. I admire and salute them, one and all. But the wonderful Wilds of Missouri will always hold a very special place in my heart.

Movers and Shakers

'Crestwood Ann'
(Fay-Griesbach)

While I was happily planting all my beloved old Wild and Hall cultivars, a revolution—not always bloodless—was taking place in the daylily world. The first shots were heard in David Hall's adopted hometown of Chicago, and they were fired by Hall's friend and next-door neighbor, Orville Fay, a production supervisor at a local candy company. To understand the significance of Fay's work with daylilies and the explosion detonated by the unveiling of his tetraploids at the 1961 National Convention requires a little background.

During the early thirties, scientists discovered that colchicine, the alkaloid derived from the autumn crocus, when applied to living cells, both plant and animal, altered their chromosome complement. Within each cell's nucleus are the chromosomes containing genes which determine all hereditary traits. During the course of normal cell division, the chromosomes are duplicated, then drawn apart and separated from each other by a new nuclear membrane. Two identical nuclei emerge, each surrounded by a new cell wall. Colchicine prevents the formation of this new cell wall.

Applied to daylilies, the action of colchicine during cell division doubles the number of chromosomes. Instead of having two identical cells, each with its complement of twenty-two chromosomes (the normal number in almost all daylilies), a single giant cell is formed containing forty-four chromosomes—or twice the hereditary material possessed by diploid cells. A few enterprising breeders were intrigued with the possibilities this increase presented.

Dr. Ezra Kraus, who must have been a very effective teacher, made the analogy that genes are to plant breeding what letters are to language or notes to music. Think how many thousands and thousands of words can be made using a mere twenty-six letters. Or the staggering number of possible melodies which may be fashioned from sixty-four notes. Consider now the allure of doubling the already mind-boggling collection of traits inherent in a plant as varied and variable as the daylily. Why, the combinations that can be made with forty-four chromosomes must run into billions! It takes an adventurous spirit to contemplate working with so many elements. It also takes unlimited patience. Nor do the qualities of audacity and forbearance often inhabit the same soul. All of which makes me regard tetraploid breeders with particular awe.

On the surface of it, daylily breeding is relatively simple. One chosen plant is crossed with another; the traits—desirable and undesirable—displayed by offspring of the cross are studied and only those plants exhibiting the most pleasing features are retained. Gradually, by selecting the best of each succeeding generation, the undesirable characteristics are eliminated and the desirable ones preserved. But how long does it take? How many crosses must be made and how many seedlings studied? In 1957, Dr. Kraus was growing seven thousand selected diploid seedlings from an unknown but doubtless unbelievable number of crosses. Had he been studying tetraploids with double the number of possible variations, he would have had to examine twice as many seedlings.

Add to the overwhelming task of selection the fickle nature of early tetraploids. They had a tendency to be uncooperative parents, and their low fertility meant that many, many crosses were required to produce a mere handful of seeds. It is no mystery, then, why few backyard breeders leapt into the field during the early days. But there was a coterie of scientifically inclined amateurs, Fay being one of the first and foremost among them, who took the plunge.

What made these people willing to go to extraordinary lengths when beautiful diploid cultivars could be produced with far less trouble? For the visionary few, it was the enormously expanded horizons—the unknown wonders that might be unlocked by virtually unlimited genetic combinations arising from tetraploidy. And there was another more accessible reason: the promise of bigger flowers in more intense colors; handsomer, lusher foliage; stronger scapes capable of holding aloft the new large blooms; greater vegetative vigor and increased resistance to disease. Here, there was a precedent for optimism. Bearded irises had undergone an earlier transformation from so-so to spectacular by doubling the diploid number of chromosomes. The route to this achievement in irises was, however, easier and far more direct.

In the wild, there are no known tetraploid species of daylily. Triploid *Hemerocallis fulva* and its variants are the only exceptions to the diploid rule. There are, however, naturally occurring species of iris that are tetraploid. In 1900, three such species were introduced into this country and used extensively in breeding. In short order, they had contributed to a new race of prima donnas with huge blossoms, tall stalks, and colors no one heretofore had thought possible. The transformation was quick and complete. At the turn of the century, all garden irises were diploids; by 1940, practically all were tetraploids.

Daylily breeders, who were familiar with the success story of the tetraploid iris, were eager to experiment with their own flower of choice. And during the fifties and early sixties, former iris breeders like Orville Fay began to focus on this new and fascinating activity—employing colchicine to produce tetraploid daylilies. Fay's collaborator, Dr. Robert A. Griesbach, had every reason to be drawn to this essentially scientific branch of horticulture. After a stint in the U.S. Army 332nd Service Band, Griesbach gave up music for science and proceeded to earn degrees in biology and botany. He completed his Ph.D. under Paul Voth at the University of Chicago—Voth, as you may remember, was one of Dr. Kraus's "bright young men." The subject of Griesbach's thesis was "Dormancy and Seed Germination in *Hemerocallis*," and from here it was a short step to hybridizing and experimenting with colchicine.

Robert Griesbach came by his horticultural leanings from a father who had been an enthusiastic grower of daylilies, roses, irises, and gladioli. Together, father and son developed popular new varieties of gladiolus. This striking member of the iris family resembles the daylily in its breeder-friendly behavior and the almost endless range of possible sizes, forms, and colors. In 1971, the younger Griesbach was awarded the North American Gladiolus Council's Gold Medal, having the previous year won the American Hemerocallis Society's highest honor in the field of hybridizing. But I'm getting ahead of my story.

In 1955, fresh from the doctoral program at the University of Chicago, the thirty-year-old Griesbach joined forces with Orville Fay to produce the first proven tetraploid daylilies that were both garden worthy and the potential founders of an entirely new breed. Fay was already an old hand at plant breeding and had received formal training in cytology (the study of cells) and genetics while at River Falls State Teachers College in Wisconsin. At the time of his retirement in 1953, he had spent twenty years of his life as a color and flavor chemist at the Nutrine Candy Company, but he had been breeding plants much longer. And like every other Chicago daylily great, he had been helped by Dr. Ezra Kraus. In his way, Fay acknowledged the debt in a letter printed in the *Hemerocallis Journal* in 1969.

> Dr. E. J. Kraus, Chairman Dept. of Botany, University of Chicago, with whom I was closely associated during all the years he bred daylilies in this area, is really the only pioneer breeder from whom I received help and inspiration. He was a scientist, so we saw eye to eye on everything. He was most generous and would give me a division of anything I admired. One day he offered me a division of #1986 (a seedling under number) which was later named 'Evelyn Claar'. He was ready to dig it when I told him I wouldn't take it as a

gift if there was a trace of *fulva rosea* any place in its pedigree. He consulted his records, which he kept in a covered garbage can in the field. After a detailed search, he assured me that there was no trace of *fulva rosea* in the pedigree, so he dug the plant and gave it to me to use. This proved to be the most valuable gift I ever received from a plant breeder. It became the starting point of my work with pinks, roses and melons—both diploid and tetraploid.

The ramet of 'Evelyn Claar' was indeed a generous gift, as Fay went on to win Stout Medals for his melon-colored 'Frances Fay' (named for his wife) and the pastel blend 'Satin Glass'. To me, this letter is indicative of a quality in Orville Fay which might not endear him to competitors. With what I suspect was inadequate justification, he clearly felt on a par with Dr. Kraus as a scientist. Moreover, his confidence makes him sound presumptuous. His daylilies did, of course, win an unprecedented *four* Stout Medals and his irises, four Dykes Medals! But tact and modesty were not Mr. Fay's long suit. His self-assurance verged on hubris—which may explain the events that rocked the National Convention in Chicago in 1961.

Leading up to all the excitement was the development of the so-called "Crestwood Series," the first successful tetraploids to emerge from the ten-year-old Fay-Griesbach program. Two methods of employing colchicine are used to bring about the conversion of diploids to tetraploids. Neither is foolproof. Curiously, with all the advances in the plants themselves, the methods of conversion have remained virtually unchanged for the last thirty years. One involves the treatment of a mature plant, the other the submersion of seeds in a weak solution of the chemical. In each case, the success rate is moderate and the mortality rate high. However, once converted, tetraploid plants can be crossed with one another, bypassing the time-consuming colchicine step.

In 1959, two years before the Chicago Convention, the Fay-Griesbach team saw one hundred colchicine-induced tetraploid hemerocallis in flower for the first time. Of these, one particular seedling was singled out and named 'Crestwood Ann'. By dusting the stigma of 'Crestwood Ann' flowers with their own pollen (a practice called *selfing* in daylily parlance), a pod containing four viable seeds was obtained. The seedlings raised from this self-cross bloomed the year of the Convention, thus establishing a new line of seed-grown tetraploids.

The significance of this achievement was not lost on Orville Fay, who described 'Crestwood Ann' as "the most important introduced tetraploid in the World today." Unfortunately, it was his attitude, along with the announcement that within ten years diploid daylilies would be obsolete, that caused a furor at the Chicago Convention. In Mr. Fay's defense, he drew this conclusion not from arrogance, but from his experience with bearded iris. Later, in an interview with A. H. Goldner printed in *The Hemerocallis Journal,* he explained his position:

> When I started breeding iris in 1930, at least 90% of iris were diploids. Ten years later in 1940, the figures were reversed, and 90% of the iris grown were tetraploid. Today, nobody grows diploid iris—unless he is running a museum and wants to show the old varieties that were the forerunners. So today we have reached the time when people can buy tetraploid daylilies. I predict that in ten years from now all the good gardens will have tetraploid daylilies and the figures will be reversed. Instead of great quantities of diploids, we will have great quantities of tetraploids.

Today, there are great quantities of both immeasurably improved diploids and tetraploids. Most ordinary gardeners wouldn't know the difference and couldn't care less as long as their plants are beautiful and grow well. Speaking for myself, I like the arching leaves and wandlike scapes of the older diploids in the section of the perennial border that slopes quite steeply. Their flowing lines are appropriate here. On the other hand, I love some of the big, bold tetraploids held aloft at the back of the garden on their strong, upright scapes. I enjoy different types of foliage, and different sizes and shapes of blossoms. For my money, David Hall had the right idea when he said, "We need variety in our gardens, and we don't all like the same flowers or girls—thank the Lord for that!"

Of course, it is easy for me with nothing at stake to see both sides of a once hot daylily issue. At the time tetraploids burst upon the Chicago scene, there were dedicated, ambitious diploid breeders with a lot to lose if Orville Fay's prophecy came true. Bill Munson of Wimberlyway Gardens, who attended the Convention as a young man, said years later that successful diploid hybridizers were, in effect, told to "go home, ignore their previous work, and start afresh with tetraploids."

The diploid versus tetraploid battlefield was the Scientific Forum, a Convention fixture presenting the latest in daylily research. On this occasion, the Forum had been arranged in the form of a panel discussion. Leading hybridizers and scientific experts were to expound upon the nature and future of colchicine-induced tetraploids. According to Virginia Peck, who became one of the great breeders of tetraploid daylilies, what was meant to be "a sort of debate, one side taking the positive view and the other the negative," became a bloodbath. "To call the debate spirited is a euphemism. At least one member on each side of the panel was known to have a short fuse. Heart failure looked possible as tempers flared and faces reddened. The scientists, however, fielded questions from the audience, explained the nature of tetraploids, methods of converting, chromosomes, polyploidy, chimeras, et cetera."

The battle lines were drawn and, in the aftermath of the debate, daylily people took sides. If you were for tetraploids, you were against diploids, and vice versa. To this day, it is Bill Munson's belief that if the tetraploid supporters had taken a less assertive position, what became a full-scale war might have been "nothing more than a minor skirmish. But most breeders saw their programs under attack and responded accordingly. Like the mother who attacks to protect her young!" Fortunately, this period in daylily history is long past. Tetraploids are gloriously here to stay, and few people can find a sensible reason not to grow them.

Roy Klehm, who raises and sells both diploids and tetraploids, has hit the nail on the head in speaking for the ordinary gardener: "I think people are going to look at a daylily and say, 'Yes, I like that' or 'No, I don't'; they're going to ask, 'Is it worth $8.95 or isn't it?' The bearded iris years ago were all diploids, and now they're all tetraploids, and nobody knows, and nobody cares. I think eventually most people are going to understand that. They are just going to look at daylilies for what they are and enjoy them. To me, tetraploids should be presented as sort of a breeding phenomenon intended to increase the potential for color breaks, new flower forms, and this kind of thing. What has happened for us is that we probably have more flowers in a clump and, oftentimes, stronger stems and larger flowers. The plant structure is different, too. The diploid has graceful, grassy foliage. A tetraploid plant is bolder and more striking with its yuccalike foliage. It gives a different landscape effect." In short, personal preference should be the gardener's guide, not the number of microscopic chromosomes secreted in the plant's tissue.

The Trouble with Tetraploids

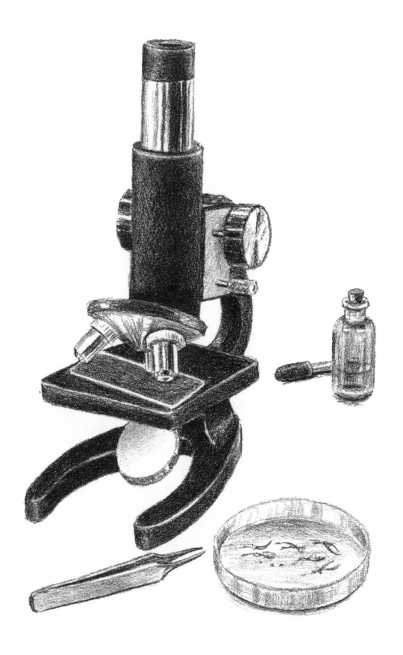

The vast majority of amateur daylily hybridizers shunned tetraploids in the early sixties. Possibly a pro-diploid backlash after the 1961 National Convention discouraged a few, but a much more telling reason was the difficulty of handling colchicine. Orville Fay was a chemist and sensible of the dangers: "Because of the exactness of weighing, measuring, and timing, colchicine is strictly a laboratory material, and is a serious skin irritant. It is not a safe material to handle, unless the user understands the danger." As early as 1964, Fay was convinced that the period of producing tetraploid daylilies by the colchicine method was drawing to a close. This prophecy proved no more accurate than the one forecasting the demise of the diploid.

The practice and process of treating plants and seeds with colchicine has remained remarkably constant. It is neither easier nor more infallible than it was thirty years ago. Few people understand the action of colchicine better than Dr. Currier McEwen. Orville Fay introduced Dr. McEwen to the technique of treating seedlings in 1960:

"I was attending a medical meeting out in Chicago and took the opportunity between meetings to call both David Hall and

Orville Fay. I was this pipsqueak who was just beginning with daylilies and irises, but they kindly permitted me to come out to their gardens. They showed me things, gave me pollen, and couldn't have been more kind. Orville Fay, at that time, took me down to his basement where he had a whole lot of seedlings coming up under fluorescent lights, and he introduced me to what he was doing with colchicine. I was delighted with the thought, so I went right home and started doing it, too."

Dr. McEwen's field of specialization was rheumatology, and he was familiar with colchicine as an ally in the treatment of gout. One of the few plant products still employed by the medical profession today, colchicine was used to relieve the symptoms of gout and rheumatism as early as 1500 B.C. Meeting this old friend in a new guise intrigued Dr. McEwen. But even with his knowledge and scientific expertise, success in raising tetraploid seedlings was not quick in coming to him. The reason soon became apparent, as Dr. McEwen patiently explained.

"When you use colchicine, the affected plants—between sixty and ninety-eight percent of them—die after about three weeks. They develop on their first primitive roots a little thing that looks like a radish. If you look at it under a microscope in sections, it resembles a cancer. The cells are not abnormal, but the growth is completely disorganized and nothing can get through in the way of nutrition. After about three weeks, the endosperm [the nutritive tissue in the seed] which nourished the plant for the first few weeks is used up. If the secondary roots develop before that happens, the plant lives. If not, then the poor things starve to death. You end up with, at the most, twenty percent of what you started with alive, and of those only about ten percent will have been affected [converted into tetraploids].

"I was using a thousand seeds at a time in order to have a reasonable chance of getting a fertile tetraploid out of it. So it was an enormous effort. Of course, once you get your tetraploids, then it's a cinch. It's just like crossing any other plant. But the colchicine techniques are still the same as they were in those early days." If this is the experience of a physician and expert hybridizer, an amateur's chances of success appear slim indeed!

W. Quinn Buck at the University of California College of Agriculture began treating mature daylily plants with colchicine in 1945. His practice—which is still employed today—was to cut out a wedge of the leaf tissue at the base of the plant, exposing the growing point (the site of all future development). A solution of colchicine was then applied with an eyedropper. By this means, Buck managed to convert some of the Stout cultivars into tetraploids. But the success rate was not high.

Most would-be hybridizers were discouraged either by the tedious methods of producing tetraploids or by the potential health hazards of working with colchicine. After all, colchicine alters cells in both plants and animals—including the human animal. As if that weren't enough, the products of early tetraploid hybridization hardly seemed worth the trouble or the risk. Dr. Hamilton Traub produced a line of tetraploid daylilies at the Plant Industry Station in Beltsville, Maryland, in the forties. He introduced 'Tetra Starzynski' in 1949, and 'Tetra Peach' and 'Tetra Apricot' two years later. But Dr. McEwen, who remembers these introductions, found them "not very handsome."

The Fay-Griesbach results were, therefore, a dramatic improvement over previous efforts. But most tetraploids of this period were far from perfect. They often had ungainly scapes which, reportedly, were subject to cracking. Other objections included a want of grace, the absence of much-sought-after ruffles which were becoming commonplace in diploids, and lack of variety. Orville Fay himself commented in 1964 on the limited color range. Reds and lavenders, he conceded, were limited in number and mediocre in quality.

In short, breeding tetraploid daylilies in the sixties was the road less traveled. The hurdles were daunting and the rewards—if there were any—were a dream in the future. To the conventioneers who had been primed for miracles, even the Fay-Griesbach "tets" were a sharp disappointment. Outspoken Annie Giles, President of the American Hemerocallis Society at the time, took one look at a field of perfectly ordinary-looking yellow and melon tetraploids and said to young Bill Munson, who was standing nearby, "You're not going to fool with these things, are you, Bill?" When he assured her that he was, she shook her head and warned, "Well, you'll be sorry!"

Why, then, would the thirty-year-old Munson, with a booming career as an architect, devote every waking moment of his free time to this new and precarious enterprise? For the same reason a mature woman from Tennessee with a Ph.D. in English literature and a full-time teaching job traveled to Beltsville, Maryland, to learn how to count chromosomes. For the same reason that an elderly monk in Illinois still pours his physical and spiritual energies into hybridizing tetraploids. And for the same reason that Orville Fay risked the wrath of the established daylily world to promote tetraploids: in his words, "The challenge to produce new things that have never existed in the world before."

The Munson Family and Their Flowers

'Ida's Magic' (Munson)

'Malaysian Monarch' (Munson)

'Emperor's Dragon' (Munson)

At the time Bill Munson (R. William Munson, Jr.) committed himself to breeding tetraploid daylilies, examples of this new race were unprepossessing, unproven, and unpopular. Moreover, they were as few in number as they were undistinguished in appearance. Today, tetraploids are numerous and beautiful. All over the United States and wherever daylilies can be grown abroad, gardeners are enjoying "tets" with stunning blossoms in every possible daylily shade and in new patterns and color combinations. The plants themselves are disease resistant and robust. They produce bouquets of flowers displayed above the foliage on strong, well-branched scapes. And this has been achieved, in no small part, thanks to the Munson family.

With tetraploids taking their rightful place in the daylily picture, Bill Munson's faith has finally been justified. But as he is the first to admit, "It has taken twenty-five years, instead of the earlier forecast of ten to fifteen. This was basically because of the limited plant material that had been converted and was available for breeders to use. However, I personally feel that the early predictions regarding the qualities of tetraploids were correct. Tetraploids do have better vigor, health, sun resistance, and an ability to achieve greater variety. But one has to remember that not all tetraploids have all the desired characteristics, and great effort is going to be required to orchestrate the now enormous gene pool that has evolved or is evolving." Nor does Munson predict the demise of the diploid. In the best of all possible daylily worlds, there will always be room for diversity.

The road to success with tetraploids was steep and fraught with difficulty. Nevertheless, after the explosive Chicago Convention, a group of second-generation breeders emerged "from the rocket's red glare," and began their slow, frustrating climb to the top. Members of this corps were pioneering spirits of a particular stamp. To a man and a woman, they were scientists, not necessarily by vocation but by inclination. Their approach was based on observation, experiment, and critical testing, and their methods were disciplined.

At this early stage, about a dozen staunch individualists espoused the tetraploid cause, among them Dr. Virginia Peck, an English professor at Middle Tennessee State College in Murfreesboro; James Marsh, who migrated from a farm in Kansas to Chicago to serve an apprenticeship in the plastering trade; Brother Charles Reckamp, sequestered in a monastery in Techny, Illinois; architect Bill Munson of Gainesville, Florida; and Munson's close friend, young Steve Moldovan from Ohio, a professional horticulturist and protégé of Orville Fay.

Of this group, no one did more to produce, promote, and popularize tetraploid daylilies than Munson and, by extension, his mother, Ida Wimberly Munson. Nor does the Munson family's contribution to the development of the modern daylily end with the sophisticated, highly refined tetraploids Bill and Ida produced over the years. His sister, Betty Hudson, is currently working on tetraploid doubles — 'Renaissance Queen' is a beauty. Her daughter, Elizabeth Hudson Salter, has created a line of diminutive, elegantly wrought diploids which have changed the faces and fortunes of the miniatures. Elizabeth is currently working on miniature tetraploids, while her husband, Jeff Salter, is noted for fine, large-flowered "tet" cultivars. Whether or not the Salters' little girl carries on the family tradition remains to be seen. At the moment, Alexandra Salter is a fairy thing of six with primrose-colored hair who likes flowers and being out-of-doors.

When Bill, the acknowledged head of the Munson clan, was elected to the board of the American Hemerocallis Society in 1970, a profile appeared in the quarterly, then called *The Hemerocallis Journal.* It was written by Wilbur Harling, Gainesville neighbor and fellow hybridizer, who, it may be supposed, knew the Munsons well. It characterizes Bill, born on June 20, 1929, as a typical Gemini. Those born under the sign of the twins are said to have two opposite sides to their personalities. I have encountered only the calm, quiet, and introverted side. However, I am prepared to believe that an extrovert lies beneath the surface. Bill told me that in college he had been attracted to the theater. "I was in the junior and senior plays and enjoyed that experience very, very much. In fact, I loved it and perhaps would have been a theatrical person had I been more outgoing at the time."

Even if Mr. Harling's assessment of Bill's character had missed the mark, he knew what he was talking about when it came to Ida Munson. He described her as a "constant source of strength" to her son and went on to say that "as a team they are unbeatable, working together toward a common goal—the best hemerocallis that can be produced!" Although this was written more than twenty years ago, it is as true today as it was then. At eighty-six, Ida is still a vital part of the family team.

A native of Gainesville, Ida is proud of her forebears. She showed me a photograph of her parents just before they were married and another of her father at the age of seventy-four. "Still quite a guy," was the way she described him. "He was originally from Maryland, but his older brother came down to Florida and started doing a little truck farming. That coaxed the other boys to come south. Soon after he got here, my father met my mother. They were married and had five children. And I'm the last of the five."

Ida's mother was a Wimberly from nearby Levy County. A born educator, she taught in the Gainesville school until she had to retire at the age of seventy. After that, she took up oil painting, turning out dozens of colorful canvases, several of which hang in the Munsons' living room. Favorite subjects were flowers and the Florida landscape. Two of the girls followed in their mother's footsteps and became teachers, but Ida's career was cut short by an impatient husband-to-be. Roswell William Munson, Sr., an engineering student at the University of Florida, got tired of waiting for his bride and insisted that she marry him at once. Instead, she promised to marry him as soon as school was out.

To me, everything about their son's life is astonishing. I was astonished to learn that by the time he was fifteen, Bill knew he wanted to be an architect. I taught for twenty years and seldom met a teenage boy who had any notion of what he wanted to be. I was even more astonished to hear that this precocious young man made his first daylily crosses while still a student in high school. My students engaged in much more run-of-the-mill activities, such as tinkering with old cars or competing strenuously and noisily on the athletic field. Bill's only sport was tennis, and while his contemporaries were dismantling jalopies, he was pursuing a very different kind of hobby.

Using an old Amos Perry cultivar called 'Queen Mary', he began breeding daylilies, not, he said recently, because he envisioned creating new hybrids but "because I wanted to produce seedlings so that I would have more of the plant to landscape our place with. And that's what started it. I was a senior in high school at the time. Then I went to college in Gainesville, and during college I lived at home. Architecture is a five-year curriculum, so I had five years to break away from crossing only the yellow 'Queen Marys' and to start buying a few newer things like Stout's 'Wau-Bun', 'Sachem', and 'Theron', which were available in the late forties and early fifties. It just emerged from that small beginning and has kept getting bigger and bigger and bigger." For the benefit of neophytes, "it" is Wimberlyway Gardens, a thirteen-acre paradise where tall pines and magnolias preside over a sea of daylilies in every color, tint, and tone known to the modern cultivar.

Little did Ida Munson know what lay ahead the day she accepted a shovelful of daylilies as a gift! Cheerfully and with-

out regret, she recalled the event which was to have such profound consequences. "One day, a neighbor of ours who lived
across the way brought me a clump of yellow daylilies. I lined
those things out on our driveway, and Bill got interested. He
was just beginning in college. He saved his money—we didn't
have a lot of money—and ordered daylilies from Russell out in
Texas. Then, he ordered things from Ophelia Taylor down here
in Ocala and from Dr. Stout and Mrs. Nesmith up north. So
that was the beginning of the daylilies." But not of Bill's interest
in flowers. That dates from his earliest childhood.

Around the turn of the century, Ida's father bought a forty-
acre farm on the site of what is now the impressive, beautifully
landscaped University Medical Center in Gainesville. Ida was
raised there and returned to the farm when Betty, her first child,
was born. Bill also grew up in this still rural world. Musing on
the early influences in his life, he attributed his youthful interest
in plants to Ida's father. "When you're a small child, and you're
growing up around both parents and grandparents, grandparents tend to be very, very important to you. They usually have
more time for you than your parents do, and I always used to
tag along behind my grandfather. Being in the fields and watch-
ing things grow, something rubs off on you. Of course, Mother
was the same way.

"Ida always had flowers—things she could grow from seed
like nasturtiums, larkspur, snapdragons. Later she became interested in roses. But I came along in 1948 with my daylilies and,
as she puts it, 'kicked' her roses out of the garden. Then she
became part of the daylily program—as much a part as I was.
Between 1960 and 1965, she helped me treat thousands upon
thousands of seeds with colchicine. We would take the tweezers
and plant them in flats and watch three fourths of them die. But
she was a great supporter of my program and still is. At eighty-
six, she goes out and makes crosses, collects seeds, and plants
them. She even lines out the seedlings. It's what keeps her
going. She says, 'Well, I've got to live at least until next year to
see these babies.'"

In truth, Ida Munson is her son's secret weapon. It explains another aspect of Bill's daylily career that astonished me. Chiefly because of his mother, he was able to concentrate on a demanding professional life in which he was genuinely interested and at the same time carry on one of the most extensive hybridizing programs undertaken by an individual breeder. He graduated from the University of Florida in 1953 and went to work for the governing body of the state higher education system. The state Board of Control was responsible for all major construction on the University of Florida's five campuses, and over the years, Bill produced master plans for four additional branch campuses.

For many years he was a long-distance commuter, shuttling between an apartment in Tallahassee where he was working and his garden in Gainesville 150 miles away. Oddly enough, it was an arrangement that worked well. Like the "Remarkable Mr. Pennypacker" in the once popular play of that name, he had loves in two cities and by keeping them apart was able to take pleasure in both. "If I had tried to do daylilies and architecture side by side, it would have caused entirely too much conflict. So I enjoyed architecture at the University of Florida in Tallahassee and commuted to Gainesville for the weekend.

"I came home on Friday evening and spent Friday and Saturday doing what I had to do in setting up the daylily program. On weekdays, we had two or three full-time employees who maintained the garden, and I would leave tasks for them. During the blooming season, I would take my vacation from the University and spend as much time as I could here in Gainesville, directing the crosses that I wanted. When I couldn't be here, Mother or my sister Betty or friends of mine would come in and make the crosses for me." For the last twelve years of his working life, Bill was director of facilities planning at the University of North Florida in Jacksonville. Despite illness (Bill suffers from Parkinson's disease), he continued to drive the seventy-three miles to and from Gainesville every weekend until his retirement in 1988.

At this writing two years later, he can no longer do the extensive foot work involved in maintaining a thirteen-acre garden. Nevertheless, he manages to keep up a rigorous schedule. I made my first pilgrimage to Wimberlyway in May 1990. The afternoon was warm, and I found Bill temporarily indoors. Having spent that morning since early dawn making crosses, he had been resting during the heat of the day. We talked in the cool, spare living room of the house he designed for his parents in 1967.

Illness has muted his voice, but there is no mistaking the inner intensity that has made his career and this place possible. "We moved here in 1968—twenty-two years ago," he began. "We had a daylily garden on the other property. But I just planted daylilies under the array of trees and shrubs that my mother and my grandmother had planted. I didn't really create the garden at the other house. But when we moved here, my parents said, 'Design the house'—which I did." By this time his father had suffered a stroke, and it was decided that the family should gather under one roof. Bill designed a house to accommodate the two households: Betty Hudson and her family and the senior Munsons. At the family's urging, he added the porte-cochère and guest house where he now lives.

After we had talked for an hour or so, he took me into the garden. Responding to my many questions had taken its toll, and his voice sounded tired. But simply being outside surrounded by the daylilies seemed to revive him, and as we toured the garden, his vitality returned. He pointed out a swath of coral pink and rosy tangerine 'Sari' and said, "I had to at least try a border of all one cultivar. And it's okay, but I kind of like the mixed colors." There were, in fact, two different cultivars in the long, narrow bed. Behind 'Sari', the slightly taller 'Magic Mandarin' picked up the tangerine shade of its companion. The effect was spectacular, but I, too, loved the random mixture of colors in the huge seedling beds—melon, red, peach, gold, cream, yellow, and purple, united by a common bond of underlying warmth.

Photographs never do Wimberlyway justice. Most photographers employ a wide-angle lens, which limits the field of vision to a horizontal slice of the garden. Dazzling as these horizontal views may be, they fail to convey the cathedral effect of the lofty green canopy pierced by vertical shafts of bare tree trunks. Beneath pines and sweet gums, a lush understory thrives in the filtered light: magnolias, camelias, many different species of holly, dogwoods, azaleas, and as far as the eye can see, an undulating knee-high carpet of daylilies. The formality of the garden helps to control the vegetative bounty. Beds, separated by broad grass paths, are laid out in rectangles edged with liriope and punctuated with dense globes of holly. The sea of daylilies is broken up by hedge-enclosed beds containing only trees and shrubs.

Bill had given careful thought to the design before a single plant was moved from the other garden. "I knew that I wanted a semi-formal landscape. At the other place, we had a very informal layout with winding paths and irregular beds. Here, I wanted something more formal because we would be planting the daylilies in rows. The design had to be useful in terms of the hybridizing program. But I wanted other seasonal plants that I particularly enjoyed: hollies with their red berries for November and December and magnolias, which bloom in January, February, and March."

Many of the beautiful trees were planted for the benefit of the tetraploid daylilies which Bill had been breeding for several years when the Munsons moved to Wimberlyway. He had learned from Quinn Buck in California that high heat causes lack of fertility in tetraploids. Buck suggested providing a little shade, and it made all the difference in the world. Bill immediately began to plant trees. Encouraged by the extra water from an irrigation system installed for the daylilies, the pines shot up. Today, soaring russet trunks rise straight up for seventy feet before interlacing their branches overhead. The trees are one of the glories of Wimberlyway, and to walk in their shade with the man who planted them is a privilege.

There are architects who have designed their own homes, gardeners who have made their own gardens, and hybridizers who have created their own cultivars. But to claim responsibility for everything the eye can see on thirteen acres must be a unique experience. When the Munsons bought the property, there was nothing here. The land had been part of a farm, and Bill described it as "just rolling hills, very attractive, but the tallest tree out here was perhaps eight feet high."

To a New Englander, the north Florida "hills" are mere ripples in the level pine- and palmetto-clad natural landscape, but the gentle rise and fall of the land west of Gainesville gives it an added dimension that is very appealing. At Wimberlyway, the ground slopes imperceptibly. Enough, however, to require the liriope edging of the daylily beds to control erosion. Once, after a heavy tropical downpour, the unconfined daylilies washed down onto the grass paths.

Strolling these same paths from one glorious display bed to another, I asked Bill to point out cultivars of which he was particularly proud. Instead, he gave me his definition of a "good garden daylily" as one that comes in as many color variations as there are, including white; that performs happily in your garden, preferably blooming twice; and that develops into a nice, symmetrical round clump. I commented that his cultivars, no matter how large their flowers, had scapes strong enough to hold them up, at which he laughed and said, "Right. You don't want creepy-crawlers!" He added that one of the most welcome compliments he ever received came from a Jacksonville daylily friend who said, "Thank you for putting the daylily back in the garden."

"For years," he continued, "we have taken the daylily out of the garden and put it on the show table where the flower, its petals, ruffling, and the novelty of its shape are very important. But these things are not important in a garden setting. These decorative details are attractive and should be there, but almost as a serendipitous surprise when you view the flower at close range. Its color, the size of the plant, and the height of the scapes are the important features in a garden."

Pressed to point out a favorite or at least one with which he was particularly pleased, he showed me 'Cartier's Gem'. "It has a pencil edging—what I call a tracery—which I think is just gorgeous." In another section of the garden, he singled out

'Francesca Da Rimini', named for one of his favorite opera heroines. "Now, here's one of my short ones that I like very much. Look at its stem—it's branched and heavily budded—the flower is held above the foliage, and the petals are overlapping. That's my kind of daylily." We also looked at 'Malaysian Monarch', a large, lush purple with a dramatically contrasting ivory-yellow center which he feels is "very special."

While we were absorbed in the daylilies, a car appeared in the driveway. The occupants were a couple in their thirties. The young man rolled down the window on the driver's side and called out, "Is this private? Or open to the public, or what? It's outrageous, it's so beautiful!" Bill invited them to park the car and come in. Upon leaving half an hour later, they expressed awed thanks and the determination to return.

After they had gone, Bill turned to me and smiled. "It happens all the time," he said. "I guess there's something about daylilies—when you're hooked, you're hooked. Of course, some people don't get hooked, but six weeks ago, a woman named Mrs. Thrasher from an outlying community happened to stumble upon the garden and just went crazy! The daylilies weren't even in bloom, so I told her to come back the middle of May. She did, and it was amazing to see her looking at these flowers. Now, she has been back five times and she's purchased eighteen to twenty cultivars. The last time she said, 'If it's okay with you, I'll come back every week until they stop blooming.' She's not the exception, either; there are lots of people who do that."

I learned from Bill that visitors come in droves to Wimberlyway—which hardly seems surprising. Indeed, the Munsons were expecting houseguests the following day, and I did not want to tire the host any more. But he insisted on telling me about the Canadian who was arriving in the morning. "I'd love you to meet Doug because he's on the threshold of breeding. It's interesting, the way we met. He was leafing through a magazine one day and happened to see an article about our garden. His mother had died recently and he was feeling depressed, so on the spur of the moment, he decided to take a trip down to Florida. He called us up, stayed at a hotel for a week, and visited us every day. He used to have lunch with us, and by the end of the week, we had become fast friends. Now he's hybridizing, growing seedlings, and bubbling over with the joy of it."

That evening after Bill had gone in to dinner, I sat on a bench at the far end of the garden. The only sounds were the patter of water from the sprinklers and birds calling among the trees. I heard mockingbirds, cardinals, bluebirds, even chickadees and wrens from up north. Bird houses hang in the dogwoods, and a feeder beside the drive is well attended. Ida feeds both the feathered and the furred creatures that share her family's sylvan world. Squirrels are not discriminated against; field mice pick up what the squirrels leave. Even rabbits have no fear of reprisal for occasionally sampling the daylily foliage in the Munsons' peaceable kingdom.

Visitors to Wimberlyway

Steve Moldovan

Fortuitously, my sojourn to Wimberlyway coincided with that of Steve Moldovan from Avon, Ohio. Every year, for longer than either cares to remember, Steve has left his own garden on the shores of Lake Erie to join Bill Munson in his for an extended visit. Later in the season, Bill makes the trek north to Moldovan Gardens. And they have been doing this for thirty years. When Bill effected introductions, he reminded Steve of their first telephone conversation. "You called me up and said you were just graduating from college and wanted to buy some daylilies from me, and I wondered, 'Who is this guy?'" They soon became friends, and ever since that time have visited each other annually.

The Munson-Moldovan relationship says more about the cooperative, generous spirit of daylily people than pages of glowing text. By rights, the two men should be competitors; instead, they are loyal confederates. At the time of the tetraploid wars, they were both in the same camp. "Yeah," Steve recalled with a chuckle, "there was just a small group of us who believed in these new things. We were the black sheep!"

Tetraploid king Orville Fay was Steve's mentor. "I was not primarily interested in daylilies, I liked bearded iris, and I'd read about this breeder of iris who lived in Chicago. Well, there was an air show in Chicago—my brother flew model airplanes, and my dad used to take him to air shows all over the country. Needless to say, when there was one in Chicago, I went along. I got to meet Orville Fay, and that's how it started. I went to help him that summer, and when I saw the daylilies in bloom, I fell in love with them. That was back in 1953 or 1954. But I've always been interested in plants, ever since I was a little tot."

Soon after Steve began helping Fay during summer vacations, the Crestwood series propelled tetraploids into the spotlight. Naturally, the young man jumped on the bandwagon. "I bought four plants of 'Crestwood Ann' at two hundred dollars apiece—and eight hundred dollars was a lot of money. I made crosses with 'Reverend Traub', an orange daylily from Dr. Hamilton Traub."

Here, Bill joined in. "The important thing about 'Reverend Traub' was that it was a seedling 'tet' from two tetraploid parents, not a conversion. Anyway, Steve had thousands of plants from that cross, and I went to Ohio to view the new seedlings— they were *all* orange!"

"Yeah," admitted Steve good-humoredly, "all shades of orange, and none were anything you'd be enthusiastic about saving."

Bill continued, "Of course, we did save some, because they were a little bit more round, or a little bit more something or other, but here was this stunning defeat for the thing we'd placed our faith in."

Bill bought 'Crestwood Ann' at just about the same time. "It was a known 'tet'—a conversion, though, and not a seedling. What I did not know at the time was that it was not necessarily one hundred percent 'tet'! Just the same, it was a beautiful plant. Branched, very round little melon flowers on it. But I would make crosses and the pods would drop. I'd do it again, the same thing would happen. It was not an easy pod parent, and many people who bought it couldn't get seed to set on it at all. You can imagine how popular that made the person who introduced it! Worse than a polecat at a picnic!"

Steve's early experience with tetraploid breeding was marginally less frustrating. "I managed to get much more seed than Bill did due to the climate." In the South, high heat adversely affects fertility. Tetraploid breeding has never been easy. Even today, it is still a challenge. Although there are hundreds of full tetraploids from tetraploid parents, some of the most exciting new daylilies are being created by converting the best diploids and crossing them with the latest and best tetraploids. One of the crosses Bill and Steve were making that morning involved a converted diploid from another breeder and a 1991 Wimberlyway introduction.

For the two men, the day had begun at the crack of dawn, and Steve was still at it when I arrived. The high, insistent whine of the cicadas promised heat by afternoon, but at eight o'clock in the morning, it was still lovely. Long beams of sunlight reached down through chinks in the soft canopy of pine branches, and birds sang from every tree and shrub. There was still dew on the grass, and Steve was barefoot, his trouser legs rolled up to keep them dry. He had a yellow bloom in one hand and was about to put the pollen from one of its anthers on the pistil of a small, pastel flower with a ruby-red eye zone.

"This one," he said, indicating the flower in his hand, "is from Bill's 'Ruffled Dude' line." Incidentally, Steve was responsible for naming this magnificent cultivar, with its deep, gold-embroidered ruffles and shallow flower cup. On an earlier visit, he had tried to write out the names and numbers of its antecedents on the identifying tag, but there wasn't enough room. Being eleven years younger than Bill Munson and of a more colloquial turn of phrase, he simply referred to it as the 'Ruffled Dude', and the name stuck.

Steve waxed lyrical on the subject of the plant he had christened. "As a breeder, it's going to go down in history as one of the great breakthroughs. Back in its day—that was five years ago—we had never seen ruffling like that. In addition, this was an incredible plant to begin with. It had branching, bud count, the opening of the flowers—*and* was dormant! Bill Munson producing a dormant!" Nearby, a clump of 'Ruffled Dude' offered up its glorious golden yellow flowers to the morning sun, eliciting a gasp of admiration from this viewer. The offspring being used that morning was called 'Comtessina'—a typically Munsonian name implying royal origins.

Steve drew my attention to its small, very round, deeply ruffled flowers. "Plus," he said, "it's very fertile, so this is one of the ones we'll be sure and get into the line—even if the ones we prefer with eyes fail. 'Comtessina' has a lot of good qualities—it has low, sixteen-inch scapes and is well-branched. We're crossing it with Pauline Henry's line, which is dormant. 'Comtessina' is very evergreen. So it's an exciting cross, I think."

By combining tender evergreens with hardy dormant daylilies, Bill and Steve have made significant contributions to gardens on both sides of the Mason-Dixon line. Many of their introductions do well over large areas of the country. Steve was prompted to try crossing dormant with evergreen after seeing his own creations in southern gardens. "This gorgeous thing that I had at home just looked like two cents down here! It wouldn't grow; it was too dormant; it just sat there! A two- or three-year-old clump often had only two or three little spindly scapes—which is the way the evergreens react for me in the North. Fortunately, this happened to me early on. That's why I thought if I got the evergreens and crossed them with the dormants, it would do the trick. And it's working. Now 'Strutter's Ball' and 'Mariska' and some of my new ones do well down in the Deep South—they have evergreen blood in them."

Steve and Bill have crossed their lines to the great benefit of gardeners everywhere. "We work as a team," Steve told me. "I got my 'Strutter's Ball' by crossing his 'Damascan Velvet'—which is half mine and half his—with my 'Houdini'. Now, he has 'Strutter's Ball' and is taking it back into his line of purples. So that's how we've done it for years—just cooperating." If you have been unable to follow the complex family tree of the Munson and Moldovan cultivars, it doesn't matter. What does matter is the mutual cooperation, respect, and affection that binds these two men in friendship.

As I was about to leave Steve to his work, he turned and

grinned. "You know, to be able to come down here and help, to see the developments ... it's just remarkable what this man has done—and on the scale he does it. I'd be insane in a day!" He threw his head back and laughed. "It's bad enough spending ten days here—all the possibilities.... It's just mind-boggling."

The Thrashers

Steve and I were not the only visitors that morning. There was also Frank Chamberlin, a daylily enthusiast whose video-taped garden tours are eagerly awaited by homebound members of the American Hemerocallis Society. As the sun rose higher in the sky, sections of the garden became exposed to its full strength, and Bill's sister Betty patiently accompanied Frank on his rounds, holding aloft a black umbrella to reduce the glare.

Betty Hudson is another remarkable member of a remark-able family. She not only pursues her own hybridizing pro-gram—she is working on doubles—but she does the bookwork for Wimberlyway, keeps the records, copes with correspon-dence, and shepherds visitors around the garden. Earlier, she had spent time showing me her new doubles and explaining that often the increase in flower segments is achieved at the expense of the pistil and stamens. "Sometimes you will not even get sta-mens. Also, the pistil will be split or twisted, and it will not take the pollen down the tube into the capsule." Whatever the diffi-culties, she is producing some lovely flowers, such as pale yel-low 'Double Dandelion' and a promising line of purples.

Having taken enough of her time, I was on the point of mak-ing my reluctant farewells to the Munson family when Bill sum-moned me. He was on his way to the airport to collect yet other visitors, but he wanted me to meet someone. "This," he said with the ghost of a smile, "is the lady I told you about who has just fallen in love with daylilies." For a moment, Mrs. Thrasher looked self-conscious and glanced toward her husband for reas-surance. Then she stifled a soft, breathy laugh. "I'm a nut, as my husband says. He tells me I love daylilies better than him!" A great deal of chuckling and tittering followed this statement, with muffled agreement from her spouse. It soon developed that Mrs. Thrasher was not the only daylily "nut" in the family. Her husband, too, had been bitten by the bug.

Oh, gentle reader, there is nothing more beguiling, more touching, or more hilarious than newly smitten daylily fans! The Thrashers are a middle-aged couple. She is a hardworking housewife who loves her garden; he is a mechanic. They have many responsibilities, including six children, ten grandchildren, and great-grand-twins soon to be born. But there they stood, shoulder to shoulder, a little foolish, a little excited, flustered and happy. They looked at one another, each hoping the other would begin.

"I was telling Mr. Munson that I get up every morning and check out the daylilies before I go to work," offered Mr. Thrasher tentatively. I asked him if he had any favorites. He nodded. "The lavenders, and then I like the ones with eyes. And you see that yellow over there with kind of a rose blush to it—it actually looks kind of cream? I like that. I like them all. These," he said, pointing to some of the reds, "are extremely eye-catching. You look at them and enjoy them—even at a distance. But these pastels and creams are elegant." Between them, the Thrashers had nineteen Munson cultivars, counting 'Renaissance Fair', a silvery mauve with a purple eye, chosen that day by Mr. Thrasher.

It was Mrs. Thrasher who told me how it all began. "One of my neighbors said they had heard about Wimberlyway Gardens. And I came up here. There was *nothing* in bloom, not a thing, except a couple of azaleas and some Japanese iris. I guess that was in April. But I saw all the plants, and they were starting to put their scapes on. And I thought, 'Oh, just look at these! It's just going to be beautiful. It's … it's going to be heavenly! And I knew I had to come back. So I got a catalog. I went home and began reading all these beautiful descriptions of my flowers."

Mrs. Thrasher sounds young, eager, and breathless. After she had placed her first order, she persuaded her husband to call the Munsons. "So we made an appointment to come up and get my plants. I've been back now seven or eight times, and I've got three of my neighbors completely, totally hooked!" Thinking of the upheaval she has caused in the lives of her unsuspecting friends made her giggle with delight.

If the Thrashers were enthralled by the daylilies, I was enthralled by the Thrashers. They are archetypal daylily people. Most gardeners are enthusiastic and optimistic. In daylily people, these qualities are raised to the nth power. Many gardeners are warmhearted and generous. Daylily people are both—in spades. But the trait that distinguishes daylily people from all other gardeners is their passionate evangelism. They won't rest until there are "hems" in every garden in the United States. After that, I expect missionaries will be sent abroad to convert the heathen.

I called Mrs. Thrasher the other day to ask if she had bought any new daylilies this year. She laughed and admitted that the collection which began with nineteen had already grown to two hundred. "I have ninety-seven of Mr. Munson's, and I'm trying to get a complete collection. I think there are about four hundred!" By now she must have been over every inch of Wimberlyway with a fine-tooth comb. But at the time we met, she had still not seen the whole garden.

"I keep saying I'm going to come up and go row for row." She sighed. "But I'll be going along, and all of a sudden, I'll see a red." Lowering her voice, she confided, "My favorites are the reds. Anyway, I'll see a red one, and I'll go, 'Oh! Oh! Oh!' I'll run over to it and forget where I was in the other row. And I don't remember to go back."

The Thrashers had to develop a system for narrowing down their wish lists, and their well-thumbed Wimberlyway catalog bore numerous hieroglyphics. Mrs. Thrasher explained her method. "If I put *xxx*, that means I'm *really* going to get it; then *xx* means it's next in line; and that's how I do it. I can't resist. Nor can my neighbor. She had been growing daylilies for years but had none of the real elaborate ones with the beautiful wide petals. She came over to our place, and I'd just gotten five. After that, every day she'd call up and say, 'What's in bloom?' Then she had to come up to Gainesville for a doctor's appointment, so she and another friend slipped over here—and bless her heart! Now they keep coming back." She paused for a moment, obviously struggling to find a suitable description for the magic of Wimberlyway. "It's absolutely ... it's ... it's heavenly to come up here and go through these flowers." With an obvious effort at restraint, she concluded in a normal tone, "I just enjoy it thoroughly." Dissatisfied, she tried again, but again words failed her. Finally, in a voice reduced to a whisper, she said, "It's something else."

Jim Marsh

'Chicago Picotee Memories'
(Marsh)

Many of the pioneer "tet" breeders are gone now. That giant, Orville Fay, died on Thanksgiving Day 1980. James Marsh, one of his many protégés, died two years earlier. Jim Marsh was everything Fay was not—amiable, easygoing, and modest to a fault. The soft-spoken farm boy from Kansas came to Chicago in 1921, leaving behind the outdoor world that he loved. He apprenticed himself to a local plasterer and for forty-one years plied this strenuous trade. But according to his friend Paul Watts, "his love of the earth and its gifts never left him during those city years." Instead, he and his wife, Searcy, set about making their long, narrow lot into a flowery retreat from their urban environment.

Mrs. Marsh, herself a country girl, planted annuals, perennials, and climbing plants. Among the latter was a particularly beautiful clematis which one visitor, Bill Munson, described as a "stunning pure chalky lavender to violet purple," a color range Munson craved in hemerocallis. Indeed, it was for developing the first lavender and purple tetraploid daylilies that James E. Marsh earned his place in the hemerocallis hall of fame.

Marsh was quick to credit his success with daylilies to the hybridizers who had encouraged him. In a letter dated March

1967, he wrote, "To begin with, the old established breeders who have given me the most help are Mr. Hall, Mr. Fay and Mr. Fischer. Without their expert advice, breeding stock procured from them, and their generosity in supplying pollen from their finest things, I could not have started this most interesting and delightful business of breeding daylilies."

Marsh came to daylilies by the same route as his mentors— first iris and then hemerocallis. But his earliest plant obsession was with dahlias. As soon as he arrived in Chicago and had a patch of earth to call his own, he began planting dahlia tubers. Soon he was a principal breeder, exhibitor, and judge of these glamorous flowers. Then, according to Paul Watts, "Jim fell in love with the iris as it moved from its old 'flag' status into the realm of modern flowers of real distinction under the local leadership of David Hall and Orville Fay. Gradually Jim was drawn into that group." Again, success attended his efforts with irises. He introduced nineteen cultivars, many of which won awards— not that he totally abandoned his first love. He continued to grow a lovely pink-quilled dahlia among Searcy's perennials.

In 1955, when his iris friends turned their attention to hemerocallis, he followed suit. And in a short time, daylily people were traveling great distances to the Marsh garden to marvel at new developments there. The speed with which Jim Marsh achieved results astounded his mentors. "Surely," wrote one admiringly, "this man must have some rare intuitive faculty that enables him to select just the right parentages to begin with and then to quickly evaluate the progeny, choosing just the right seedlings to advance his program with the least possible waste of time and energy."

Marsh seldom used the first person singular in comments about his breeding program, preferring to include his wife's contribution. For example, in describing his pink line for *The Hemerocallis Journal*, he wrote, "Our pinks have come primarily from seedlings and pollen from Mr. Hall's garden plus 'Frances Fay' blood. Our biggest lift came in 1960, the first year 'New Love' bloomed in Mr. Hall's garden. He very generously gave us pollen from it which produced for us some 2,500 seedlings that bloomed in 1962. One, 'Prairie Melody', was introduced in 1966." All Marsh cultivars of diploid breeding are identified by the prefix "Prairie." From that period came the lovely 'Prairie Moonlight', a huge, flawless pale yellow which I still grow and treasure.

While Marsh had no desire to confine himself to one color and said that he liked to work with all the available daylily colors, his greatest ambition was to produce a blue daylily. And by 1967, he pronounced himself "very much encouraged as every year the lavenders and purples get bluer and better." The first lavender seedling for which he expressed enthusiasm was introduced as 'Prairie Mist'. From this stepping-stone came 'Prairie Thistle', and from 'Prairie Thistle', a raft of promising lavenders and purple diploids, culminating in the introduction of 'Prairie Blue Eyes' in 1970. 'Prairie Blue Eyes', already more than twenty years old, is probably still the bluest daylily in cultivation. To me, it appears a soft blue-lavender, but the halo in the center is considerably bluer than the background color.

When it came to tetraploid daylilies, Jim Marsh was more open-minded than most of his contemporaries. As soon as the methods pioneered by Orville Fay and Dr. Robert Griesbach made breeding tetraploids a practical reality, he embraced the new technique. In 1965, he treated three thousand sprouting seeds with colchicine. Of these, about four hundred were from a cross between Edna Spalding's 'Lavender Flight' and his own 'Prairie Thistle', which he believed to be his best breeder for lavender and purple. Alas, he lost eighty percent of the treated seeds from this cross. Disappointed but not downhearted, Marsh planted the remaining seeds, which bloomed two years later.

Disappointingly, only about thirty percent of the seedlings bore the telltale marks of tetraploidy. Nevertheless, there was one that observer Bill Munson called "a magnificent purple of startling clarity and intensity." This history-making plant was a chimera. The colchicine treatment had doubled the chromosomes in some but not all of its cells, resulting in two genetically distinct tissues. However, all was far from lost; seedling #TR67-90, as it was known, produced tetraploid offspring and, crossed with one of Dr. Griesbach's proven tetraploid seedlings, it gave rise to two landmark purple "tets"—'Chicago Royal' and 'Chicago Regal'. Munson predicted that these two would in time "make a fantastic splash."

Using the name "Chicago" for his tetraploid series, Jim Marsh went on to produce dozens of fine purples and lavenders, some with dark eye zones and ornamental edgings in the same shade. Crossed with Munson cultivars, the Chicago purples and lavenders produced the extraordinary "watermarks" for which Wimberlyway is famous. Bill Munson, who pleads guilty to dubbing the chalky patterns "watermarks," says they look as if the color had been "lifted off," leaving behind a pale eye zone.

For his contributions to the daylily world, Jim Marsh was awarded the American Hemerocallis Society's highest honor for hybridizing. He was presented with the Bertrand Farr Medal on September 21, 1974—his fifty-fourth wedding anniversary. According to all who knew the Marshes, their marriage was remarkable no less for its happiness than its length. Having been high school sweethearts and having exchanged vows before their eighteenth birthdays, the durability of their union is the more noteworthy.

Before his death in 1978, Marsh made an arrangement with the Charles Klehm and Son Nursery to acquire his stock and to introduce the selections he did not live long enough to name, retaining the Chicago prefix. Young Roy Klehm was in a curious position with regard to Jim Marsh and the other elderly Chicago breeders who entrusted their daylilies to him. Having grown up in the nursery business, he had accompanied his father on expeditions to the gardens of these local hybridizers.

"It's ironic," he said recently. "I can remember as a little kid six years old complaining from the backseat of the car about wanting to go home or being hungry or needing to go to the bathroom, and then having to wait until the men got done with their flowers." Now the men whom he looked up to all his life turn to him for the reassurance that he will perpetuate their efforts. Roy has been as good as his word. As recently as 1987, he introduced show-stopping 'Chicago Picotee Memories', a pale, creamy flower with a rich purple eye zone and a thread of the same color around the edges of the petals.

"The Chicago prefix has only been broken twice," Roy told me in a phone conversation. "When Jim was dying, his son suggested that he name one for Searcy and pick out a namesake for himself." Thus, 'Searcy Marsh', a beautiful pink, joined the distinguished company of Chicago tetraploids. To Roy's surprise, Marsh chose a red for himself. "Even though he broke the mold with his lavenders and purples, he told me he was still proud of his reds." And so it was done, and a fine scarlet tetraploid bears the name 'James Marsh'.

Brother Charles Reckamp

Brother Charles Reckamp

W̲hen I first began perusing nursery catalogs, I used to come across the daylily introductions of Brother Charles Reckamp offered by Wayside Gardens. In those days, I was far more interested in the gorgeous color reproductions of flowers than in hybridizers, but the idea of a tonsured monk engaged in the mysterious craft of plant breeding appealed to me. I had visions of a medieval cloister and the figure of Brother Charles, robed and barefoot, moving softly among the daylilies. However, this quaint image was dispelled by the publication of Jim Wilson's admirable book, *Masters of the Victory Garden*. Wilson had the good fortune to visit Brother Charles at the Society of the Divine Word in Techny, Illinois.

Wilson had his own preconceived notions about Brother Charles. "Figuring that he had to be in his eighties, I expected to meet a frail, elderly man." Instead, he found "a bright-eyed, vigorous man who, while small in stature, was doing his share of the grunt work" involved in transplanting a large serviceberry tree. Shod and hatted, Brother Charles Reckamp toils happily in the service of his fellow brothers and the genus *Hemerocallis* on the grounds of the mission's headquarters. During the growing season, he may be found in his garden at dawn soon after morning devotions. His equipment consists of a tomato basket with a wire handle, which rests over one arm. In it is everything he needs for making the crosses that have established him as one of the premier breeders of tetraploid daylilies in the United States.

Accustomed to early rising and hard work, Brother Charles grew up on a farm fifty miles northwest of St. Louis, Missouri. "We had a large family," he said in a recent phone conversation. "Everybody had to work from early in the morning until late at night. Nobody had time for flowers then. But at the time I joined the order, there was a priest who had trained in Europe. Father Peter Oswald was a member of our order, Divine Word Missionaries, but he had studied biology under the Benedictine monks. He taught in our seminary and knew quite a bit about botany. It was his idea to start a garden and sell plants to help support our seminary." And that's how Mission Gardens came to be.

It almost seems like divine providence that Father Peter Oswald came to Techny in the first place. As a young priest, he was assigned to missionary work in Papua, New Guinea. "He was already on a ship on his way there," Brother Charles relates, "when orders came from that government that German citizens would not be permitted to enter the port. This was shortly after World War I. So Father Oswald, being German, was denied entry. His orders were changed, and he was left off the ship in New York, then assigned to our U.S. headquarters here in Techny."

Although he never attempted plant breeding himself, Father Oswald kept up with the latest developments. He made daring acquisitions for the fledgling nursery and propagated new and unusual varieties to sell. An enterprise that began in the twenties with a few gladiolus corms wound up in 1975 with fifty acres of general nursery stock—shrubs, flowers, and trees; an enormous planting of tree peonies; Brother Charles's magnificent daylily introductions; and two thousand tetraploid seedlings.

Even before the daylilies brought national recognition to Mission Gardens, the nursery had become a gathering place for the region's avid amateur horticulturists. Among the regular visitors was that ubiquitous pair, Orville Fay and David Hall. The two men befriended Brother Charles and urged him to try his hand at hybridizing. "I started with a few irises because at that time our nursery was small and I could spare the time. But as the nursery business developed, we got so busy just when the irises bloom that I didn't have much time for hybridizing. So my friends said, 'Why don't you switch to daylilies? They bloom in July and August when you're not so busy in the garden.' So I started making some crosses. Then Mr. Fay and Dr. Robert Griesbach converted some diploids into tetraploids and that was the beginning of great improvements in the daylily."

Although there was considerable expense involved in a tetraploid breeding program, Brother Charles was convinced that hybridizing tetraploids offered "greater potential for genetically different colors and a broader range of form." Fortunately, his superiors believed in him and made it possible for him to purchase one plant of Orville Fay's 'Crestwood Ann'. Through the generosity of veteran hybridizer Fay, he also had access to the pollen from other cultivars which he would have been unable to afford otherwise.

Meanwhile, he found a young brother at the mission with enough scientific background to experiment with the colchicine treatment. Using the Fay-Griesbach method, Brother Daniel Yunck managed to produce a few tetraploid seedlings. These, crossed with 'Crestwood Ann' and others of the Crestwood Series, gave Brother Charles the foundation stock for his breeding program. Later, Brother Daniel succeeded in converting several of the best Reckamp diploids, including 'Milepost'. As a tetraploid, 'Milepost' passed on its beautiful pink coloring to the now famous pastel blends for which Brother Charles is known.

If by any chance you have never gazed upon the pale countenance of a Reckamp pastel, you have a treat in store for you. Be warned, however, that to describe the color will be impossible. The general difficulty in pinning down daylily colors was best explained by Dr. Ezra Kraus in an article written for the 1957 yearbook issue of *The Hemerocallis Journal:*

The hues of the flowers are of two distinct types. One type, such as most of the oranges and yellows, is due mainly to small colored granules inside the cells. The same is true for the green color in the leaves and flowers. The various hues of red, purple, pink and so on are known as sap colors, as they are not generally in the form of small granules but are in solution in the cell sap. Furthermore, these sap colors are mainly in the superficial cells on the upper sides of the sepals and petals, rarely on the backs of the same structures. Thus it is difficult to evaluate the true color of the hemerocallis flower. Generally the basic color is yellow or orange overlaid by various quantities or degrees of redness, resulting in the pinks, reds and purples. Anyone who has used any of the more readily available color charts will understand this difficulty.

Most amateurs do not have access to the expensive Royal Horticultural Society color chart or the American-produced Munsell Color Chart of a thousand or more number-coded shades and tints. (These charts consist of an index of color "chips," rather like the swatches produced by house painters for a client's consideration.) In any case, Brother Charles's pastel daylilies, with their opalescent layers and multiplicity of glints and gleams, would surely confound the color charts. Pioneer breeder Ralph Wheeler observed that daylily flowers can have a base of one hue and a "bloom" or "pile" of another. No one has exploited this two-dimensional color scheme the way Brother Charles has. Forget about trying to describe his complex blends of apricot-cream washed with a transparent layer of scintillating pink. Instead, give yourself up to mute admiration and leave the descriptions to fools like me who rush in where angels fear to tread.

I spoke to this Old Master of my admiration for the subtlety of his pastels, and he told me about a new one. I could hear the pleasure in his voice. "I have a new little one called 'Angel's Smile', and I would say it is the loveliest little thing I have ever seen. It's creamy white in the center and lavender toward the outside. Some lady from Vermont—or perhaps it was Connecticut—saw it on the Convention tour, and she said it was the most outstanding, interesting, and most beautiful new daylily of the whole tour! Now, I thought that was a nice compliment."

Important as these delicate color combinations are to Brother Charles, he has a farmer's appreciation of health and vigor in a plant. He is known for producing daylilies with good branching and a high bud count. Another of his claims to daylily fame is the introduction of exquisite ruffles. States Roy Klehm, who introduces the Reckamp daylilies through Klehm Nursery, "Brother Charles should be given credit for putting ruffles on daylilies. People told me he saw them even before they were there!" Roy could barely contain his excitement about some of the upcoming Reckamp introductions. He described one as a "baby-shell-pink with a gold picotee edge." When I made appreciative sounds over the phone, he chuckled and said, "Ooooooh, is right!" Brother Charles has great expectations for the two thousand seedlings that will bloom for the first time in 1991. Many of them have parents that exhibit this edge of gold.

I learned, to my surprise, that decorative edges and even fringes on the petals are not a new phenomenon. They were turning up in Orville Fay's garden by the early sixties. At that stage, however, they did not appeal to Brother Charles, who found the ruffling too irregular and untidy. "I wish you could see the difference between the nice ruffles now and the things that showed up then. Every generation is a little better and a little better and a little better."

He has always had a clear picture of his ideal daylily. "What I'm after mostly," he says, "is wide petals that are round and sepals that are not rolled back. I think it is unfortunate if the sepals or the petals roll back because the only way you'll see them is to go behind and look at the flower from the back! If the flower opens up as if it's facing you, smiling at you, you can see the entire petal and the entire sepal. And that's a quality I have been working for—fairly wide petals and wide sepals, if you can get them, and segments that are rounded, not coming to a point. That's my favorite. That doesn't mean the others are no good, but that's what I like."

That seems to be what many other people like, too. Roy Klehm liked what Brother Charles was producing at Mission Gardens so much that when the nursery closed, he offered to handle all future Reckamp introductions. Mutual admiration and affection between the nurseryman and Brother Charles has been long-standing. "I knew Roy's father and his grandfather," said Brother Charles. "I knew them very well. And they don't make them any better. Roy's the same." Grandfather Charles, for whom the Charles Klehm and Son Nursery is named, supplied shade trees for the mission grounds. Unfortunately, many of these were elms, which have since succumbed to the Dutch Elm disease, but the maples are still extant.

Brother Charles was eager to accept Roy Klehm's offer to market his introductions. But there was one hitch. "Formerly, our nursery was across a very busy highway. And with all the traffic now, it's almost impossible to get across the road. I told Mr. Klehm that I wouldn't think of doing the work on that side of the property. And he said, 'How about starting a garden on your side of the road?' I said, 'Well, it's all heavy, poorly drained clay.'"

"Right!" said Roy Klehm, and promptly sent over a commercial tiling truck and a crew to lay hundreds of feet of drain tile. Next, the Klehm trucks hauled load after load of good, black soil from the former nursery and spread that as a foundation. The mission had literally received a windfall from the nearby village of Wilmette—their accumulation of autumn leaves. When these had partially decayed, Brother Charles himself tilled a five-inch layer into the rich soil from the nursery. A dwindling mountain of Wilmette's bounty stands at the far end of the new 85-by-125-foot garden. In the summer, pumpkin vines festoon the mound of rotting leaves and produce huge fruits. According to a local garden writer, one of the "exceedingly well-fed pumpkins weighed in at an impressive (or alarming) 159 pounds."

Since 1975, Brother Charles's daylilies have been offered for sale by Roy Klehm, hence the designation (Reckamp-Klehm) after the cultivar name. Many of Brother Charles's cultivars are further identified by the prefix 'Heavenly'—not, he hastened to tell Jim Wilson, because he considered himself any closer to the angels than anyone else, except in terms of his age, but because he feels at home with "heavenly" names.

Sometimes choosing names is a joint effort. "It turns out to be an ecumenical process," Roy says. "The funny thing is that he's Catholic; and I'm not, I'm Protestant. But I sit in church and look through hymnbooks and make a list of possible names, then he picks out what he wants." The hymn "Silent Night" proved to be a gold mine, furnishing no fewer than five cultivar names. Occasionally names occur spontaneously. Recently Roy and Brother Charles were looking over the new crop of seedlings when the breeder spotted something he really liked. "That's right smart," he enthused. "Pretty!" And that cultivar will be introduced by Roy as 'Right Smart Pretty'.

Almost as enthusiastic as Brother Charles himself, Roy says, "He's got so many good ones coming…. He works with all those delicate colors: delicate creams, pinks, pastel yellow with pink. He says they carry better in the garden, especially in the late afternoon and evening. The thing about his daylilies is that they change color during the day. A normal July summer day, they're one color in the morning. Then the sun pulls out the pinks and creams. They get better and better, and by evening they're often a beautiful pink."

While beauty is God-given, Brother Charles does not rely on divine intervention alone in his hybridizing program. He is a meticulous record keeper and has documented the family history of every variety he has ever produced. For this reason, seeing his seedlings bloom gives him a special thrill. "Going through in the morning, you don't know what to expect. Then, all at once, there is one—you see it in bloom and you look at the tag. You see the parentage in it, and you realize that you have accomplished something of what you had in mind when you made the cross. That's what gives me the most pleasure."

Virginia Peck: One of a Kind

Virginia Peck

In the early days of gathering material for this book, Ned Irish, a former President of the American Hemerocallis Society, said to me, "I wish you could talk to Virginia Peck. I think she's one of the true wizards of the Society. She looks like an Okie with one of those long, mournful, tired faces—like the Dust Bowl portraits of the thirties. But she was a professor of English and her husband was chairman of the department at Middle Tennessee State University. Virginia lost her husband some years ago, and she wrote me the loveliest letter when my wife died— the most understanding, the most sympathetic; she knew what I was going through."

Peck Hall on the campus of the university where Virginia and Richard taught was named for this remarkable husband-and-wife team. The Program of Dedication stated, in part:

> Dr. Richard Peck brought with him to the MTSU faculty his wife, Dr. Virginia L. Peck, who also was an excellent teacher. The two were a pair. They worked together, talked and listened and advised together, and savored living together. Her international renown as a hybridizer of tetraploid daylilies consumed many of the couple's off-campus hours, and specimens from her gardens have for many years enhanced the campus landscape.

In 1965, Dick Peck provided us with a charming introduction to his wife and himself in *The Hemerocallis Journal.*

> My first experience with flowers of any kind was with sunflowers in Kansas, the seeds of which I fed one at a time to impatient chickens. Mother's gardening efforts were limited to petunias and nasturtiums, both of which grew leggy, and African violets which usually developed leaf spot in the winter.
>
> My education was nothing out of the ordinary, and it certainly had no connection at all with horticulture, much less floriculture — except that I collected more peach pits to be used in gas masks in World War I than anyone else in my room at school.... Virginia and I met when we were both in graduate school. She was working on her Ph.D. at Vanderbilt at the time, and after a couple of years, one of which Virginia spent teaching at Montevallo in Alabama, we decided, mistakenly it turned out, that two could live as cheaply as one, and were married.

For two years, the newlyweds lived precariously on Dick's fellowship, supplemented by fatback and turnip greens provided by Virginia's father. Then the bombing of Pearl Harbor signaled the entry of the United States into World War II, and Dick was called up. A bit too old for combat duty, he was posted to an Army air force base in Arkansas. Virginia came with him and here, the young couple set to gardening with a will. "We gardened," Dick tells us, "for the sake of our stomachs, not our souls, raising vegetables exclusively."

After the war, the Pecks returned home and joined the faculty of Middle Tennessee State University in Murfreesboro, Richard as chairman of the English Department, and Virginia as a member of his department. Once settled at MTSU, both with full-time jobs, the Pecks bought what Dick describes as "a farm of sorts — that means it has many acres but not much arable land." It was here that they began gardening in earnest. Name a flower and they grew it. They planted seventy-five rosebushes and twenty-five tree peonies. They also had herbaceous peonies; irises, dahlias, and mums; and annuals and vegetables.

Then one season during the mid-fifties, Bob Hill, a fraternity brother of Dick's from the University of Kansas, sent the

Pecks a present of five daylilies. Bob and his father ran a nursery in Lafontaine, Kansas, and the Pecks always ordered their peonies and irises from the Hills. By 1946, Bob and his father had become intrigued with daylilies. Virginia tells the story in *The Hemerocallis Journal:*

> He and his father, H. M. Hill, were producing and introducing new varieties each year, and Bob was so enthusiastic about the future of daylilies that a little of it rubbed off on me, and I inquired about the process of hybridizing daylilies. Bob's wife Harriet laughed and said, "Don't ever put your first seed in the ground. If you do you're a lost soul. No matter how many acres you have, you'll never have enough to plant your seeds."

Despite this warning, Virginia Peck sallied forth into the garden one day, allegedly to admire a bloom of her favorite Peace rose. En route, she made a fatal mistake. Instead of making straight for the rose, she took a detour, pausing beside a clump of Hill daylilies. Heedlessly, she plucked a stamen from 'Redwood' and brushed the pollen-laden anther against the pistil of another Hill offering, 'Bold Beauty'.

The following week, this rash woman happened to notice that a seed pod had formed on the scape of 'Bold Beauty'. She made a mental note of this development but thought no more about it until a few weeks later, when she observed that the pod had turned yellow. Cracks had appeared at the top of the barrel-shaped pod, and she could see the gleam of black seeds within. Like a fairy-tale princess who cannot resist the magic draught, she bent down and with a stick scratched a little trough in the soil. Shaking the shiny black seeds into her hand, she popped them in the ground and filled the trough again with her stick.

Some years after the fact, she wrote, "Little did I dream when I made this first careless daylily cross that within several years there would not only be no Peace rose to look at but no corn in the barn nor potatoes in the bin because all of the garden space was taken up with row upon row of daylily seedlings — I, who took such pride in my two-pound tomatoes and exhibition mums and roses!" Out went the seventy-five rosebushes, twenty-five tree peonies, and two hundred clumps of iris. Out went the mums and dahlias. Only a few petunias survived the purge. The perennials lay on the compost pile, soon to become organic matter for the ever-expanding daylily garden. Let Dick Peck take up the story at this point:

> Even more upsetting to our way of life than the gift of daylily plants was Virginia's dawning interest in attempting to develop tetraploids. Had I known just what would come about with the arrival of that first bottle of colchicine, I think I might have diluted it with acetic acid. I did not know, and I didn't dilute it. To make a long story short, among other things there came into our lives a greenhouse (Orlyt), that we put up ourselves; approximately $4,000 worth of the finest introductions by the best hybridizers to provide seeds to be treated, and later, a fully equipped laboratory, since to fiddle with polyploidizing without the means of checking the results is both a waste of time and a hazard to the future of tetraploids.

Naturally, 1961 found the Pecks at the now famous Chicago Convention. As we already know, Orville Fay and Dr. Robert Griesbach were reporting on their successes in treating germinating daylily seeds with colchicine. However, another of the principals was young Dr. Toru Arisumi, a plant geneticist for the U.S. Department of Agriculture.

Born in Hawaii, Arisumi did his undergraduate work in agriculture at the university there. After graduation, he came to the University of Illinois, where he studied genetics and cytology and specialized in fruit breeding. Ultimately, he received his Ph.D. in horticulture from the University of Illinois and joined the U.S. Department of Agriculture as a plant geneticist in 1955. After a stint at the Columbus, Ohio, station, he was transferred to the Plant Industry Station of the USDA in Beltsville, Maryland, where he was put in charge of developing research programs in African violets and daylilies. The emphasis of these programs was on the development of techniques and materials that would be of use to the amateur and commercial breeder, rather than on producing new varieties.

Young Arisumi's boss, Dr. S. L. Emsweller, head of the

Ornamental Plants Research Group at the station in Beltsville, was also on the Convention panel. As part of the Scientific Forum, Emsweller held a meeting expressly for hybridizers and growers, at which he showed slides to explain and demonstrate the clonal method of conversion. Virginia and Dick Peck had never seen this performed and were fascinated.

Many years later, Virginia recalled the highlights of the occasion for readers of *The Daylily Journal:*

> The Pecks attended this Convention basically with the hope of meeting the scientists and talking tetraploids with them. We were lucky enough to do just that, and established a long and rewarding friendship with two of them. One of them was George Darrow, former Chief Horticulturist at the USDA, and the other was Toru Arisumi. Dr. Arisumi was to research daylilies, but he had no stock to work with. So we—and others—selected suitable modern diploids and sent them to him. The people at the USDA sort of adopted us as novelties. They could not understand how a little lady English teacher from the backwoods of middle Tennessee wanted to learn how to count chromosomes. They sent me reprints of all their papers, as well as those of Haig Dermen, the world's foremost authority on polyploidy. A correspondence grew up full of questions from me and answers from them.

By 1963, Virginia had learned enough about polyploidy and plant structure to present a paper entitled "Introduction and Identification of Tetraploidy in Daylilies" at the Scientific Forum that year. With this paper, she established her credibility as a scientist. By dint of hard work and application, the dedicated amateur had all but acquired professional standing. Three years later, Middle Tennessee State University relieved Dr. Peck of part of her duties as professor of English and awarded her a faculty research grant to experiment with cell-altering chemicals less hazardous than colchicine. It is interesting to note that, to date, none have been found. Colchicine is still the only effective substance for inducing tetraploidy in daylilies.

Following the presentation of her first paper, Dr. Peck and her friends from the USDA held a workshop demonstrating methods of colchicine conversions. And at this time, the participants were instructed in the mysteries of tissue development. The labor of building a plant falls to three separate layers of cells located at the so-called "growing point" or "apical dome." The outermost layer is responsible for the epidermal tissue of the plant—its skin, so to speak. The second layer manufactures the pollen grains and egg cells and part of the internal tissues of the leaves, flowers, and stems. The third and innermost layer produces the internal tissues of the leaves, flowers, and stems.

For tetraploid breeders, understanding the way in which the cell layers function is important because colchicine treatment of daylilies frequently results in "chimeras," or partially affected plants. In a given chimera, if the layer responsible for the pollen grains and egg cells has been successfully converted, the plant will be valuable for breeding. But to ascertain which layer or layers are affected requires skill and knowledge. Participants learned that the flower segments of a tetraploid are noticeably larger and thicker than those of a diploid, and that the pollen grains in mature tetraploids are significantly larger than those of their diploid counterparts. While microscopic examination of the tissues is the only way to be absolutely certain about tetraploids, these visual methods of identification were offered as guidelines.

Dr. Peck was elated by the response to the workshop and later wrote: "This program aroused a good bit of interest and we were swamped with requests for copies. Walter Hava, Director of the Science Committee, got us to tape the narrative for the slides and make duplicates of the slides. He then had a number of copies made of all of it and put it in the slide library (of the American Hemerocallis Society), charging $5 rental." The original paper was also printed in the *Hemerocallis Society Yearbook of 1964*.

What self-taught Virginia Peck did in writing for the Society publications and presenting demonstrations was to put the tools for converting diploids into tetraploids in the hands of any amateur willing to take the time and trouble. She had done the dog work. In sharing what she had learned, she advanced the cause of tetraploid daylilies almost single-handedly. That she managed to learn enough herself while maintaining a full teaching schedule and growing thousands of seedlings in her garden is the more to be wondered at. The woman was a marvel. "It's a life of dedication," she once said. "You couldn't pay me enough to do it."

To the sorrow of her many friends in the daylily world, Virginia Peck died in the fall of 1990. Not long afterward, I asked Van Sellers of Iron Gate Gardens in Kings Mountain, North Carolina, what place he would assign to her in daylily history. Van was not only Dr. Peck's friend of many years, he also introduced her cultivars. His response to my question was immediate and unequivocal: "She was just without a doubt, not the first, but *the* major contributor to the 'tet' gene pool in this country. She was a front-runner in every color. She was the first to do the whites. She was the first to work on reds. Now, when I say *work*, I mean to work intensively for major improvements. In every category, she concentrated intensively until she reached what she felt was a plateau. If she could not improve upon that category further, she moved on to something else."

In 1986, Virginia Peck was interviewed at length during the National Convention. When asked about her future goals, she replied:

> I've started many things, but as time moved on, and as I moved on, I found out I couldn't do everything. Right at present, I have homed in on white.... I have been working in white for several years now. I started a line with 'Astolat'. That was very white. It was a big flat flower, but it didn't have wide petals. And nowadays, if it doesn't have wide petals and ruffles, it's not a daylily. I worked around with 'Astolat' for awhile, and then, I felt I'd better get some "style" in it, so I treated Sellers' 'Iron Gate Glacier', which was a very nice, not a large flower, but quite ruffled and very white and pretty, nice scape. So I worked a long time crossing that into my whites.
>
> I see Mr. Durio back there. [Kenneth Durio is a professional horticulturist and highly successful daylily hybridizer whose fine cultivar 'Joan Senior' is among the whitest of the whites.] I thought I'd gotten as far as I could get with what I was doing, so I converted 'Joan Senior', and last year was able to cross it into my line of whites, and they are going to bloom next year. I want to live that long. After that, I don't care.

I don't know whether or not any of the progeny from this cross were introduced, but by the time of her death, Virginia Peck had focused the high-powered beam of her bright mind on other challenges. Having seen the wide petals, ruffles, and round flower shape become commonplace, she turned to the development of tetraploid spiders and doubles. In the course of more than thirty-five years of hybridizing, the childless English professor became the "super mom" of the daylily world.

She did it all—narrow petals and wide, the reddest of the reds, lovely near whites and ruffles. The public went mad for 'Dance Ballerina Dance'. Even I had heard of 'DBD', as it was invariably called by the cognoscente. This ruffled apricot-pink cultivar appears in the family tree of countless cultivars and in the early seventies was the most sought-after daylily in the world. Dr. Peck herself told me that "a hybridizer from Ohio said he'd crawl all the way to Tennessee to get a plant of it!"

In every color category, there are distinguished Peck introductions that have contributed to generations of outstanding daylilies. And thanks to this intrepid groundbreaker, modern tetraploid breeders have a bountiful supply of genetic material on which to build. As a hybridizer, Virginia Peck was a giant figure. In person she was the reverse—small, thin, and frail-looking, with a tanned, wrinkled face. "She looked as if she had just come in from chopping cotton," recalled Ned Irish affectionately. "But she was an absolute darling. One of the great ladies of the world."

The Eden of Louisiana

In the eighteenth century, French settlers deported by the British from Acadia (now Nova Scotia) made their tortuous way south to Louisiana. According to *Evangeline*, Henry Wadsworth Longfellow's narrative poem, they found themselves at last in a landscape of "devious waters" where Spanish moss and mystic mistletoe festooned the trees. The bayou country of southern Louisiana, where Evangeline sought her ill-fated lover, became home to many exiled Acadians. And "they who dwell there have named it the Eden of Louisiana!" In the twentieth century, the Eden of Louisiana has appropriately become home to some of the most beautiful daylilies in the world, including no fewer than eight Stout Medal winners.

From the little town of Iowa, Louisiana, came Miss Edna Spalding's exquisite 'Luxury Lace' and 'Lavender Flight', winners in 1965 and 1973, respectively. 'Lavender Flight' was one parent of Jim Marsh's 'Prairie Blue Eyes' and must surely be in the background of every lavender and purple cultivar we have today. During the 1950s, Miss Edna often had a visitor from Abbeville, an hour and a half away by car. Her visitor, Mr. W. B. MacMillan, was then approaching seventy and had only recently become interested in daylilies. However, he had already established an impressive reputation in horticulture as a hybridizer of Louisiana irises, *les gles de marais* ("the glads of the marsh"), as they were called by the local fishermen.

An astute, intelligent man, he had no difficulty in recognizing a good daylily when he saw it. Miss Edna's favorite colors were lavender and pink, which happened to be his, too, and he always came home with a number of her best seedlings and named cultivars. In his hands, these and their progeny gave an entirely new look to the daylily blossom. MacMillan's only hybridizing excursions outside the Spalding line were to Orville Fay's diploids, 'Frances Fay', 'Cartwheels', and, providentially, 'Satin Glass'. According to Louisiana native Clarence Crochet, a former President of the American Hemerocallis Society and frequent caller at MacMillan's House of Macs Garden, "'Satin Glass' was a big break in wide petals. Mr. Mac used it extensively and got spectacular results."

I asked Mr. Crochet, a well-known hybridizer himself, how he would rank MacMillan's contribution to the daylily world. He stated without reservation that "W. B. MacMillan was the father of the modern daylily as we know it. He was the very first person to increase the petal width to three inches. His work in this respect placed him as the pioneer in developing the full daylily form, particularly in the Deep South." With 'Satin Glass', the candy chemist from Chicago broke the narrow petal syndrome. But it took the Louisiana sales executive to make the most of the wider petals.

Called Billie by his intimates and Mr. Mac by devoted but respectful daylily groupies, W. B. MacMillan was born in 1883 not far from Austin, Texas. He began his education in the local one-room schoolhouse. Later, he continued his studies by riding horseback the five miles to Burnet, where he attended high school. He finished his secondary education at the preparatory school of Southwestern University in Georgetown, where he alternately taught and attended the university. (He became principal of the preparatory school as a college senior.) At the same time, he embarked upon the ardent courtship of a local girl named Bessie Belle Cooper, "Peggy" to her friends. Being a girl of uncommon common sense, Peggy wouldn't marry him until he had completed his master's degree in school administration at Columbia University in New York City and had found a job.

Neither school administration nor the Northeast appealed to Billie and his new bride, and they were relieved when a member of the school board with connections in Louisiana made it possible for him to switch careers. He joined the Louisiana State Rice Milling Company, Inc., as director of sales and sales promotion manager and prospered in the rice business. Indeed, he became a figure of considerable importance in the industry. But Mr. MacMillan was concerned with other things besides work.

He was fascinated by the landscape of his adopted state and took a keen interest in the wilderness that lay just beyond his doorstep. The marshy islands of the Mississippi Delta support many unique plant species, among them the beautiful Louisiana irises. Lured by their jewel-like colors and velvety petals, MacMillan began venturing deep into the swamps in search of different varieties. In the company of Caroline Dormon, an accomplished naturalist, writer, and artist and a close friend of the MacMillans, he explored the bayou country by boat and on foot. In 1939, he made a major contribution to horticulture in the discovery of *Iris Nelsonii,* with which he began to hybridize. Many of his hybrids represented breaks in form and color, and the flower he named for his wife was the first to display the flaring, overlapping form that is still much admired in Louisiana irises.

In 1941, MacMillan and Ms. Dormon and other devotees of the native iris formed what is now known as the Society for Louisiana Irises, and he served as its first president. Later he became the second president of the Louisiana Camellia Society and first treasurer of the Louisiana Society for Horticultural Research. This background helps to explain how a man who didn't discover daylilies until he was in his late sixties and introduced his first cultivar at the age of seventy-seven succeeded within fifteen years in producing three Stout Medal winners and in winning the Bertrand Farr Award for achievement in hybridizing.

The purchase of $28 worth of daylilies from Russell Gardens in Texas launched Mr. MacMillan's career. In 1960, a friend and fellow hybridizer, Louise Simon of nearby Layfayette, wrote an article about the MacMillans for *The Hemerocallis Journal.* At that time, in addition to maintaining a camellia collection and hybridizing Louisiana irises, the MacMillans were getting more and more absorbed in their newest plant diversion. "In spite of (or perhaps, it's because of) earlier gardening interests, the MacMillans have recently expanded their planting area and have literally 'gone overboard' as they call it, in daylilies. They will tell you that they have been 'playing around' with hybridizing hemerocallis for quite a while, but now, although still devoting full-time to business, they are doing some serious hybridizing in daylilies."

By this time, Clarence Crochet and his wife, Beth, had not only discovered daylilies, they had also discovered Mr. MacMillan and began making regular trips to Abbeville. As their home was not far away, proximity and their own escalating absorption in daylilies established a bond between the Crochets and the MacMillans. Crochet observed the demise of Mr. Mac's iris hybridizing in favor of daylilies.

> Realizing the limitations of time and space in trying to pursue the work involved in hybridizing irises and daylilies, Mr. Mac settled for the daylily, and for these reasons: he knew that the very best iris hybrids could be purchased for only $10, while the best daylily hybrids sold for $25 or more; the daylily seemed much more popular and enjoyed a more widespread demand than did irises. Therefore, the profit motive plus his realization that the daylily had tremendous possibilities for improvement led him to discard or sell nearly all his iris plants.

Mr. Mac wasn't put in charge of sales for nothing!

Shrewd as he was, MacMillan could also be very generous. He used to give divisions of his best cultivars to his gardener, Olivier Monette, and to Lucille Guidry, the loyal nurse who joined the household to look after Peggy MacMillan when she became disabled by a household accident in 1969. Before her accident, "Peggy Mac" used to accompany her husband on his hybridizing rounds with pencil and notebook in hand. She was the record keeper, and her entries provided him with the information he needed to select future parents. The Crochets would often find the MacMillans companionably seated in the gazebo consulting the "stud book" in order to plan the work of the day. Having no children, the MacMillans were very close and mutually dependent. It was, therefore, a dreadful blow to Mr. Mac when Peggy became incapacitated.

However, the MacMillans were blessed with the arrival of Lucille Guidry. Born and raised in Abbeville, Mrs. Guidry virtually joined the MacMillan household. "I felt as if they were my family and I was their family," she says simply. "I was with them for two years before she passed away. For a while, he thought he could take care of himself, but he really couldn't. Oh, he came near dying many times during those years."

Fortunately, Mrs. Guidry, her husband, Gabriel, and their son lived only a mile away, which made it possible for her to look after Mr. Mac and still manage a semblance of family life. It was during this time that she learned to hybridize, and gradually she and Monette assumed more and more responsibility. But MacMillan continued to take a lively interest, issuing instructions from his wheelchair. Sometimes he would give them plants to take home. "Here," he would say, "let's see what each of you can do with it."

What they did was imprint the indelible MacMillan stamp on generations of Louisiana daylilies. In this process, Olivier Monette became the first internationally known black hybridizer and won many awards for his beautiful cultivars, including the prestigious Annie T. Giles Award for the small, round, near white 'Little Infant'. Sadly, he died in December 1985 before some of his most promising seedlings ever flowered. Only a few months before his death, Roswitha Waterman of Long Island had visited the Monette garden and singled out one of his new crop as a future great, "a gorgeous glowing salmon pink seedling with an orange throat, thick, crisp substance, ruffling, and wide petals and sepals."

Lucille Guidry has gone on to win Stout Medals for 'Janet

Gayle' in 1986 and 'Becky Lynn' the following year. Clarence Crochet recounted the story of 'Janet Gayle'. "She brought MacMillan a bloom to see and asked for his opinion. He replied, 'Lady, you've already outdone me with this one.'"

Soft-spoken and modest, Mrs. Guidry demurs. "I learned by being with him," she says. "He would show me what he wanted. He never wanted any space in between the sepal and the petal, and he said that I had to keep selecting and crossing for wide petals and wide sepals. He would show me with his walking cane. I sort of took up where he left off because I could have anything he was working on. I'd bring some over here and start making crosses. You have to learn a little something in ten years!" She finished with a quiet laugh.

Asked which MacMillan cultivar she considered the pinnacle of MacMillan's achievements, her reply was swift. "From the time I was with him, I'd say it was 'Moment of Truth', a near white with a little bit of cream in it."

Clarence Crochet agreed with her choice. "His 'Hope Diamond' opened up near whites to the hybridizer, but he really hit the jackpot with 'Moment of Truth'." Another that Mr. Crochet admires is 'Sabie'. Named for Mr. MacMillan's sister, who used to come from Texas every summer to spend the bloom season with him, this cultivar won the Stout Medal in 1983. Of this huge, wide-petaled yellow flower, Crochet wrote, "If there was any daylily which stood as a veritable landmark in hybridizing, it was 'Sabie'."

When Mr. MacMillan died in 1978, a tribute appeared in *The Hemerocallis Journal* one line of which jumps off the page. The writer was Martin Standard, a Kentucky hybridizer: "I dare say that there is not a hybridizer in America who has not used MacMillan seedlings in his breeding program, which means that virtually all modern daylilies own a part of their beauty to Mr. Mac."

Eden Update

Beautiful daylilies are still being produced in Abbeville and Iowa, Louisiana. Although Mrs. Guidry lost her husband,

Gabriel, in November 1989, she is going forward on a reduced scale with the help of her son Davis. A choice pink daylily will be named in honor of her late husband. "He discovered this one in the last year of his life," she told me. "The seedling number is written in his own handwriting—'cream-pink 10/87.' The flower is flat and has a wide, spread-out, ribbed throat. And the edging is so pretty, it's picoteed all around. It's a beautiful thing. I haven't measured it yet, but I'd say it had a twenty-four-inch scape and about a seven-inch bloom. I might introduce it this year—it depends on how well it increases this summer. I usually prefer to wait four or five years because then I have enough so that I don't disappoint so many people."

Mrs. Guidry's description of the daylily she considers worthy of naming for her late husband tells you something about her criteria for introduction. In the late seventies, an admiring Texan visitor, hybridizer Mildred Schlumpf, summed up the elements that give Guidry daylilies their distinctive style. "For Lucille to look at them twice they must have wide, overlapping segments, ruffling, and firm substance. She has her preference as to form. She doesn't care much for the spider type of pinched petals. She wants them open-faced with a flat, round form. Most of Lucille's daylilies are in the eighteen- to twenty-six-inch range in height. She does not like the tall ones. Another quality I found in her daylilies was fragrance, which I feel will become more important in the future."

The ample, overlapping form developed through the years by Mr. MacMillan is still being refined by Mrs. Guidry. And the attribute of fragrance noted by the visiting Mrs. Schlumpf continues to give an added dimension to Guidry cultivars. In general, scent is once again emerging as a desirable trait in daylilies. It was one of the attractions of the lemon lily (*Hemerocallis Lilioasphodelus*). New Englander L. Ernest Plouf, who endowed an award for fragrant daylilies, must have remembered their sweet smell from the old days when they were common in northeastern gardens.

A charter member of the American Hemerocallis Society who started hybridizing daylilies in the 1920s, Plouf made breeding for fragrance worthwhile. In 1979, he established a $10,000 trust "for the purpose of stimulating the development of consistently very fragrant daylilies of the dormant variety." In 1989, the Plouf Award was won by Mrs. Guidry's 'Golden Scroll' and in 1990 by another Guidry cultivar, 'Smoky Mountain Autumn'.

In 1968, Elsie Spalding, Miss Edna Spalding's niece by marriage and legatee of her daylily collection, was stunned by the news of her inheritance. "When my Aunt Edna passed away, we found out she had left the home to us. We didn't know this until the will was read. So the daylilies were just dumped in my lap! The hard thing about it was that I had my poor mother in a wheelchair, which took a lot of my attention. But I had always loved flowers, ever since I was a baby. So I went to work with the daylilies because they were so beautiful."

Earlier, Mrs. Spalding had assisted her aunt in the garden, more out of kindness than any serious interest in the daylilies. "When I started helping her, I didn't know anything, and she didn't tell me anything, either. I suppose that she took it for granted that I was learning a lot, but that wasn't true. Believe me, I knew nothing. When Aunt Edna died, I went to the library and said, 'Please give me a daylily book.' The librarian said, 'Well, honey, I don't have one. But I will get you one.' So she called me, and I went over, and there was this hemerocallis book [a copy of *The Journal*]. Lord, I already had boxes of them that belonged to Aunt Edna. They were in the top closet. I knew they were up there, because I put them away to make room for my stuff when I moved in this house. Anyway, I dragged them down. But they didn't tell you all that much.

"So then I called Mr. Tanner and I'd ask him first one question and then another. Oh, he was wonderful because I knew nothing! And bless his heart, he'd answer me just the best he knew how." It seems that the patient Mr. Tanner was a Louisiana hybridizer who lived in the little town of Cheneyville, not far from Mrs. Spalding. Helpful as he may have been, he cannot have taught her very much over the telephone. Nor had she any other tutor. It is possible, of course, that more of Aunt Edna's expertise rubbed off on her than she realized at the time. Edna Spalding's sheer ruthlessness with her butcher knife when it came to inferior seedlings did impress Mrs. Spalding. "Everything that my aunt kept had good texture and branching. If a good seedling didn't, over the fence it would go!"

In an interview conducted at the time Mrs. Spalding won the Bertrand Farr Medal, she described her kind of daylily for *The Hemerocallis Journal:* "I like scapes of about fourteen inches with four-way branching and at least eighteen buds, if it's without rebloom. This is not easy to get." If a daylily reblooms, she finds twelve to fourteen buds adequate. As to colors, she prefers pastels for the very good reason that her exposed garden gets the full brunt of the southern sun. She used to experiment with some of the dark hues but found that "By noon they were wilted and black instead of being the color they should be." Texture is important to her, and she is pleased when a seedling displays thick substance and a smooth, waxy finish. "When I see this feature in a seedling, I know that it will hold up in the hot sun."

From this corner lot enclosed by a chain-link fence have come some of the most beautiful daylilies imaginable. Everyone knows small-flowered, pale pink 'Lullaby Baby', winner of the Annie T. Giles Award in 1982; and lovely, lovely buff pink 'Martha Adams', the Stout Medal winner of 1988. But remember, I am new to the wonderful world of the modern daylily. I discovered Mrs. Spalding at the time of the 1990 National Convention in Pennsylvania. I didn't consciously look for Spalding introductions. It wasn't until I was studying the Convention brochure later that I realized how many of the daylilies I found irresistible were Elsie Spalding's.

My notebook is full of her flowers. Looking back at my scribblings, I find that I was bowled over by the combination of 'Lullaby Baby' paired with a small flowered grape-purple cultivar. I yearned for 'Homeward Bound', a "huge cream-melon with a wide spread flower and wide, wide ruffled petals." For

'Priscilla's Rainbow' there was this note: "fascinating for its curious subtle colors." On the subject of 'Elsie Spalding': "gorgeous cream, as round as a cookie." And 'Jerome': "a beautiful shade of tangerine with a brushed halo." 'Ruffled Original' drew the following: "Heavenly blend in the indescribable range of pink through yellow." There were four stars beside 'Jolyene Nichole' and the description: "Huge, flat pink—lovely!" And perhaps best of all, at one garden enormous clumps of exquisite 'Yesterday Memories'. Here my notes wax positively fevered: "Must have! Branching and bud count! True pink with a wide lemon yellow throat. Magnificent!"

The secret of Mrs. Spalding's success is just that, a secret. She is not a record keeper, and she does not plan her crosses. Do you believe in magic? I do. Suffering from arthritis herself and with a husband slowed down by knee surgery, Mrs. Spalding's life is not easy. She wanted to open her garden to visitors this summer but made no promises. I was sad to hear her say, "It's time I was quitting, anyway." I said I hoped that she would still be able to do as much hybridizing as she wanted for her own pleasure. Her reply was cheerful. "I'm going to keep my best daylilies, you bet. And as soon as I can walk a little better, when I see one that I know *needs* to be crossed, I'll do it—even if I don't plant the seeds!" So that's how it's done, folks. You look for the one that *needs* to be crossed. If that's good enough for Mrs. Spalding, it should be good enough for you!

The Modern Daylily

Youthful as he seems to me, Van Sellers of Kings Mountain, North Carolina, has been around the daylily world for a long time and is a keen observer of trends and events. During the past quarter of a century, he has grown and sold hundreds of different cultivars from dozens of different hybridizers. His tastes are eclectic, and in his own hybridizing program he has pursued a wide range of objectives. In the mid-seventies, he took a near-white MacMillan cultivar and produced nearer whites that represented a giant step in that direction. He has bred for size in red tetraploids and interesting patterns in small-flowered diploids. His 'Exotic Echo' reminds me of a pheasant-eyed narcissus. The segments are cream to white and the eye zone has three distinct bands: a burgundy-purple ring surrounded by a lighter shade within a thin pencil line of the darker color and, at the very heart, a glint of vivid green. In short, he has done it all, and his achievements as a hybridizer were recognized in 1987 with the Bertrand Farr Medal.

I asked Van if it would be fair to say that by 1980, the modern daylily had arrived. His reply was:

"Yes, and it was during the eighties that we saw a rapid rise of interest and many new members joining the American

Hemerocallis Society. Until quite recently, the daylily world was stable—in membership, I mean. The same people went to the National Conventions, and everybody knew everybody else. Then, about ten or twelve years ago, a new generation of daylily people joined the Society—became part of the daylily world.

"These people are not aware of how long it took to widen the petals of old 'Painted Lady'. They're coming into the daylily world at a time when there are round, ruffled daylilies, because now everybody has them. That's what we all sought for twenty-five years. Because new people are coming into the daylily world when there is already this thing available to them, they're seeking other shapes and forms and colors. And that's why the spider and the variants have had a revival.

"People already have the round, ruffled form. So they want other things. They want spiders; they want fragrance; they want early openers in the morning and those that stay open at night; people in the north want the ones that start opening the previous night so that they will be open even if the morning is cold. In other words, they want everything today, because they were not in on the background of the daylily."

The large, luscious modern daylilies, with their flat, round segments, intricate ruffles, and shallow profiles, are now a familiar sight to this new generation of devotees. But as we have seen, this form and the expanded color range now taken for granted were a long time in coming. The aims of mainstream hybridizers, from Stout to MacMillan, remained remarkably consistent, and today's improvements represent the life work of many people over a period of many years.

Although Dr. Stout set about his hybridizing as part of a study of "physiological incompatibilities in the process of fertilization," he immediately foresaw the possibilities of certain species of *Hemerocallis* as garden plants. He was, after all, a gardener himself, as his beautiful backyard in Pleasantville, New York, proved. He was convinced that daylilies could be made more beautiful by thoughtful hybridizing and careful selection. Not long ago, his daughter, Elizabeth Rausch, happened to be in a Florida shopping mall where a daylily show was in progress. Out of curiosity, she stopped to look at the flowers that had been so important to her father. She was amazed by what she saw. "My father would have given anything to have been around today to see these glorious things—glorious things—I mean, they almost make a gardener out of me! They're just magnificent!"

Dr. Stout had been working to overcome the obstinate sterility of the brightly colored *Hemerocallis fulva* for ten years when he wrote:

> A cross that failed when made directly was sometimes made indirectly, so to speak, by using a third type as an intermediate parent. As a result the gayer and somewhat bold colors of the orange daylily have been both subdued and intensified in combination with shades of yellow, golden-yellow, and orange. This has also been done with the red tint of *H. aurantiaca*. A color pattern rather closely resembling that of the commonly cultivated form of *H. fulva* has actually appeared in the flowers of certain hybrids between species other than *H. fulva*.

Ten years to get shades of red, yellow, and orange and to imprint eye zones on species other than *H. fulva!* In 1925, Dr. Stout had about fifteen hundred hybrids from different crosses. Upon careful study, he concluded:

> The flowers of these hybrids taken collectively exhibit a wide range of colors from light lemon-yellow to very dark rich orange. Nearly all these shades are to be seen both in clear uniform color and in combination with various degrees of the red seen in *H. fulva* and in *H. aurantiaca*. The red may be rather uniformly dispersed over the outer half or two thirds of the petals, or it may be in streaks, in bands or halos, or in blotches.

Van Sellers has a hybrid for introduction in 1992 from Elsie Spalding's breeding, which is pink stippled on white—"like a plicata iris."

Even the reserved Dr. Stout betrayed excitement about his 1925 crop of seedlings. He was encouraged by their size, forms, and clear colors:

The best of the flowers are 'full,' with broad overlapping petals that are improvements on many of the older types. Thus the clear yellow shade of color seen in *H. Thunbergii* is obtained in certain hybrids in flowers that are fuller, larger, and more attractive. Increase in the size of flowers is to be had: some hybrids have flowers nearly twice the size of any of the species or any of the older varieties thus far seen by the writer, and in a few cases, the size is combined with rare beauty and fullness of flower. The most showy and floriferous plants are those that stand with flower stems about three feet tall and only slightly overtopping the leaves.

There, except for the height, which by today's standards would be considered too tall, you have a blueprint for the modern daylily. Stout set the course for everything that has happened in the last sixty-five years. What he wrote in 1925 could, with only the most minor changes, have been written anytime between then and 1979. Today, I still hear the litany—full, flat form, wide, overlapping petals, clearer colors. Nor is this beautiful, decorative garden form going to suddenly give way to fads and fancies. The daylily that Dr. Stout imagined and that hybridizers spent years striving toward has, at last, been gloriously realized. And it is here to stay. Even in the ever-changing world of daylilies, the classics are honored.

The daylily of the eighties and nineties is the work of many. There are the breeders who have created irresistible flowers; and the gardeners who have been happy not to resist them. There are the collectors who have driven hybridizers ever onward in the search for the new and different; and the scientists who have given amateur breeders the tools with which to pursue their work. But among this cast of thousands, a few have already left their indelible stamp.

Mr. MacMillan gave us broad petals and flat, round blossoms. From Mrs. Elsie Spalding and her aunt before her, we have finely crafted flowers in mouth-watering pastel shades. Virginia Peck's red tetraploids changed the way gardeners felt about reds, and the whites owe a debt to several southern breeders: Mr. Kenneth Durio, whose beautiful 'Joan Senior' was for many years the nearest thing to a pure white; and MacMillan, for 'Robert Way Schlumpf'; which gave Van

Sellers 'Iron Gate Glacier' and 'Iron Gate Iceberg'.

We remember Jim Marsh of Chicago when we admire today's lavenders, purples, and the edged cultivars which have posthumously emerged from his breeding. Marsh's neighbor, Brother Charles Reckamp, must be credited with trapping the rainbow in his pastel blends and for putting ruffles into the mainstream. Orville Fay and Dr. Griesbach led us, albeit protesting, into the tetraploid era, while Munson, Moldovan, and others refined and legitimized this newcomer to the daylily world. In the pursuit of increased flower size, Van Sellers has produced gorgeous big things like 'Brazilia', one of the first huge red "tets."

These and dozens of other gifted hybridizers wrought the modern daylily from materials inherited from the pioneers. By 1980, Cinderella had come out of the kitchen, flung down her apron, and kicked off her clogs. Slipper-shod, she was ready for the ball. It takes time, however, for new daylilies to find their way into local garden centers and the consciousness of the general public. It was thus, dear patient daylily friends, that I was able to remain ignorant until the 1990 National Convention. Here, I discovered the new, newer, and newest.

For the first time, I met a modern spider — 'Pink Super Spider', ten inches across! A huge windmill of narrow, peach-colored blades invaded by a spreading throat of creamy yellow. The petals boasted ruffles, and the strong scapes carried masses of huge buds. In my day, spiders were shy bloomers with weak-willed stems that could barely support the flowers! This miracle of strappy pastel segments was a stunning garden plant. The work of Kate Carpenter, it was only one of the revelations of the Convention gardens.

At the opposite stylistic extreme, I met 'Charlie Pierce Memorial', with the widest petals imaginable. The big, beautiful flower commemorating its late hybridizer was as flat as a plate and just as round. Registered as a six-inch flower, it appeared much larger because the segments were extended to their horizontal utmost. The garden effect of such flowers is quite different from the picture created by trumpet-shaped daylilies.

There is, to be sure, charm and grace in long tubes and flaring segments carried at right angles to the scape. However, the flat, open flowers present more petal surface to the viewer. They are therefore more colorful and, as a result, more eye-catching. In my heart, I find no difficulty accommodating both shapes; in my Connecticut garden, it is not so easy. But believe me, I am working on it. At the very time in my gardening life when I should be cutting back, I find myself digging into the unwilling turf and rocky New England soil to make room for some of the exquisite things I saw last summer.

The new pinks are partly responsible for the latest scar in my lawn. When I began buying daylilies, not one of the pinks that I could marginally afford was, by today's standards, pink. I did not love 'Bright Spot', 'Coral Mist', 'Sweetbriar', or 'Pink Damask' any the less for the reminder of their yellow forebears. Their soft colors blended well with the golds and even some of the reds, just because their varying degrees of pinkness overlay a yellow base. Today, pink *is* pink, which is *not* a color that belongs in the "hot" scheme of my perennial border! Moreover, my long, undulating flower bed, contoured to fit the east-facing hillside, unrolls to the north. It is intended to be viewed not broadside, but from one end and at a distance.

From the house and terrace, the eye blends the colors, rising to the exclamation marks of vertical flower forms, easing over the colorful masses of daylilies and weaving them all together. As the daylilies face downhill and toward the viewer, the surface of their rather narrow segments receives the maximum amount of exposure, and their trumpet-shaped blossoms are very effective. But I was spoiled by the National Convention. Now I expect *more* of daylilies.

The wide-petaled flowers with their intricate ruffles demand close observation in order to plumb their subtleties: the changes of color created by the depth of the ruffling; the minute projections that fringe the edges of some cultivars; the thread of gold or purple or red trimming the segments. Daylilies with these embellishments require a different stage on which to perform. Members of this glamorous new race should be buffered from the prickles of echinops and separated from the coarse, hard-working rudbeckias and echinaceas. In fact, the modern daylily should be treated like the queen that she is. How to use this aristocrat in my sprawling country garden remains to be seen. But I do know that the bed I gouged out of the lawn last summer presents a challenge.

Whatever the complexion of this addition to the garden, it will contain new daylilies. With congenial neighbors? Possibly. Please note that I *will not* call perennials of which there are thousands of different species "companion plants." However, I am prepared to admit that the daylilies of today must star in the garden in a way that their ancestors never expected, much less demanded. The queen is a bit of a snob when it comes to bedfellows, and her preferences will have to be respected. So it is going to be interesting to see how this bed evolves.

At last I understand how a daylily fancier can be mesmerized by a single blossom. Ned Irish, friend of Virginia Peck, former President of the Society, and an artist by early training, told me that he could stand and look at a single daylily flower all day without ever getting tired. And if the truth were known, so could I. Until I began to really *look* at the flowers, especially some of the pastels, I had not realized how exquisite the anther filaments could be—delicate as Venetian glass and suffused with color, often deepening toward the ends. They are in themselves works of art.

At the gardens on the Convention tours, I encountered flowers that were a revelation to me. 'Sweet Shalimar', a guest plant from the hand of Florida hybridizer Ra Hansen, brought me to my knees. The blossoms were the width of my hand and absolutely flat with broad, fluted segments the color of blushing cantaloupe ice cream. Georgeous pink 'Dream Awhile' from Ed Brown's Corner Oaks Garden in Jacksonville, Florida, beguiled me with its perfectly formed flowers and the rose-tipped stamens which stood out against its yellow-green throat. 'Silent Wonder', the creation of Alabama hybridizer Sarah Sikes took my breath away, but not that of a fellow admirer who turned to me and said, "Now, that's really got energy!"

'Unique Purple' from the late Frank Childs displayed colors entirely new to me. The flower is smoky lavender with a deep magenta-purple eye and matching stamens. I discovered another marvelous blend of smoky colors in 'Seductress', the handiwork of Louisiana hybridizer Lee Gates. The background color is a hard-to-describe beige with lavender accents in the edging and eye zone. 'Super Purple' by Texas hybridizer Bob Dove may have been introduced in 1981, but it, too, was new to me and super handsome.

Of the small flowers that I saw, I wanted everything! *Cute* is the only word for *tiny* 'Siloam Tom Thumb'—far tinier than any miniature I had ever seen—gold with a red halo. Nothing could be more charming than neat little 'Siloam Doodlebug', round as a button and pale primrose yellow with a purple eye. Golden 'Siloam Special'—so small and so wide open—won stars in my notebook and in capital letters, "A MUST." The same, alas, was noted of 'My Melinda', a much-branched plant bearing neat pink flowers of impeccable shape. Bred by veteran miniature hybridizer Lucille Warner and named for her daughter, 'My Melinda' is a small-flowered tetraploid. Little "tets" are a new direction for daylily breeders.

Asked once to name some unexplored avenues of daylily hybridizing, Van Sellers replied, "Everything!" Recently he singled out sunproof red tetraploids as a "for instance." "All the red tetraploids are of two types. There are the ones with a blue base and there are the ones with a yellow base—red over yellow. The tetraploids with red over yellow hold up in the sun. But those are not the ones the public wants. The public wants the good, velvety blue-red tetraploids with green throats. And at the present time, these do not hold up in the sun. It takes the yellow base to be sunproof. They're fiery, they are loud, they look good in the garden. But that's not what the public wants. So the reds have extensive work to be done."

Nor is there yet a blue daylily, though genetic engineering may offer one route to that goal. Already genetic engineers in Germany have succeeded in changing the pigment-making chemistry of the petunia. "Lab notes" by Jerry E. Bishop in a

1988 issue of the *Wall Street Journal* reported that the German experiments were good news to Calgene, Inc., a California genetic engineering company. Calgene owns a one third interest in an Australian horticulture firm that has cloned the gene that naturally produces blue in petunias. Scientists are now hopeful that this gene can be transferred to ornamental plants that don't ordinarily have blue flowers.

Whatever the future holds, it will be as adventurous as the past. No single flower has lent itself more graciously to the manipulations of hybridizers than the daylily. Having metamorphosed from scullery maid to pretty belle of the ball to fascinating woman of the world, the daylily of today rivals Shakespeare's Cleopatra: "Age cannot wither her, nor custom stale / Her infinite variety."

Miniatures

As my daylily enthusiasms seem to have run anywhere from ten to fifteen years behind the times, it follows that I only became aware of miniatures during the last ten years. Having spent the sixties in pursuit of the new colors—pink and anything resembling white—I next turned my attention to size, the bigger the better. During the seventies, I would greedily run my eye down the pages of every catalog in search of adjectives like, "huge," "massive," and "immense." In restrained brochures that confined their descriptions to a number of inches in diameter, I would look at nothing under eight.

How thrilled I was with the large-flowered tetraploids! I loved (and still do love) Virginia Peck's bold golden 'Bengaleer' and her rosey red cultivar 'Cherry Cheeks'! But my real find in terms of size was 'Yellow Pinwheel'. Created by the late Don Stevens, a noted and well-loved New England hybridizer, I rejoiced in its huge, sunny blossoms. Even the buds of 'Yellow Pinwheel' are the size of small bananas. In bloom, it can be seen from the adjoining county. But in their nocturnal decline, the spent flowers sprawl across neighboring buds and inhibit their opening. And removing the deadheads leaves behind noticeable white scars. So it was the excesses of my beloved 'Yellow Pinwheel' that drove me into the arms of the miniatures.

In the river of daylily cultivars that has flowed into commerce during the last twenty-five years, the swiftest current has always been in the middle of the stream. Here, the competition to produce wider petals and bigger flowers engaged the majority of hybridizers. During the last ten or fifteen years, however, there has been a growing interest in miniature daylilies. Indeed, the history of the small-flowered and miniature daylilies would provide enough material for another book. But suffice it to say that the little ones have always had their champions.

In the American Hemerocallis Society lexicon, *miniature* is the correct description of a flower less than three inches in diameter. *Small-flowered* is the designation for those from three to four and a half inches across, and anything over four and a half inches falls into the *large-flowered* category. The term *dwarf* refers to height, not flower size, and can be applied to a short plant (with scapes under twelve inches), even if the flower is full-sized. Plants of relatively small stature with three- to four-inch flowers have acquired the informal name *pony*. And they are popular enough to be the subjects of a "Mini-Pony Tet Robin." Defined for the baffled public, this round-robin is composed of letter writers who eagerly exchange news about small-flowered tetraploids.

During the hundred-year history of daylily hybridizing, friends of miniature and small-flowered daylilies have been loyal, if few compared to the number favoring large flowers. Cast your mind back to 1925 and the New York Botanical Garden, where Dr. Stout had just received plants of a new small-flowered daylily species from China. Stout responded at once to the charm of the dainty little yellow flowers of late-blooming *Hemerocallis multiflora*. He foresaw a new type of garden daylily which would extend the blooming season and provide a wealth of small flowers on a tall plant. Remember that in those days, height was regarded as an asset in some daylilies. Other little ones in which Dr. Stout saw possibilities were the lower growing and earlier blooming *H. minor* and *H. Middendorffii*. While he, like every other hybridizer before and since, strove to increase the segment width of the large-flowered daylilies, he never lost sight of miniatures as a desirable addition to the gardener's repertoire.

Like Stout before him, Dr. Ezra Kraus liked the little ones. His 'Autumn Daffodil' is an oldie but a charmer—if you don't mind its height. The well-branched, thirty-six-inch scapes rise very straight from its upright foliage and carry as many as forty small, creamy yellow flowers on a single stalk. Its height, late blooming habit, and myriad of miniature blossoms are hand-me-downs from its not too distant ancestor *H. multiflora*. The Kraus cultivars 'Ringlets' and 'Curls' are not miniatures by definition, but they are small-flowered and can be found in the ancestry of innumerable later and smaller cultivars. After all, you have to start somewhere.

Stanley Saxton of Saratoga Springs, New York, started right at the bottom with the species *H. minor* and spent years developing better garden varieties of small-flowered daylilies. His true miniature, little golden yellow 'Pinocchio', was the proud parent of far more famous 'Bitsy'. 'Bitsy', hybridized by Lucille Warner of Dallas, Texas, figures in more miniature pedigrees than you can shake a stick at—including that of 'Stella De Oro' and all Stella's many kith and kin. In 1966, Mrs. Warner's bright, precocious seventeen-year-old daughter, Melinda, who had been hybridizing since she was eleven, paid Mr. Saxton a fine compliment. Melinda wrote an article entitled "Breeding Miniature Daylilies" for *The Daylily Handbook* (a special issue of *The American Horticulture Magazine* devoted entirely to *Hemerocallis*): "In our garden we grew almost all the miniature cultivars of Stanley Saxton. Therefore, I feel that I started 'at the top.'"

If Melinda was not a typical teenager, nor was her mother, Lucille Warner, a typical housewife of the 1960s. Lucille had married her college sweetheart, Jay, and moved with him from their native Oklahoma to Dallas in the early fifties. Not long afterward, she contracted polio. During her convalescence from this crippling disease, she immersed herself in horticultural literature and even managed to crawl into the garden to pull weeds. Meanwhile, in the course of her reading, she had discovered daylilies, and the fateful purchase of a few named cultivars from Russell Gardens sealed her commitment to the genus *Hemerocallis*.

Mrs. Warner attended her first National Convention in 1957 and began hybridizing in 1959. Like Virginia Peck and the rest of the audience, she became aware of tetraploids at the Chicago Convention in 1961. Afterward, she made three trips to the tetraploid stronghold of Mr. Fay and Dr. Griesbach and found that after each successive visit, the progress in tetraploids seemed "more exciting and stimulating." By this time, she knew that she wanted "to be a part of the experimental work in these 'new fields to conquer.'" As early as 1968, Mrs. Warner was expecting to see bloom on the tetraploid miniatures which were to become her specialty and which were described by Bob Bearce in *The Daylily Journal* (Summer 1990) as "The Cinderella Flowers of the Nineties."

In young Melinda Warner's article of twenty-five years ago, she wrote, "Miniature daylilies provide an exciting new frontier for the ambitious hybridizer." What needed to be done to make miniatures competitive, according to this singular girl? First, produce colors other than the familiar golds and yellows; second, reduce the flower size; and third, shorten the scapes. "At the present time," wrote Melinda, "the smaller ones do not have the variety of color possessed by larger daylilies. The second goal is self-explanatory. The third goal, short scapes, is important because, proportionately, small blooms are set off to the best advantage when the bloom-scapes are under 24 inches in height." This wisdom from the mouth of a babe has guided the efforts of miniature hybridizers ever since.

Another bit of wisdom dispensed by Melinda Warner addressed the problem of acquiring stock with which to effect the desired changes. Clearly, the wild species had been thoroughly mined, and improved miniatures in yellow and gold were available. In order to extend the color range, small flowers of other colors would have to be employed, even if they were larger in size than the ideal miniature. Please remember that Melinda knew whereof she spoke. She had already been hybridizing for six years and had seen the results of her theories. "An idea which produces favorable results is the crossing of daylilies with flowers 2–3 inches in diameter with flowers 3–4 inches in diameter. This procedure proves to be a good beginning because by using both flower sizes, more of the desirable characteristics are in the genetic make-up of the resulting hybrids. The smaller flowered plants of the progeny are selected for continued inbreeding." This is still how it is done.

Although Melinda Warner went on to other interests, her mother stayed the course and is considered one of the pioneer breeders of miniatures, both diploids and tetraploids. It is entertaining, if not significant, that three of the foremost breeders of small-flowered daylilies should share the same Christian name. Members of this impressive trio, Lucille Warner, Lucille Lenington, and Lucille Williamson, were hard at work during the sixties producing new colors and even new patterns. Thanks to the incentive of Hubert Fischer's Donn Fischer Memorial Cup, the breeders of beautiful miniatures were receiving recognition for their efforts. And in the seventies, miniatures began to take their rightful place alongside the large-flowered daylilies. In 1975, an entire issue of *The Hemerocallis Journal* was devoted to the miniatures and their makers.

Two years later, in another issue of *The Journal,* the following evaluation of Lucille Williamson's contribution appeared, written by fellow hybridizer and "mini" enthusiast Edna Lankart (Ms. Lankart also introduced Mrs. Williamson's daylilies): "Before Lucille started seriously working on miniatures and ponies, as we like to refer to them, there were mostly yellow, melon, orange, gold and rust miniatures and many of these were much too tall for their small blooms. She also added many eyed miniatures."

Another contribution from this modest lady, who seems never to have written for *The Journal* or called attention to herself in any way, was to bring shades of purple into the miniature fold. Indeed, if she had produced only 'Little Grapette', many of us would recall her with gratitude. What a lovely small plant this is! The neatly turned flowers are the color of Emperor grapes. I have a large, very floriferous clump of 'Little Grapette' next to airy, primrose-yellow *Coreopsis verticillata* 'Moonshine', and I enjoy this pair tremendously. But far more significant than Mrs. Williamson's contribution to my gardening pleasure was her development of the eyed miniatures. These were cornerstones in the breeding endeavors of the amazing Mrs. Henry of Siloam Springs, Arkansas.

It has been said that Pauline Henry achieves her outstanding success rate by "crossing pretty on pretty." However, there is more to it than meets the eye. In the course of twenty-eight years, Mrs. Henry has named and registered more than three hundred cultivars—the majority of them small-flowered and many of them true miniatures. The small, immaculate blossoms of Henry cultivars appear to have been cut from some miraculous crystalline substance by a master craftsman. Of the introductions that I have seen with my own disbelieving eyes, each new one seems more perfectly formed or more startlingly colored than the last. Many are embellished with contrasting eye zones. The plants themselves are vigorous, floriferous, and, fortunately for northern gardeners, cold tolerant.

In the comparative isolation of northwestern Arkansas, Mrs. Henry regularly churns out gem after gem. Having used up the available space in her own garden, which is 125 feet square, she manages with the help of neighbors who let her use theirs. Who wouldn't welcome a garden full of Henry cultivars? And every year there are new ones. Said one awed colleague, "I'll bet if the good Lord spares her for ten more years, she'll have another three hundred! And she does it all by putting pretty on pretty. But she's got the eye and follows a train of thought in her head, I think."

I think so, too. She works like a bread maker who knows from experience how long to knead the dough and how much flour to incorporate. The feel, the degree of elasticity, the appearance of the surface—this is all the information that is necessary. Appearing to follow no recipe, a good baker knows exactly what he or she is doing. And so, I'll warrant, does Mrs. Henry.

If she has a secret, I suspect it is vigilance. "I throw away so many," she says. "And I'm sure I've thrown away a lot of good ones. But I try not to keep any that I don't think are pretty fine." In developing the style, which even a neophyte such as myself recognizes as "classic Henry," she began with some of Lucille Williamson's small ones. Having no small-flowered stock of her own, she used Williamson cultivars with what she did have: Dr. Kraus's 'Curls', Mr. MacMillan's 'Clarence Simon', and introductions from various other hybridizers.

Eventually the smaller ones began to come. And as the seedlings chosen for their diminutive stature became parents, there were more little ones. Of the forty-two Henry introductions registered between 1957 and 1973, only *one* was under three inches in diameter. The majority were between five and six inches. By the time the next checklist of new daylily cultivars was published, the vast majority of the 131 Henry cultivars were in the three-inch range and more than a few were in the two-inch-plus range. This phenomenon could hardly be accidental.

In 1983, Dr. Arthur M. Kroll of New Jersey wrote: "Mrs. Henry has introduced a new series of miniature and small flowers, particularly in red, yellow, cream, pink, rose and lavender shades, many with either subtle halos or shockingly pronounced eyes and strong green throats, that has set a new standard in those classifications." Four years later, Mrs. Henry was awarded the Bertrand Farr Silver Medal in recognition of her achievements. Best known for her varieties with eye patterns, she acknowledges a debt to Mrs. Williamson, whose eyed cultivars she used in her first crosses. The source of her doubles remains a mystery. "They just started to come," she told me. "And I started crossing them and just working like that." There was pardonable satisfaction in her voice as she said, "They tell me now that my doubles are taking over."

Siloam Springs, the name of the town where Mrs. Henry lives, provided her with the prefix for her many cultivars. I wondered but did not ask if she knew the lines penned by Anglican bishop and poet Reginald Heber: "By cool Siloam's shady rill / How sweet the lily grows!" It seems appropriate.

Even in the rather specialized world of breeding for small-flowered daylilies, there have been many more able hybridizers than I can possibly mention. Indeed, it is quite probable that I don't even know the names of many worthy breeders, let alone their unique and valuable contributions to a flower type of which I have grown particularly found. But it would be difficult not to recognize the name Elizabeth Hudson Salter.

The daughter of Betty Hudson, granddaughter of Ida Wimberly Munson, and niece of Bill Munson, Elizabeth has been around daylilies all her life. However, to attribute her talent to exposure alone would do an injustice to this young hybridizer. Of course, there's nothing like a favorable environment and a good teacher—both of which she had. Her grandmother began working with small-flowered daylilies in the sixties, even before the Munson clan moved to their present location in Gainesville, Florida. As an only child, it was natural for Elizabeth to amuse herself by trailing after the adults while they were engaged in their garden activities.

"For years, she'd follow Bill everywhere," her grandmother reported. "Wherever he'd go, she'd go." From observation or osmosis, a curiosity about hybridizing began to stir in the youthful acolyte, and she expressed an interest to Ida, who said, "Elizabeth, if you're interested, you just take over the minis." Like a child star who has to make the transition to adult performer, Elizabeth pursued a less direct career route than might be imagined. At the University of Florida, her major was journalism. Nevertheless, in her early twenties she assumed responsibility for the miniature program at Wimberlyway Gardens, and the die was cast. Even at that time she had clear objectives, one of which was to reduce the size of her little flowers. "I wanted to breed what I considered to be true miniatures," she wrote in a 1986 article for *The Journal.* "Flowers that could be registered at two-and-a-half inches and would not exceed that measurement."

Another goal she wanted to achieve was a broader and clearer range of colors in the miniature daylily. "I wanted to be able to grow more than just yellows—I wanted clear reds, pinks, purples, whites and a multitude of eyed varieties. I also wanted to achieve a very full, compact, round form, which in the early 1970s was not widely available in miniature and small-flowered daylilies." Now, of course, there are miniatures as round as buttons, with all manner of ruffles and frills, and an extensive color range.

Today, Elizabeth Salter has set her sights on a new goal — miniature tetraploids measuring under the three-inch limit. "I haven't totally given up the diploids," she said recently, "but you can only do so many small, perfectly formed, two-and-a-half inch yellows, and then, you look for a different challenge." The tetraploid miniatures offered that new frontier. Moreover, the widely held belief that producing a truly miniature "tet" was impossible egged Mrs. Salter on. "Somebody telling me I couldn't do it!" She laughed. "Well, I've done it now, so I know that it is possible." Not that it has been either quick or easy.

Like Melinda Warner, she had to start with flowers of a greater size than her ideal: "We had to start with the small flowers first. Then, in order to get them down in size, we had to cross them with something smaller. So we took some of my diploid miniatures, like 'Munchkin Moonbeam', 'Knickknack', and 'Moonlight Mist', and converted them. Getting them into the lines brought the size of the larger things down."

Whittling down the size of tetraploid miniatures is an ongoing project because conversion tends to increase the size of the colchicine-treated plant. However, progress is being made. As smaller flowers turn up among the seedlings of the converted "tets" and selections are made, the size will diminish. "We're just now getting the true miniature in tetraploids," she told me with ill-concealed excitement. "We had one bloom in 1990 that for the very first time was only two-and-a-half inches across! So they're coming."

If miniature and small-flowered tetraploid daylilies live up to expectations and earn their title the "Cinderella Flowers of the Nineties," it will be thanks to people like the three Lucilles, Pauline Henry, and Elizabeth Hudson Salter.

Spiders

'Kindly Light' (Bechtold)

In 1982, a serious-minded article appeared in *The Daylily Journal* entitled: "Can You Mistake a Spider?" The following year, there was another: "What is a Spider?" As these titles are apt to draw a snicker from outsiders, let us clarify the issue once and for all. To daylily people, a spider is a flower style, originated in the early forties by LeMoine J. Bechtold on his Colorado property nine miles south of Denver. He had chosen this location for its beautiful setting with a view of the Rockies and for the stream which would provide water for his numerous horticultural enthusiasms and experiments.

Bechtold's Christian name was the inspiration of a plant-loving mother who insisted on calling him after French horticulturist Victor LeMoine. As a boy, young LeMoine may have found the name a burden, but it proved suitable after all. He grew up to love plants and soon became involved in hybridizing. His earliest love affair was with dahlias. Later, he embraced gladioli, peonies, irises, and even lilacs, and then he discovered daylilies. In fact, he found so much pleasure in this new hobby that it often took precedence over his music business, and for this, fanciers of the spider daylily can be grateful.

Of the daylily world's father figures, LeMoine J. Bechtold

was probably the most self-effacing and is the least well known. No one would be more surprised than he by the current popularity of his daylilies, which fell out of favor during the sixties. In 1922, he had ordered every variety of *Hemerocallis* in the Gilbert H. Wild and Son catalog: *Hemerocallis minor, H. Midden-dorffii, H. Thunbergii,* and a few garden varieties of *H. fulva.* These he crossed among themselves and by 1936 thought some of his seedlings an improvement on their parents. He wrote the Wilds and asked if they would be interested in listing a few. They were, and thus begins the history of the spider.

Bechtold's first introduction appeared in the Wild catalog in 1936. It was called 'Golden Wings', and the flower was described as "a large, twisted petaled, lacquered yellow." Soon after the debut of 'Golden Wings', an unusual seedling turned up in his garden. Its long, narrow, recurved petals were different enough to catch his eye, and he saved it for breeding purposes. Called 'Harem Girl' but apparently never registered, he used this early spider type to produce his classic arachnids: 'Blythe Lady', 'Kindly Light', 'Shirley Wild', and 'Lydia Bechtold'. To my shame, I have grown and, ultimately, lost the last three.

At the time I began ordering from the Gilbert H. Wild and Son nursery, I was looking for size. By measurement, spiders have very large flowers, but their narrow, wind-blown petals and sepals have far less impact in the garden than smaller flowers with broader segments. Anyway, having read the vital statistics of 'Kindly Light', I was determined to have it. I anticipated a sort of giant version of 'Hyperion' and was disappointed in the wispy, albeit graceful flower that arrived. I made a similar mistake with the other spiders that I ordered. The flowers were not showy enough to suit me, and were few in number. And on the rare occasion when more than one flower opened on the same scape, the combined weight brought the stalk nearly to the ground. The upshot was that eventually spiders were phased out of my garden.

Now that my daylily consciousness has been raised, I am much more attracted to spiders than I ever was in those days.

And I welcome their resurgence. Their creator, Mr. Bechtold, who seems to have been a most kind and sweet-natured man, was honored for his achievement with the Bertrand Farr Medal in 1960. He died soon afterward, before his dream of producing a pure pink spider could be fulfilled, but also before his flowers were abandoned in favor of those with wider petals. For the most part, although the Wilds continued to list Bechtold's introductions long after they had gone out of fashion, spiders had become forgotten except by a few loyal fans.

Rosemary Whitacre of Columbia, Missouri, has been devoted to daylilies for more than forty years and is an authority on spiders. "They were kept alive," she says, "by people who truly loved them—little old ladies in blue gym shoes or dirty moccasins—like mine—who kept these flowers since the day they bought them in 1945." She also credits the Wilds for the survival of spiders and attributes to Lois Burns of Exeter, New Hampshire, their current renaissance. "She was responsible for rounding up the old spiders and educating people to appreciate them."

Mrs. Burns's interest stemmed from the chance gift of a spider as a bonus plant in 1978. It came with the other daylilies she had ordered, and she liked the unusual form. "I began talking about it, and all of a sudden it sort of caught on a little bit. A few people wanted to be in a spider robin, and so we started one. It took off from there." In recent issues of *The Daylily Journal* there have been feature articles by Mrs. Burns and Mrs. Whitacre, and in the fall of 1991 a spider actually made it to the cover. How gratified LeMoine Bechtold would be to learn that cover girl 'Jan's Twister', an introduction from Joiner Gardens in Savannah, Georgia, is the result of a cross between 'Jean Wise' and his prototypical 'Kindly Light'.

My friend Greg Piotrowski has become intrigued with spiders. "I don't think when they were introduced they were particularly popular," he says. "Certainly they were an oddity, but I doubt they were as popular as they are now. Daylilies then—as now—were money-makers, and hybridizers try to breed and introduce types that they think will sell. Oftentimes they will be led by the taste of the collectors in the Society. So at that time, tastes were changing. I guess one of the driving forces behind hybridizing has always been wider petals, ruffles—whatever. So these narrow-petaled things—not necessarily the spiders, but the parents that produced the spiders—were tossed aside. Once the parents were tossed aside, we no longer saw the spiders being produced. Now, to get spiders, it seems you either have to go back to old material or use current spiders."

Talking to Greg, I feel vindicated to some extent in my assessment of old-fashioned spiders as poor garden plants. In his view, very few of the original spiders are really good performers. "Most spiders do not have good branching," he admits. "They only have a cluster of buds at the top, and a high bud count for a spider is fifteen." In addition, the scapes are usually tall and weak. As for the ruffles that are so popular in other daylilies, they are absent altogether in spiders.

Now, having heard the downside, it is only fair to present the opposite view. Arachnophile Lois Burns writes: "Almost without exception, spider plants bear fair to large size flowers when they reach maturity. Many of them can be described as being lyrical, animated—fluttery, swirling, twisted. They usually ride atop tall, graceful, multibranched scapes that are constituted to carry a respectable quota of buds, several of which generally bloom at once."

As more and more people become interested in the spider form—and they will—improvements will be made in branching and bud count. According to Greg, breeders are already addressing the problem of reducing the height of the scapes. And more colors are available. For example, 'Wind Frills', a ruffled, twisted pink introduced in the seventies, has become popular. Not technically a spider, it is sufficiently spiderlike with its narrow segments and airy, open form to satisfy spider enthusiasts and to make converts among the uncommitted. Greg says this one is quite popular and "the sort of thing that helped bring back interest in spiders."

A flower that succeeded in winning me over was 'Peacock Maiden'. Again it isn't a true spider—the segments are too wide. But it is open in form with pinched segments, and the color scheme is stunning—a white starry center and white midribs against a background of deep red-purple. Another admirer described it as "an ooh, aah type of daylily." Moreover, according to Greg it's a wonderful garden plant.

So what is a "true" spider? Two round-robins devoted to spiders worried this knotty question for years. There were the classicists, who stringently adhered to the five-to-one ratio—petals five times as long as they are wide—and no overlap of segments at the center of the flower. "But," wailed the romantics, who love anything informal with long, narrow petals and a spidery appearance, regardless of measurements, "only a handful of spiders qualify!" And so the lines were drawn and battle commenced. Then, in 1989, the new Harris E. Olson Spider Award was established. A decision had to be made. So the ontology of the spider was left to the board of directors of the American Hemerocallis Society. They, in turn, entrusted this task to the Awards and Honors Committee, and guidelines for determining the essential nature of a spider emerged.

The official definition of a classic spider is also the definition of a classic "star." Uh-oh, what's this new designation? Patience. One of the problems with which the spider round-robins struggled was how to stop hybridizers from giving the name "spider" to flowers that were not bona fide spiders, thereby, confusing the public. The case for sparing us confusion is sound. Any cultivar which is *called* a spider will sell in today's spider-conscious market. Moreover, the hybridizer can ask whatever the traffic will bear, and often that is plenty. Collectors are avid for the new and different. And certainly spiders are a complete change of pace from the round, ruffled, full form of the eighties. If you are paying for a spider, that's what you should get. But what to call these other spider-like flowers?

Rosemary Whitacre puts the hybridizer's problem in a nutshell: "Everyone who makes any attempt to hybridize spider daylilies finds out right away that this is no easy task. Resulting seedlings are rarely, if ever, classic spiders. You will in the course of the work, however, come up with some beautiful and dashing specimens, and again the question arises: What are they, if they don't fit the classic proportions?" Well, the official spider rule, which still needs further clarification, is flexible enough to include variations on the spider theme while maintaining the five-to-one ratio as the classic spider measurement.

The rule arrived at in 1989 and printed in *The Journal* says this: "Length to width ratios can be as high as 5:1 or higher, as is the case with classic spiders which bear ribbon-like segments." But the next item makes provision for nonclassic spiders. Here the ratio may be four-to-one. "This group of nonclassic spiders includes those spiders generally referred to as stars, pinwheels, crispatas (with segment edges that curl under), and spatulates (spatula or spoon-shaped segments that become markedly wider at one point)." There is more, but if you can absorb one more detail, you will know a classic spider when you see one: "In classic spiders, petals do not overlap petals, and petals overlap sepals only at the base."

It all boils down to this: There are spiders, and there are spiders. The classics are mostly old-timers, whose creators are long gone. LeMoine Bechtold's 'Kindly Light', registered in 1949 and introduced by the Wilds in 1952, is still the standard for spider daylilies. 'Scorpio', introduced in 1952 by Florida hybridizer Ralph Wheeler, is another classic and a good garden plant to boot. Hugh Russell produced 'Silver Drops', which also fits the classic mold. Then Lois Burns tells us there are "the 'fancy' spiders whose narrow segments can be spatulate, elliptical, straplike, or asymmetrical in character, and at the same time may twist, curl, spiral, ruffle, be pinched or fluted, or recurve — whatever, singly or in combination." Spider daylilies have become many-splendored things. So take your pick.

Doubles

'Betty Woods'
(Kirchhoff, D.)

In the case of double-flowered daylilies, I must once again confess to a former prejudice. It was based on an unhappy experience with a cultivar whose name I have conveniently forgotten. The flower was gold in color and clumsy in shape when it actually *was* double—which was not often, but often enough for my prejudice to become established. Why, you will ask, did I not just cut my losses and throw it away? In the first place, I am a child of the Depression era and do not throw things away easily. In the second, the catalog made this flower sound so appealing that I kept hoping it would live up to its description. It never did. It sulked and flung its blowsy double blossoms to the ground and eventually wound up on the compost heap. After that I was never tempted to look at another double daylily— until I saw photographs of David Kirchhoff's cultivars and met in person the spectacular 'Betty Woods'. But I am way ahead of the story.

Double daylilies have been in cultivation since the eighteenth century. Karl Peter Thunberg, star pupil of Linnaeus, saw the double-flowered version of *Hemerocallis fulva* growing in Japanese gardens on his visit in 1784. There may be modern gardeners who have never seen the robust, handsome plant that

Thunberg saw. It is not nearly as common as the single form. However, it, too, has naturalized in some spots. Despite its colorful flowers, which are an eye-catching muddle of orange and red segments, few today would welcome it into their flower beds. It is a coarse plant well equipped to carry out its territorial ambitions by spreading underground rhizomes. Like the single *H. fulva*, it is a triploid and sterile. Propagating itself vigorously by runners makes up for its inability to set seed.

All double-flowered daylilies originated as "sports" or, more properly, mutations. Their extra segments are hereditary abnormalities resulting from a genetic glitch. Some of the abnormalities are very attractive, others are not. Sometimes there will simply be twice the usual number of segments. In my garden, the old cultivar 'Hyperion' sometimes produces a few big flowers with four sepals and four petals. This type looks almost like a large clematis blossom.

In other doubles, the stamens become extra petals (petaloids). In another form, there may be two sets of petals, one on top of the other, like a cup and saucer. This arrangement is sometimes called "hose-in-hose," for an imagined resemblance to Elizabethan doublet and hose. In still others, there may be many extra segments resulting in a lovely, fluffy blossom called "a peony-type double." Not surprisingly, there is a price to pay for this excess. The reproductive organs get shortchanged. And those with deformed or aborted stamens and pistils are more difficult to breed than their single-flowered counterparts.

Dr. Stout became very much interested in doubles—at first as a scientist investigating sterility, and later as a hybridizer. At the time of his retirement from the New York Botanical Garden, he was working on a new strain of doubles he had developed from mutations which had turned up in the course of his experiments, and he continued his efforts to improve their form during his retirement. At the time of his death, he had selected twelve seedlings for introduction. Of these, four were offered posthumously by the Farr Nursery: 'Arlow Stout', 'Doublette', 'Gold Bouquet', and 'Zelda Stout'. The colors were, respectively, golden yellow, gold, deep gold, and light yellow.

The multiple segments in Dr. Stout's cultivars resembled the daffodil form called a "split corolla." In this type, the familiar trumpet is blown wide open and flattened against the ring of sepals and petals called the perianth. In the Stout daylilies, the doubling occurred as a flattened, irregularly shaped smaller flower within a normal flower. Whatever their shortcomings as to fullness and beauty, these cultivars at least produced their extra segments regularly. Many doubles are, at best, intermittently double.

Whatever the aspect of daylily hybridizing and whatever the flower form, the omnipresent Dr. Ezra Kraus seems to have had a hand in it. And during the fifties, he took a keen interest in doubles. Among the thousands of seedlings he grew, doubles occasionally cropped up, and if he thought they might have garden merit, he saved them. By the mid-fifties, he had a few he thought good enough to introduce. I will name just one — 'Double Eagle'. Kraus spotted this yellow-flowered double in 1946.

There is something haunting to me about the discovery that this flower is in the family tree of David Kirchhoff's modern cultivar 'Betty Woods'. Only a few short daylily generations ago, 'Double Eagle', even then a venerable plant, was crossed by Betty Brown of Texas with one of her own seedlings. This cross produced 'Double Cutie', a landmark in the breeding of double daylilies. In its turn, 'Double Cutie' became one of the founders of the Kirchhoff line that has given rise to such lovely things as 'Betty Woods'. Thus, through their flowers, we are — often without knowing it — brought close to men and women who died many years ago.

Returning to the past, improvement of the existing doubles presented a formidible challenge. Dr. Kraus was delighted when 'Double Eagle' proved to be double up to seventy-five percent of the time. In those days, it was the rare double that produced its extra segments consistently. And how about the color range? You guessed it — yellow, orange, and gold. The forms were nothing to write home about, either. They generally had a messy, accidental look, with distorted petals and sepals. In short, there was a great deal of room for improvement. So while one valiant band of daylily breeders ventured into the field of tetraploid hybridizing, another tackled the doubles.

Dr. James Miles of Clemson, South Carolina, believed in a "no holds barred" approach that included X-ray treatment of the flower buds. When his efforts in this direction failed, he was stuck with the tried and true but time-consuming method of crossing daylilies which occasionally or consistently produced double or semi-double flowers, and selecting the most promising seedlings. In 1962 Dr. Miles, an upbeat, optimistic man, announced in *The Hemerocallis Journal:* "There are in the making, beautiful new daylilies so different in form that one might have some trouble at first classifying them as daylilies."

He excitedly described the types of doubling. "Some are flat with the extra petaloids lying one upon the other. Another form of doubleness gives the pom-pom effect of a carnation or marigold. Others are more irregular, informal or shaggy." He alerted the public to the impending arrival of "startlingly new and beautiful 'double' daylilies." Who knows how much of the perceived beauty was in the eye of this enthusiastic beholder? While he was obviously thrilled with the new developments, he remained sensible of the problems that still existed.

Doubling remained inconsistent throughout the sixties. And even the ebullient Dr. Miles was cautious about improvements in the color range. "Progress has been satisfactory," he reported in a later *Journal,* "It will take time, but the pinks will get pinker and the reds redder. It takes a long time or a great deal of money to get enough double daylilies to cross in order to produce seedlings of various colors, sizes, forms, etc. But it can be done. It is being done."

Miles invited doubting daylily enthusiasts to stop by his garden and see for themselves. "Draw your own conclusions about the progress made in developing pretty double daylilies. Or better still, let me walk you around and point out the various features of them which I cherish, and thus see them as I do, and I know you will like double daylilies." The invitation would have won my heart, even if his daylilies didn't. Dr. Miles never, to my knowledge, received any prizes for his efforts, but he should have—for persistence, if nothing else.

Meanwhile, Betty Brown in Orange, Texas, was really beginning to make progress. She took the curse off the old partial doubles with their narrow segments and chaotic flower forms by crossing them with 'Double Decker', the first consistently double daylily then available. And for the sturdy virtues of big, gold 'Double Decker', she had the late Benton Thomas to thank. Mrs. Thomas was a Florida hybridizer who also concentrated on improvements in double-flowered daylilies.

By the early seventies, Mrs. Brown had managed to weed out the losers and come up with winners like bright rose pink 'Double Glamour', peach pink 'Double Love', salmon pink 'Double Vision', and the small, light yellow treasure called 'Double Cutie'. In the awards department, 'Double Cutie' swept all before it, culminating its triumphs by winning the first Ida Munson Award. Bill Munson established the award in 1975 in honor of his mother to recognize cultivars that displayed consistent doubling. Mrs. Brown not only advanced the cause on this front, her shades of pink also represented a breakthrough. In addition, her cultivars were already suggesting new directions in shape. They had multiple segments that were broader, fuller, more regular, and more overlapping than their forebears.

Into this promising picture, stepped young David Kirchhoff of Sanford, Florida. A daylily buff since his school days, David grew up in a world of plants. His mother gardened, his father gardened, his grandfather and great-grandfather gardened. "My father's grandfather hybridized gladiolus. Then my father and his uncle were in the gladiolus business for about thirty-five years. When my father retired from that, he founded Daylily World." But David's interest in daylilies predates that of Edward D. Kirchhoff. "I purchased daylilies way before my father ever did. I grew them in my section of the garden and actually hybridized them as a youngster. My interest was always there. And I used to read plant magazines when I was in college, instead of practicing music."

David returned to the family fold by way of the retail music business. A music major at college, he played woodwinds and the piano, but afterward went into retailing keyboard instruments. It proved to be so competitive that he began to think wistfully of the very different lives his father and grandfather had led. "I remembered what I was brought up in, which was plants. I was surrounded by plants my entire youth, and I missed that. So when my father invited me to join him in 1971, it sounded wonderful to me." Today, David and his partner Mort Morss run the large commercial nursery founded by Edward D. Kirchhoff and carry on a hybridizing program that covers the daylily spectrum. Doubles, however, were David's first love and have remained dear to his heart ever since.

His interest in the doubling phenomenon was aroused not long after he joined his father at Daylily World. The growing season of 1973 had been spectacular. Rain that year was plentiful and, for a wonder, came when needed; the planting was done on time; and everything in the garden was growing at peak performance. Then, late in the season, David began to notice that instead of their usual single flowers, many of the daylilies were displaying a pronounced tendency toward multiple segments. "Many, many," said David. More than a decade later his voice betrayed the excitement and surprise that attended this discovery. "I mean, almost everything reblooming out there was presenting a double bloom." Seeing a whole garden full of beautiful double flowers did the trick. He vowed to breed doubles that would incorporate all the forms and colors that had already been achieved with singles.

"At that time, almost every double we had ever seen had awfully, awfully narrow segments and most of them were not symmetrical and tended to bloom a different face almost every time. They weren't consistent at all in their appearance. So one of our goals was to widen those outer petals and sepals and to fill up the inside with some symmetry." During the wonderful summer of 1973, he seized upon every occurrence of doubling among the singles and crossed them with three key doubles that he already had: 'Double Cutie' and 'Double Razzle Dazzle' from Betty Brown, and 'Double Decker' from neighboring breeder Benton Thomas.

The first step was to build up the meager gene pool of doubles, and that took time. But within six to ten years, David was well on his way to accomplishing his initial goals. In 1980, he introduced 'Betty Woods'—to me, the acme of perfection. The yellow blossom is as round as a coin, each ruffled segment neatly overlapping its neighbor and layered like a dancer's tutu. Quite simply, it's a knockout. Now there are others, like a delicious pastel confection called 'Nagasaki', which puts one in a dilemma—do you eat it or pick it? 'Bed of Clouds' is a pink that presents the same problem. To me, it seems as if David has gone about as far as you can go with doubles. That is not, however, how he sees it.

"On the diploid level, I think we'll see a great deal of subtle refinement, and I think the tetraploids may show us yet another phase. We'll bloom our first seedlings out of tet 'Betty Woods' this year and I'm so excited.... I think 'tets' will give us a whole new bunch of directions that we can go in with doubles. I think the diploids are ... I don't find them as exciting anymore as I did the 'tets' last year. And so with this new influx of genes to work with on the 'tet' level, I'm more excited than I've ever been!"

As David is generally known for his excitement about his work, that means he is very excited indeed. Before I met him, he was given the following introduction by a fellow member of the American Hemerocallis Society. "David is a whirlwind, second-generation daylily addict and very successful hybridizer who gives talks to groups around the country. And he is enthusiastic about daylilies to the point of frenzy." I haven't found that summation too far off the mark. He is, in addition, a warm, entertaining fellow and modest about his accomplishments, which include the 1986 Bertrand Farr Award for outstanding results in hybridizing.

Guiding Lights

The daylily world is a real place. It has a geography: There are certain states, like Georgia, Florida, Louisiana, and Texas, that are hotbeds of daylily enthusiasts. It also has a language and a vocabulary: *tets* and *dips* (for diploids); *spiders*; *minis* and *ponies* for the small ones; *sibbing* means breeding two seedlings from the same parents with one another; while *selfing* refers to the practice of pollinating a flower with its own pollen or with pollen from another flower of the same plant.

In 1991, the population of the daylily world consisted of 6,702 diverse souls and 33,368 named daylilies. The governing body is the American Hemerocallis Society, with its rules and registration procedures for the flowers, its Awards and Honors system, and other rites and rituals. The daylily world also has its own folklore and heroes. There are names that *everybody* knows and tales related by firesides whenever daylily people gather. In this relatively small but ever-widening world, nearly everyone knows everyone else. And even if daylily people are strangers to one another, they do not remain so long. It takes one to know one. En route to the tour gardens one morning during the National Convention, a station wagon passed our bus. My seat companion looked down and immediately spotted daylily foliage in the backseat. "One of us," she exclaimed with satisfaction.

The person who eased my entry into this world was Sally Millman of Gansevoort, New York, and a kinder, more warm-hearted guide it would be hard to imagine. At the time I began my daylily adventures, Sally had just become the editor of *News From Region Four* (Region Four of the American Hemerocallis Society includes the six New England states and New York). She introduced herself to regional members in this way: "I am a teacher, writer, gardener, ex-modern dancer (amateur!), and appreciator of the arts and literature. I have enjoyed teaching fifth and sixth graders for many years. In addition to the usual curricular pursuits, my classes and I have enjoyed developing and maintaining perennial and shrub borders around the front of the school. Together we have developed annual musical and slide programs." Sally's bachelor's and master's degrees are in education from SUNY (State University of New York) at Plattsburgh and Albany, but her heart and soul are with the dancers of the New York City Ballet who summer in nearby Saratoga Springs.

Some people may know Saratoga Springs in another con-nection. During the month of August, it is the lively horse-racing capital of the Northeast. At the turn of the century, it was an even livelier place. "Races every day, gambling, millionaires and pickpockets and sporting people and respectable family folks and politicians and famous theatre actors and actresses, you'll find them all at Saratoga," according to Edna Ferber's hero Clint Maroon in her book *Saratoga Trunk*. Today you will also find the Saratoga Performing Arts Center and, of course, Saxton Gardens, where Sally Millman succumbed to the charms of the daylily. "I moved from a love affair with Modern Dance (I still enjoy attending concerts) to one with daylilies and gar-dening on an exciting mid-July day in 1978 as I was dazzled by peak bloom in Stanley Saxton's garden."

Olive Jones from neighboring South Glens Falls, New York, was partly responsible for diverting Sally's affections from dance to daylilies. Miss Jones, now ninety-two and nearly blind, lives by herself, shovels a little light snow if she has to, and still does what she can in her garden. "The younger people on this street think it's very odd," she told me with a chuckle. "They talk about 'that old lady down on the corner who digs in the garden all the time.'" The garden used to be full of every kind of plant, including a great many daylilies. Miss Jones, who has a master's degree in nutrition from Cornell University, came down with TB as a young woman, and as part of her rehabilitation the doctors recommended outdoor work. "Well, it was just as if I had been made for it!" she said. "I made the garden and had a small business right here selling daylilies and other perennial plants."

Olive and Sally had been friends for years, and when the younger woman first became interested in gardening, Miss Jones shared her expertise. "I think of Olive as my gardening mentor," Sally says. "I used to follow her around and just listen to her and ask her questions. She was a complete gardener, but she *loved* daylilies. She was growing them before the American Hemerocallis Society was founded and joined very early on. She kept up her membership until she couldn't read *The Journal*s anymore." A mass of daylilies in bloom in Miss Jones's back field set in motion a chain of events that led to Saxton Gardens. In an issue of the Region Four newsletter, Sally stated flatly that "Stanley Saxton, and the person with whom I had traveled to Saratoga to see his daylilies, Olive Jones, were more influential than perhaps they realized in my ensuing daylily addiction—mania—fascination."

By the time I met Sally, she had been enthralled by daylilies for some time and had taken out a life membership in the American Hemerocallis Society. She had attended National Conventions, and generally knew the ropes. In short, she was just the person I needed. I told her the sort of book I had in mind, and before I could even ask, she offered her help. Like an indulgent grown-up conducting a child through an unfamiliar woodland, she has taken me by the hand and led me step by step into the wonderful world of daylilies and daylily people.

There is something engagingly youthful about Sally. Perhaps it is her buoyant enthusiasm. "You'll have great fun writing this book," she told me. "The daylily network is dense and there are some fascinating people in this group. It's a mixed bag. There are the collectors. Certain people, like the Wattses, are famous throughout the country for their collections. Some of the daylily people are garden designers and others are growers, sellers, and propagators. Then there are the hybridizers and the nursery owners. A lot of daylily people are scientists, botanists, and geneticists. There are the people who grow daylilies and have a kind of 'mom and pop' mail-order business. And, of course, there are the evangelists."

No one preaches the daylily gospel with greater verve and conviction than Sally herself. And like a repentant sinner, I have been swept into the daylily fold. Through my mentor, I have been passed from one daylily person to another, and everywhere I have met kindness. One of my first outings was a meeting of the New England Daylily Society in Massachusetts. Sally explained that within each official region of the American Hemerocallis Society there are subgroups. Daylily people who find the long months between National Conventions intolerable band together for mutual support and refreshment. The New England group is particularly active, and Sally urged me to go to a meeting.

She prepared me by describing a meeting she had attended. "It was an absolutely gorgeous day in September—the most wonderful gardening weather you can imagine. The kind of day when you'd really want to be working outside. But we were in that meeting from ten A.M. until four P.M.!" She laughed tolerantly, marveling at the pleasure it afforded members to sit in the darkened room, eyes glued to the screen, while slide after slide of daylilies flashed before their eyes. "I don't think anybody missed being out-of-doors for a minute! They all seem to enjoy each other very much—there's a real family feeling about them. They're nice people." And so they are. I was welcomed with open arms.

My next assignment from Sally was to call Ned Irish, a past President, former Round Robin Chairman, and stalwart of the American Hemerocallis Society. She told me that in his everyday life he had been in public relations. He was also an artist and had a taste for music. "He is extremely bright," she added, "and I think he'd give you ideas and inspiration." I felt quite unnerved at the thought of announcing to this paragon of the daylily world that I was writing a book about his flowers and his people. But I took courage in hand and found myself on the phone with an enchanting stranger who within minutes had become a cozy friend.

I found my new guide charming, irreverent, and funny, and our discussion ranged across the board. On the subject of the modern flower form, Ned observed: "This is the passion of the moment, you know, everybody wanting ruffles, everybody wanting a round flower. I think they're beginning to look like powder puffs. They're losing some of that essential elegance that some of the old species had—some of the delicacy and the lovely curve of a petal. Some of the round ones are just blobs, but they are very effective in the garden because they're massive and make a very strong statement of color."

Color has been a persistent theme in our conversations and letters over the last eighteen months. It is a subject on which Ned has earned a right to his strong views. Color has always been one of his great loves. "I just adore color," he says. "I always wanted to be a designer for the theater, but at the time I graduated from art school, the scene designer's guild only took two out of five hundred applicants. I was a good workman and had some skill and some ideas, but I was not a blazing star, by any means. So I just gave up." The theater's loss has certainly been the daylily world's gain. And fortunate daylily friends are privileged to own portraits Ned has done of their best cultivars.

He works like an eighteenth century botanical artist, building up layers of opaque watercolor. It takes from fifteen to eighteen hours to execute a flower portrait in this style, with every tiny detail lovingly and accurately limned. Pink daylilies are among the hardest subjects. "Pinks are the biggest trouble because the ruffles on a modern daylily vary from silver-gray to violet.... Sometimes they have a little light showing through them so there's sort of a yellow cast ... each ruffle is a portrait!"

The painters whose flowers Ned admires most are the impressionists, whose unfettered style is the antithesis of his own. "I've often wanted to cut loose," he says. "But I can't. I want every detail to be there." Not one to take himself too seriously, he laughs when teased about his obsession with verisimilitude. "I know, but I get so fascinated by the light coming through a petal and trying to catch that porcelain sort of feel and also the refraction of light. Really, I think flowers are such miracles, anyway, that I've just got to put every stinking little detail in there!"

One of his pet peeves is the wording of color descriptions in daylily catalogs. Some years ago, he was behind a short-lived movement to persuade the American Hemerocallis Society that a definitive color chart was necessary. The cost of one similar to the one used by the Royal Horticultural Society proved an insurmountable obstacle. But a frustrated Ned continues to inveigh against the "color illiterates" who dream up catalog descriptions. He finds abuse of the word *red* particularly flagrant.

"Just think," he fumes, "of all the more specific red color names. Crimson, scarlet, blood, rose, flame, vermilion, maroon, fire engine—to mention a few that come to mind. If the daylily purchaser should happen to be designing a harmonious garden, he or she deserves a decent description! One that will bring the correct visual impression to the mind's eye. Even yellows are subject to the same hazy nomenclature. The word *gold* can be anything from ocher to orange, and so it has proved to be."

Ned's bark, however, is a good deal worse than his bite. A much-beloved figure in the daylily world, he was given a life membership to the Society by grateful constituents of his region. The citation read: "To Ned Irish, Region 3's Resident 'Teddy Bear' for the following services rendered." The first letters of the services enumerated spelled out the words "LIFE MEMBER-SHIP" and included "Lectures given, Incentive offered, Free plants donated, Exhibition judging." One service had particular resonance for me—the next to last in the list—"Inspiration to beginners."

A man of many parts, there is more to Ned than meets the eye at meetings and National Conventions. Resident teddy bear and Society wit he may be, but few of his daylily friends are aware of his war record. As an engineer captain with the Third Army during World War II, he was awarded the Distinguished Service Cross, a Bronze Star, and the Purple Heart. After the war, he worked in New York City for a Madison Avenue advertising firm, which appreciated his efforts enough to send him off to England to open the agency's first overseas office in London.

Today, he is retired and a widower living in a new town house in Hanover, Pennsylvania. The walls of his living room are painted a dazzling wild yellow, which gives him sunlight all night long. Although he is isolated from other daylily people by many miles, they visit him by mail through the round robins of which he was Chairman a few years ago. The importance of this network was brought home to me by an exchange with Ned a few weeks ago. He belongs to something called the Pizzazz Robin, which covers a multitude of topics and even includes nondaylily items of mutual interest. He was feeling vexed the day I called him because it was a holiday and there was no postal service. "I took the Pizzazz Robin to the post office today and it was closed. I'd spent all weekend writing the doggone letter and was so pleased with myself for not delaying the robin. Then I get to the post office, and they won't let me mail it!"

Robins Are Still Flying

When Ned Irish accepted the assignment of round robin Chairman of the American Hemerocallis Society in 1975, he began his first report: "Well, here I am, ready or not. Being really ready for this fascinating new job would seem, even from my brief acquaintance with its functions and responsibilities, to require the combined talents of Solomon, Winston Churchill and Houdini." In other words, he found the responsibility for coordinating this program, which today has a roster totaling almost five hundred names, a sobering prospect.

Each robin has from eight to twelve members, with one leader. As of 1991, there were forty-five flights aloft. Some robins are of general interest, and the letters winging their way between far-flung members cover any and all topics relating to daylilies. Others are more specific. Here is a random sampling: a Fragrance Robin, whose members relish the scented daylilies and compare notes on those with the sweetest perfume; True Blue, which circulates information about progress in the direction of the first blue daylily; and Tet Robins, which deal with growing and hybridizing tetraploids. Double Crossers are not as shifty as they sound—these folks are committed to the growing and breeding of doubles.

There really is something for everyone in the round robin program, no matter what size or shape of daylily you prefer. Spiders? Oh, yes. In fact, you'll find Spiders I and Spiders II. In addition to the special interest groups, there are round robins devoted to local pleasures and problems. For instance, growers and hybridizers in the Pacific Northwest have cultural conditions different from their counterparts in Florida. So Washington and Oregon have a round robin of their own. So does the vast state of Texas. Georgia General is an all-around southeastern round robin that also accepts outside members; so does the Georgia Mini Robin.

As you may recall, *Hemerocallis* round robins predate the founding of the American Hemerocallis Society. Through the good offices of *Flower Grower* magazine, Mrs. Olive Hindman released the first coast-to-coast flight in 1943. These early birds, along with flights sponsored by radio station KFNF, came to roost in Shenandoah, Iowa, in 1946 and formed the Midwest Hemerocallis Society, forerunner of the national organization. On July 21, 1990, Mrs. Hindman died at the age of ninety-six. But a new generation of fledglings takes to the air annually to bring news, humor, information, inspiration, and camaraderie to scattered members of the daylily family.

"The round robin program was much of the basis for the whole Society," Annie Weinreich reminded me. As immediate past president and a former robin chairman, she should know. I asked her to explain the workings of the robin flights and learned that each member in turn receives the package of letters. The recipient reads the letters—one from each member— responds to the comments of the other members, and adds his or her own letter to the package, along with slides or photographs, if the mood moves. The entire package is then dispatched to the next member of the round robin. Members type their letters, which may be anywhere from four to eight pages in length! The receiver has one week in which to read the material, add a letter, and send the packet on.

Each member sends a copy of his or her letter to the flight leader, who has to keep track of the flock. And the copies are passed on by the leader to the national round robin chairman, who reads five hundred letters quarterly, excerpting comments for publication in *The Daylily Journal.* "It is a wonderful program," says Annie. "Friendships are made that last for years. Also, the members tell it like it really is, and, while reading the copies, I would often find a line which read, 'and don't you dare quote this in *The Journal.'* Though occasionally tempted, I never did."

Complete flights take three or four months and invariably arrive on the beleaguered robin chairman's doorstep at the most inopportune moment, "be that peak bloom, tax time, Christmas, vacation, or whatever." Nevertheless, these letters are the lifeblood of the Society, and the round robins have never entirely lost their essentially midwestern character. The sharing, caring American heartland origins of the Society linger on in these warm, friendly, funny, informative exchanges.

It was the sly, sweet-talking Ned Irish who persuaded neophyte Annie Weinreich to join a round robin in the seventies. She and her husband, Bill, had recently become members of the Pittsburgh Iris and Daylily Society. The structure of the Pittsburgh group provided for an overall President, an Iris Vice President, and Daylily Vice President. Spotting them as promising new blood, somebody immediately asked if either of the Weinreichs would be willing to run for Daylily Vice President. Annie laughed as she recalled the occasion. "We agreed that we would do it jointly. Of course, when you agree you're going to run, it means there's nobody running against you! They've gotten to the bottom of the barrel by the time they're asking the new person!"

Meanwhile, the daylily collection in the Weinreichs' Pennsylvania garden was growing by leaps and bounds. Having begun with twelve cultivars, they were adding to it as fast as a limited budget and an unlimited appetite permitted. Their first daylilies were a gift from Annie's *Hemerocallis*-loving parents. Later, Annie and Bill went overboard and spent $6 for Orville Fay's 'Mary Todd'. "I just thought we'd be eating baked beans and baloney for the next three years to make up for the deficit!"

she confessed cheerfully. This lavish expenditure and meeting Ned Irish proved the turning point in the Weinreichs' daylily career. Ned got them into a round robin on the national level, and before she knew it, Annie found herself the head robin.

The next event in the already eventful life of Annie Weinreich, round robin leader, mother of two daughters, and collector of daylilies, was a move from suburban Pennsylvania to the high desert of Idaho. Bill Weinreich, who holds a Ph.D. in nuclear engineering and works for Westinghouse, was transferred to the company's naval reactor facility in Idaho Falls, Idaho. Here, a thousand miles from the nearest drop of salt water, stunned naval personnel found themselves training in prototype nuclear submarines. Here, also, 125 stunned daylily cultivars found themselves five thousand feet above sea level in a place where summer is defined as "two weeks of poor skiing."

In Idaho Falls, it is perfectly normal to experience frost through the Fourth of July, and traditionally the first snow arrives the third week in September. Growing daylilies in this climate proved a challenge to the plants and their owners. The first year, Annie and Bill covered the plants with blankets until they had a chance to get established. "It looked like a patchwork quilt if you looked out of the upstairs window at this collage of blankets spread all over. But the daylilies did well that winter with four feet of snow on top of them."

During the long, harsh Idaho winters, Annie learned firsthand just how much the round robin program, of which she was chairman, could mean. "It was really rather neat," she reminisced, "because it brought the whole daylily world as close as my mailbox. Even being in the hinterlands with the nearest American Hemerocallis Society member a hundred and ninety-five miles away, I had three hundred friends and their letters came every day. This is what kept me sane up there in the northland." For the four and a half years that she was in the West, Annie kept in touch with her daylily friends through the lifeline of round robin letters.

When the Weinreich family left Idaho for Ohio in December 1985, the snow was already twenty-seven inches deep. But the previous summer, Annie and Bill had dug, divided, and labeled all their daylilies. They had given many of them to the Denver Botanical Garden. Others they had shipped back to the National Arboretum in Washington, D.C. Having given the balance of their best to friends and neighbors, they launched their second "Great Plant Giveaway." The first had preceded their departure for Idaho. At that time, there had been 500 or more cultivars. Of these, 375 had been donated either to the National Arboretum or to a Display Garden and regional plant sales. The rest were left in the ground for the fifty local members of the Pittsburgh Iris and Daylily Society, who were invited to come with picnic baskets, shovels, and paper bags to dig their own daylilies. "It was like locusts descending on the garden," Annie remembers. "They just absolutely stripped it!"

At this writing, the peripatetic Johnny Appleseeds of the daylily world have moved again, and there may well have been yet another "Great Plant Giveaway." But the Weinreichs never lose touch with their friends or their daylily "children." People from Region Nine (Idaho, Montana, Utah, Colorado, and Wyoming) are still writing to tell them how their daylilies are faring in the Rocky Mountains. As for Annie, she manages to be philosophical about the family's many moves. "It is hard to leave friends. But with the daylily group, you can just about pick up with some of these people midsentence. The camaraderie is wonderful. You feel a real kinship. I keep tabs on how people's kids are doing, how their mothers are doing, and everything else. You just form those kinds of friendships." Daylily people may not have a lot in common other than daylilies. They are a group with diverse backgrounds and few common interests, except the plants they love. But it is enough. "Love of the daylily and love of the people," says Annie. "That's the glue that holds it all together."

Woodside: Darrel Apps

Darrel Apps

On the occasion of my first conversation with Ned Irish, he offered a suggestion. "Do you think you could make the time and effort to come to the Convention? There are some very, very attractive gardens on the tour. One of them belongs to a fellow called Darrel Apps. Darrel is an old friend of mine. We met on a bus in Florida at a National Convention and we've been friends ever since. He's a hybridizer and doing very well. He's going for small flowers and minis more than he is for full-sized ones. And he has got some *beautiful* seedlings!"

The next time I spoke to Ned, I told him that I had taken his advice and would be attending the Convention in Pennsylvania. "Good," he said. "You'll be seeing Darrel Apps's patch at Chadds Ford. He was education director at Longwood Gardens for seventeen years and then decided to try on his own as a lecturer, writer, and hybridizer. He's been so busy ever since that he doesn't know whether he's coming or going! But he's a delightful person and has a beautiful, beautiful garden."

Although he is a respected figure in the daylily world and a bona fide daylily person, Dr. Apps has worn many horticultural hats. Equipped with a Ph.D. in horticulture from the University of Wisconsin, he first accepted a teaching position at the University of Kentucky. Before coming to Longwood, he also taught at Penn State University and began developing the daylily hybridizing program that has won him many awards. He has published articles on daylilies for professional journals and was responsible for the introduction to the 1986 revision of A. B. Stout's *Daylilies*. Recently, he provided splendid color photographs for a new book, *Daylilies — The Perfect Perennial* by Lewis and Nancy Hill. An inveterate traveler, Apps has also hunted for plants in Korea in 1984, lectured in Britain, and spent time in France studying the gardens of the great designer Andre Le Notre. Now this all-round horticulturist is operating a consulting business, Garden Adventures, and a mail-order daylily business, Woodside — which explains why he is busy.

As usual, I wanted to know how he got into this predicament, and he told me. Ironically, his early career bears more than a passing resemblance to that of Dr. Stout. Darrel grew up in Wild Rose, Wisconsin, a little town about a hundred miles north of Stout's hometown of Albion. "My childhood was spent on a farm, and boy, if it hadn't been for trees and shrubs and stuff," Darrel says candidly, "I would have died of lonesomeness. I had a twin brother, but there was nothing for either of us to do, other than work. So all three of us — there are three boys in the family — became very interested in natural history."

Even Darrel's introduction to daylilies was similar to Stout's. A clump of *Hemerocallis fulva* grew on the south side of the little one-room schoolhouse where he received his early education. "I got on my bike when I was ten years old and rode out there in the summertime just to see what those flowers were like. I was fascinated with them, and that was my first interest in daylilies." Darrel was always interested in plants and in planting seeds. "I remember our veterinarian telling my parents, 'Now, that boy ought to go into horticulture.' But I never knew horticulture existed until I switched from accounting to agriculture at the University of Wisconsin."

Upon graduation from high school, the reasonable Darrel convinced himself of the need to make money and chose accounting as a means to that end. Before long, the prospect of a lifetime spent in the dusty back rooms of a bank began to pall. Knowing by this time that his real interest lay with plants, he transferred to the School of Agriculture. It was here that he learned about the horticulture program. "When I found out about horticulture, I knew that was exactly what I wanted to do."

His farmer father, supportive but dubious, observed, "You know, you could starve doing this." Darrel laughs and insists that he is doing just that. But for better or for worse, his niche has always been in horticulture.

His first teaching job brought him to Lexington, Kentucky, which in July is unbelievably hot. The normal daily temperature is often in the neighborhood of ninety-five degrees Fahrenheit, and Darrel was trying to put in a garden. "Most gardening was very difficult in those temperatures. But the daylilies survived. They were one of the few plants that were able to make it in the heat." However, it wasn't just their heat resistance that impressed him; it was their beauty.

A local hybridizer, Mrs. J. C. Lamb, had learned via the horticultural grapevine that a new young instructor at the university was interested in daylilies, and she invited Darrel to stop by her garden. Frances Lamb recognized a budding daylily person when she saw one! She sealed his fate with the gift of 'Hortensia', a handsome green-throated yellow cultivar. When 'Hortensia' bloomed in his own garden, Darrel was hooked. Furthermore, in hybridizing he suddenly saw an opportunity to create new colors with which to paint the complex planting schemes he was already imagining. Forthwith, he began his breeding program.

Early on, he established several goals, one being to extend the range of reblooming cultivars and to work for a longer season of bloom. "I shoot for a plant that stays in bloom four weeks and preferably six; a plant that makes at least three new fans per year and has at least twenty-five buds." His own 'Happy Returns' is one such. By crossing reblooming 'Stella De Oro', that first-class miniature with bright gold flowers, with pale yellow 'Suzie Wong', he obtained a small, soft yellow which brought together the best features of both parents, combining rebloom with a gentler color. He was pleased with this one. It also exhibited the quality that impressed him about the daylilies in his Kentucky garden. It was a survivor, shrugging off both heat and cold. He inadvertently left a large pot of 'Happy Returns' out-of-doors during a particularly cold winter. The temperature went down to minus ten, but the plant came through unscathed.

During his Kentucky sojourn, Darrel made another discovery about daylilies. I hope I am not revealing a guilty secret in quoting the 1987 lecture Darrel delivered at Wisley (the display, experimental, and teaching gardens of the Royal Horticultural Society in Surrey, England): "My early garden contained only hemerocallis because I was very busy in my job. This well pleased the American Hemerocallis Society but was very boring. Over the years I have experimented with all sorts of planting and now have a garden of much wider interest. Altogether I garden about one and a quarter acres of mixed planting."

Darrel is an anomaly in the daylily world, a grower and hybridizer who talks about "annuals" and "perennials"—and not about "companion plants!" His own garden, Woodside—one of the gardens that National Convention visitors were privileged to see in 1990—was a tribute to his enormous knowledge of horticulture, his eclectic tastes in woody and herbaceous plants, and his artistic sensibilities.

I am sorry to report that after the Convention, Woodside underwent a drastic reorganization. Hampered by local ordinances restricting nursery operations, the Apps had made an offer on a small farm in Lancaster County, Pennsylvania. An excited Darrel described the new venture for his daylily customers: "My plans for the new property are to increase seedling production to 10,000 plants a year and continue the mail order business with both my own seedlings and those of other hybridizers; grow several of the newer cultivars in containers for walk-in retail sales from June 15 to August 1; and, if all this works, start selling container plants wholesale to landscape contractors." Regrettably, this dream became a victim of the economy. Instead, the proposed expansion has been confined to the present property—at the expense of the glorious perennial borders Convention visitors saw.

My own memories of these borders remain vivid. The first stunning example of Darrel's skill at combining plants hit you between the eyes on arrival. A "hot" bed along one side of the driveway blazed with orange butterfly weed (*Asclepias tuberosa*); tall red lilies *Lilium* 'Red Knight', the orange-red daylily 'Tropical Glow', golden 'Cornwall', and Darrel's 'Mexican Maiden', a gorgeous shade of rosy brick red with Day-glo orange at the throat; and the whole bed was held in a net of delicate threadleaf foliage spangled with the pale yellow stars of *Coreopsis verticillata* 'Moonbeam'.

When I had recovered from this display, I sank into contented contemplation of matched borders in pastel shades of pink, lavender, silver, purple, and primrose. Three compatible daylilies enhanced each other and all their neighbors—gorgeous tall purple 'Catherine Neal' was paired in one corner with the blue-pink 'Siloam Tee Tiny', which has a purple eye zone, and in the opposite corner with 'Siloam Merle Kent', another cool pink with a purple eye. Add to this bed clouds of silver and blue-gray foliage and masses of the tiny lavender-blue flowers of catmint; tall, narrow spikes of lythrum in a vivid, bluish pink; and pink bee balm and I can't tell you what other wonderful things.

Everywhere one looked there was a commingling of plants—woody and herbaceous. A red, green, and white trio caught my attention: a shrubby red twig dogwood (*Cornus alba* 'Elegantissima') with white-edged leaves rising from a flat silver and green sheet of *Lamium maculatum* 'Album'—which was also pierced by the sword foliage and arching stems of incandescent red *Crocosmia* 'Lucifer'. Elsewhere, the new German yarrow, *Achillea taygetea* 'Heidi', which is a soft peachy color, was combined with matching daylilies and spiky blue veronica for an appealing perennial threesome. I couldn't scribble down ideas fast enough!

This is Darrel Apps's kind of gardening. The changes that have been wrought since the Convention are temporary. "I will go back to displays with other plants," he says, "because I think the real way to sell daylilies is to have people see how fascinating they can be when they are worked in with other perennials." Until the happy day when these tapestries return to the garden, Darrel has to make do with the memory of a visitor who stood transfixed before the pastel borders. "I have never in all my life seen anything as beautiful as this," he murmured. "These colors together just give me goose bumps!" And this is exactly the effect the designer intended. "But it was a great kind of feeling for me to have him so taken by it," said Darrel. "He really loved it."

Southern Charmer

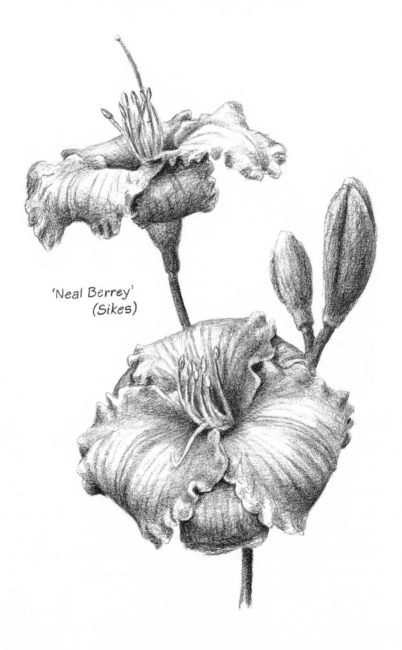

'Neal Berrey'
(Sikes)

Having already committed myself and a hefty sum of money to the 1990 American Hemerocallis Society Convention, I had no other plans to attend distant daylily functions. Then I talked to Sarah Sikes of Windmill Gardens in Luverne, Alabama. If you are a daylily person, Sarah needs no introduction, but for the benefit of neophytes and "civilians," Mrs. Hugh Bach Sikes is an eminent hybridizer, sought-after speaker, former Regional Vice President, daylily judge, and an excellent photographer. She has been and done and won nearly everything there is to be or do or win in the daylily world. She will tell you that daylily people are all "a little bit weird."

"We are!" she insists, laughing. "This daylily has pulled together a group of people from all over wherever; from all walks of life, all levels of intelligence, all levels of culture. And together, we work. I mean, it all works out. It is a marvelous common bond, and it has certainly enriched my life."

A great many things that I have done in the course of writing this book have been done at Sarah's behest. "When I was chairman of the Regional Vice Presidents of the Society," she told me, "we invited the Munsons—Bill and his mother—to the second annual RVP interview. [Every year, an important hybridizer is interviewed at the National Convention by the Regional Vice Presidents, and the assembled membership eagerly attends. Sarah herself was interviewed in 1988.] The Munsons graciously accepted, and we had two hundred and forty people there. You could have heard a pin drop! It was one of the most wonderful things I've ever participated in." It was then that I knew I must go to Florida.

When I returned, I talked to Sarah on the phone. "Now," she said, "you must come to Charlotte, North Carolina, for the Region Fifteen meeting. The chairman has all sorts of mini-programs planned: converting diploid daylilies to tetraploids, breeding daylilies, soil testing, pesticides. They have a line-up of well-known people to do these demonstrations, and you should be there to check it all out." There is no denying Sarah. I went.

Recently, Ned Irish urged me to make a pilgrimage to Windmill Gardens. "I know I'm not advancing the cause of your marital status," he said gleefully, "but I wish you could make it to Sarah's garden in bloom season. I've never been there when there wasn't a carload of people coming from somewhere. She has an open garden day once a year and gets three hundred or four hundred people there. They walk through the seedling patch and pick out their favorites. You put a little bamboo stake by the ones you admire—everybody who visits does that. When a seedling collects two or three bamboo stakes, she'll consider it as a possible introduction. But she's very decided in her own mind. Out of thousands of seedlings, she picks only six or seven every year. And it has to have everything—form, vigor, buds—or Sarah won't introduce it."

As you may have gathered, Mr. Irish is an unabashed Sikes fan. Before I ever met Sarah, I knew from him what to expect. "She's bright, she's attractive, and one of the most charming people I know. In fact, her husband was quite suspicious of me because I was so much in her corner!" It is doubtful that Hugh Bach Sikes was unduly worried. Having singled her out in high school, he clearly has the prior claim. Sarah believes they have been married forty-three years. "I can't remember," she says. "I have to think how old our oldest son is, and then add a year. But

I think it'll last." It has so far, and together they have succeeded in raising three grown sons of whom they are justifiably proud. But the spectacular success of Windmill Gardens is Sarah's alone. As Ned puts it, she has made "quite a name for herself" in daylily circles.

It was inevitable that Sarah and I would meet. Her name came up in my first discussion with Sally Millman, who said, "Be sure to call Sarah Sikes in Alabama. She can clue you in on the southern scene." When Annie Weinreich learned of my interest in the daylily world, she had the same advice. "You should talk to Sarah Sikes. She's vivacious, gives lectures all around the country, and is a successful hybridizer of great note."

After numerous phone conversations, Sarah and I finally came face to face at the airport in Charlotte, North Carolina. Naturally, I had acted upon her suggestion about attending the Region Fifteen meeting, and we were both en route there. My flight arrived before hers, and we had arranged that I would meet her plane. Having often seen her photograph in *The Daylily Journal,* I recognized her at once—fair-haired and youthful, with the peaches-and-cream complexion of a coed and a delightful smile. Sarah has all the obvious charms of a southern belle, but during the course of the weekend, I discovered that she also has the tact and tenacity of a statesman, and the insight and humor of the worldly, highly intelligent woman that she is.

As usual, her handbag was full of airline tickets to destinations where she would be giving daylily talks. "I'm not really a speaker," she said with a winning schoolgirl giggle. "I never know what I'm going to say! But people keep asking me, so I must be doing something right." Having since heard her speak, I can describe what she is doing right—presenting, without notes, a cohesive, enlightening, entertaining program illustrated with gorgeous slides. What I wanted to know was how a soft-spoken southern girl brought up in a village of a hundred people came to be in demand all over the United States as a lecturer.

"Well, it amazes me," she said, "how this [daylily] thing has developed. It started off as a hobby. I started growing daylilies just for the sheer pleasure of it. In fact, early on, I had a neighbor who was always trying to get me to grow some rather common-looking daylilies. And frankly, I didn't think they were very attractive. But I joined the garden club when my youngest child was about three years old. I loved flowers and had studied art at the Advertising Art School in Nashville, Tennessee. I wanted to be a fashion illustrator, but then I married this wonderful man in the country, and there's not much call for a fashion illustrator on a farm."

Sarah and I belong to a generation of women whose career expectations were rather circumscribed. Young women were programmed to look after their parents, honor and cherish their husbands, and bring up 2.5 children to be decent, civilized human beings. "For years," says Sarah, "I was the all-American wife and mother. I did all of those things women of my generation did and really enjoyed them. But now, I'm doing this for myself. It is a way of self-expression."

Breeding daylilies has become a satisfying career for this amateur-turned-professional. Sarah got her first look at some of the newer daylilies in the early sixties after she joined the garden club. "The club went on a tour down to south Alabama to a couple of daylily gardens," she remembers. "All these women were walking up and down the rows oohing and aahing, and I thought they were a little bit crazy. I must confess, the flowers were more attractive than any I had seen before, so I bought some. And then, the next spring when they bloomed, I absolutely lost my heart to them."

Sarah recalled the names of cultivars I remember from the same period—musical names like 'April Breeze' and 'Cradle Song'. 'Frances Fay' was one of her first purchases, and 'Ruffled Pinafore'. When these bloomed, she felt that she had to have every daylily she had ever heard about. At first she bought only the inexpensive ones for anywhere from $1 to $5, and then she began looking at the new introductions that sold for $25 and $50. That was when she started selling daylilies. "To buy my first fifty-dollar daylily, I dug fifty clumps of things I had and sold them for a dollar each. The daylily I bought was 'Moment of Truth'." Which indeed it was for Sarah, because the plant died!

"My love affair with daylilies never has run smooth," she admits with a rueful laugh. "To make this garden, I bought and sold daylilies, and all the money went back into the garden. It was that way for years—and I sold a lot of dollar daylilies! Then all of a sudden, I started hybridizing. I think it was in 1975."

At first, Sarah used whatever daylilies she had, making crosses, harvesting the seed, and planting it in rows. The flowers that bloomed weren't anything special but she persevered. "One of the things you learn," she continued, "is that you need to get the best material available. And sometimes that means you've got to put out money. You want to use some of the latest stuff, otherwise the material may have been exploited to its fullest already. So you start off with something, and eventually get your own line going. It's pretty exciting! I tell you, I thought I'd had fun gardening—until I started hybridizing. But when you walk out in the morning and there's something blooming that has never bloomed before ... I don't know ... it's a very special feeling. It's a very humbling experience."

I found it a humbling experience to meet this small, energetic woman who with a minimum of help does all the work in a two-acre seedling patch, maintains a beautiful display garden, tours the United States to give lectures about the plants that have so dramatically changed her life, and still runs a house and cooks meals. And that's not all. She often cooks for busloads of "hem" people who visit from neighboring states. "They're our home folks," she says with a shrug.

Daylilies may be a serious business at Windmill Gardens, but Sarah remains lighthearted. "Back in 1984," she says with another trill of laughter, "I was the leader of a round robin that Ned Irish was in. In one letter, he went into a long tale about visiting here and about my husband insisting that biscuits have to be served hot. To do that, I just pitch 'em across the kitchen straight out of the oven. But I told Ned, 'Here I am trying to create a different persona, and there you are trying to put me back in the kitchen—where most men want women, anyway!'"

Southern charmer, hardworking gardener, gifted hybridizer. Sarah is all three. Her flowers are unusual and exquisite. Her

1991 introduction 'Designer Image' rendered Ned rhapsodic: "I saw it as a seedling in her garden, and I've been frothing at the mouth ever since, pestering the daylights out of her: 'When are you going to introduce it? When are you going to introduce it?' The base color is almost a cream with a faint lavender wash over it. It really is an overlay—like a watercolor wash. And it has black-purple edging all around the petals and this huge black-purple eye. It is the most elegant, the most luxurious-looking daylily—it is absolutely stunning!"

Big Dave Talbott

Dave Talbott

As my first assignment from Sarah Sikes, I went to visit the Munsons in Gainesville, Florida. While I was there, Bill made the comment that Dave Talbott over in Green Cove Springs would be a great addition to this book. "Dave is delightful and just the most comical man you've ever seen in your life. I mean, the overalls, the straw in his teeth—the used car salesman who is now selling daylilies! Just wonderful!"

A Yankee visitor returning from a swing around the southern daylily circuit used almost the same words. "Dave's a great big guy. Funniest man you ever want to meet!" And so I was not unprepared on arrival at the Talbott garden to find a vast man in bib overalls holding court beneath a pair of live oak trees. At his side was a little gray waif of a dog appropriately named Toto.

It was after midday and the Florida sun beat down on the level, sandy growing fields. Pop music blared from a shed in the fenced yard beyond the sales area, where named cultivars and Dave's best seedlings were grown in rectangular beds. Seedlings occupied a field on one side of the unpaved driveway; daylilies for sale by the clump were arranged on the other side, according to price. In a patch of shade under the trees, Dave sat at a table with the cash box in front of him, exhorting and cajoling the customers while his girls scurried around digging the daylilies.

The whole scene suggested the hand of a skillful director. The setting was perfect: the pool of shadow cast by the live oaks, the hot Florida sun blazing down on the colorful daylilies. Costumes and casting were impeccable; the affable star in his shirtsleeves surrounded by hardworking extras in shorts and running shoes. Even Toto looked as if he had come straight from the William Morris Agency. The customers and I filled supporting roles and had our scenes to play. The first was a three-character interlude.

My arrival coincided with that of a young woman who had recently moved up from southern Florida and wanted to buy an orange tree. Dave was scandalized. Oranges are not hardy in northern Florida, he insisted. She wouldn't take no for an answer. He demanded to know if she was a "cracker" and she allowed that she was "afraid so." Dave: "Why are you afraid? That's wonderful! You're an endangered species! [Turning to me] A Florida native is a 'cracker!' I'll bet you didn't know that." I recognized my cue and asked where the expression came from.

"At one time, Florida had a large cattle industry—as large as Texas. I know because I worked cattle when I was thirteen years old, and I hated it. I hate cows to this day! In Florida, you drive cattle with dogs and whips—long whips. A cracker can take that whip and, boy, it sounds like a shotgun going off! You pop that over the cows' heads a few times and they'll move!"

Cattle herding was not Dave's only job as a young man. The pines of northern Florida are tapped for turpentine in much the same way maples in New England are tapped for their sweet syrup. Thirty or forty years ago, turpentine was a big industry in the South. I can remember noticing spouts attached to the tree trunks on my first visit in the mid-fifties. In his youth, Dave spent many months working for a local turpentine company as a "woods rider." The woods rider is a sort of foreman, and at the end of the season he was put in charge of the "tally men."

"The workers all had distinct specialties. There were the 'chippers'—the guys who had a little piece of metal, real sharp, and they'd cut a slash into the trees every week. They had to work a 'crop'—that was ten thousand trees. About as much as a man could work would be one or two crops a week. Then there were 'pullers'—they'd strip the bark away—and 'dippers', who'd collect the turpentine out of the little cups. At the end of the season, they'd have a 'tally man' out in the woods, and he'd add up the total. Each turpentine camp had a different name, and one man from that camp would call out the name to the tally man. As each person finished, he'd shout out, 'New Glimpse of Glory!' That was the name of one of the camps." Dave called it out on a long, haunting upward curve of sound that silenced customers and helpers alike.

After his adventures as a woods rider, Dave sandwiched a foray into the car business between stints with two different finance companies. "Now," he says with obvious pleasure and relief, "we do the daylilies. And I like it. It's kinda late in life. My legs are kinda going bad on me, basically because I'm fat and need to lose some weight, so what else is new? But the mail-order business is real good. And it's the blessing of God to be able to step out into the garden every morning and drink a cup of tea. During the winter months, I kinda sleep in a little bit because at this time of year I don't get much sleep. I'm often up at four or five o'clock."

There is even more to big Dave Talbott than meets the eye. During a lull in business, he told me that he was a pastoral elder. "I felt the call to pastor, and I've built two churches—very small. The first one I left in good hands, and they have about sixty people now. The new one, the Good Shepherd Ministry, may only have five people, maybe ten on a Sunday. But we don't worry about numbers. God never worried about numbers—he started with twelve!"

Long before Dave's call to the ministry, before he rode the woods for the turpentine company, and even before his cattle-driving days, he grew flowers. "I just always liked to raise things," he said. In those days, everybody raised vegetables. There wasn't much money, and people lived off the land. After he married Reba, he was the one who did the outdoor work while she kept house. Having always liked flowers, he was interested in an ad for Russell Gardens in Spring, Texas, and he ordered some daylilies. "Hugh Russell," he recalled nostalgically. "Greatest promoter of daylilies who ever lived! Probably started everybody! Then I heard about Merle Kent." Dave's voice softened at the mention of Merle Kent, whom thereafter he referred to as "Mo." The late and much lamented Mr. Kent was the owner of Big Tree Daylily Garden in Longwood, Florida, a short distance from Orlando.

"Mo Kent had an ad in the Florida Market Bulletin back in 1955. As Reba's people live in the Orlando area, we made frequent trips down there. One weekend, we went over to Big Tree Daylily Garden and bought some things. I went back that Sunday and bought some more. That day, Mo took me over to meet Mr. Wheeler." Wheeler had a lavender flower that instantly captured Dave's fancy, and after some soul-searching, he bought 'Prodigy' for what was then a staggering sum — $25. He kept the price a secret from Reba for years. With the purchase of 'Prodigy', Dave became a hybridizer and began his pursuit of a blue daylily. But he was unable at this stage in his working life to combine daylilies with his job. Commuting the twenty-eight miles to Jacksonville meant leaving home early in the morning and not returning until nine o'clock at night. And for a time, the daylilies were put aside. Then he started over again in 1973 and has been producing fine new cultivars ever since.

'Time Window' is a lavender-blue that Dave is pleased with. The segments are veined in blue, which strengthens the overall impression of a shade nearing true blue. 'Gulf Skies' represents another step toward the azure dream. Again, the blue veining is very effective. In other colors, he likes 'Golden Fountain' for the lavish number of round yellow flowers it produces, and the double 'Rachael My Love', which is named for his granddaughter. "We've also got 'Karen My Love' and 'Reba My Love'—all three are real good doubles. And I like 'Hamlet' and 'Pandora's Box'. They've been good to me." 'Pandora's Box' is one I have always admired, a lovely near white with a deep purple eye zone. And 'Hamlet' is a royal purple knockout with roots in the

Midwest—one grandparent was James Marsh's 'Prairie Blue Eyes'. "We're still line breeding a lot of blues," Dave says, "and I perceive a little bit more blue than we had twenty years ago, but nothing really blue yet."

For the last five years, Dave has made his livelihood in daylilies and is a contented man. Sitting at his table under the live oaks with his scruffy little dog beside him, he jokes with customers, puts the young people who work for him through their paces, and watches the till. "I enjoy every minute of what I do, and I've got some good help from these kids. We have a lot of fun with it. Reba, she enjoys it, too. You know, I'm happy with my life. We play around with the daylilies. We don't have all the money in the world, but it's just a real fulfilling business."

Corner Oaks:
A Family Affair

Before quitting Florida, I made one last stop. My friend Greg Piotrowski had been especially enthusiastic about the Browns' Corner Oaks Garden in Jacksonville and urged me to spend a little time there. "It has been designated as an American Hemerocallis Society Display Garden," he said, "and it's well laid out with grass paths and beds edged in mondo grass. Ed Brown's things are very refined in form and ruffling. I was impressed with a lot of the plants I saw." Dragging myself away from the lively carnival atmosphere of Dave Talbott's establishment was difficult, and I did not arrive in Jacksonville until early evening. I had arranged an appointment with the Browns for the following morning, but because I would have to fly back to New York that afternoon, I decided it would save time to locate the garden immediately.

Finding the garden on a corner suburban property proved easy. Blessed as it is with magnificent trees, you couldn't very well miss it or the brilliant mosaic of daylilies. At the 110th Street entrance stood a giant live oak with great spreading limbs that arched across the street and reached out over the garden. The centerpiece of Corner Oaks Garden is an attractive six-sided gazebo designed by a friend of the Browns. Ed told his crony, Stan Walker, "I want to be able to sit here and look out of that window and out of this window and out of that door and see everything." The plan devised by Walker gave him just what he wanted—four splendid views of the daylilies, plus storage, a utility room, and camouflage for the garden's watering system.

The gazebo is at the heart of a maze of daylily beds that radiate from this central pavilion and its adjacent brick terrace. The narrowness of the paths and the smallness of the individual beds make it possible to see every plant and permit alternate views of the same plant. Under a second huge live oak on the Wesconnett Boulevard side of the property, a rustic bench invites sated daylily folk to rest their feet and gaze upon the garden. I sat here for a while that afternoon and contemplated the beautiful display.

Nearby, there was constant activity around an elaborate martin house placed on a tall pole. I discovered later that the birdhouse had been Ed's retirement present from colleagues at the elementary school where he had been principal for thirty years. His wife, Janice, also a retired elementary school principal, received an even more unusual retirement gift—a ride in a hot-air balloon! There is nothing run-of-the-mill about the Browns. Their son, Collier, has chosen a Yamaha scooter as his mode of transportation. He has recently joined his father in the daylily business and has already put a thousand miles on the scooter rushing back and forth between the Display Garden and the growing field a few blocks away. Technically speaking, the growing field belongs to Janice. Her parents bought the property from Ed's grandfather.

As you may have already gathered, Corner Oaks Garden is very much a family enterprise. But on the evening of my arrival, no members of the Brown clan were about, except for a black chicken and her retinue of five chicks belonging to Collier's two young sons. Collier and his wife, Mary, his teenaged stepdaughter, and the couple's little boys live right next to the garden with the pet chicken and her consort, a flashy green and black rooster with feathered legs and a brilliant red comb. The boys also had four kittens, which they brought to show me—one long-suffering kitten in each fist—and a guinea pig. At the time I visited Corner Oaks, Mary was the only adult Brown not involved in the daylily operation. But I have since learned from the 1991 catalog that she, too, has finally caught the bug and joined the family business.

Janice is the reluctant bookkeeper. "Reluctant," she says, "because the only bookkeeping I had ever done was keeping the teacher's register, so I had to feel my way. It was difficult for me, but the IRS says I'm doing okay." In addition to doing the books, she also helps with the shipping and works a full day on Mondays and most Tuesdays during the daylily season. "Then I'm in and out. We live just six houses down the street, so I just stop by frequently, in case there's something that needs to be done."

Little did this chic, pretty woman know what lay in store for her when her family moved into the neighborhood forty-odd years ago. She and Ed met when they were both in sixth grade. But according to Janice, he didn't like girls at that point, so it took a while for romance to blossom. "It was after he had gone into service and I had gone away to college that he really noticed me. Our mothers were co-hostesses for a Garden Circle meeting. He had just gotten out of service, and I was home on spring break from Florida State College in Tallahassee. He came down with his mother to help make chicken salad. That's how it really got started."

The daylilies did not come until much later. "Ed was into camellias prior to the daylilies, so he already knew a good bit about plants and their habits of growth. He was also involved with breeding homing pigeons which seems a farfetched hobby for a daylily person. But he was interested in creating a better strain. He's gotten into pigeons again and spends hours studying scientific books on them." Although the scientific aspect of breeding obviously appeals to Ed, it was the eye-catching beauty of the modern daylily that lured him into the hobby that has now become the family business.

"On a Saturday morning in May," he recalls, "I think it was in 1974, I was shopping at the mall, and there was a daylily show in progress. I just discovered daylilies then and there, right on the spot. I didn't know they had such beautiful forms and colors. I thought they had narrow petals and deep throats and only came in yellows and golds. I was really taken aback— especially by the forms. I guess I've been form conscious in my hybridizing ever since the beginning. Anyway, when I saw these flowers, I thought, 'Gee whiz, this is just what we need—some splashes of color to brighten things up at a time of year when everything is green. A clump here and a clump there would really spiffy up the garden. So I started buying daylilies and joined the Society."

As the number of daylilies in his collection increased, Ed began to notice an interesting pattern in his selections. At first he simply bought those whose looks appealed to him most. But gradually it dawned on him that he habitually selected cultivars bred by either W. B. MacMillan or by Mrs. Elsie Spalding. So the next two or three bloom seasons he packed his bags and took off for Louisiana, where he visited the hybridizers and their gardens. It was during these trips that he began thinking that if they could do it, he could, too. "I really began to select for form and dabbled best on best, and so forth, and I guess I got addicted in the process."

Novice though I am, I think I might be able to pick an Ed Brown cultivar out of a group. His focus on flat, wide petals and perfect symmetry seems to have given his flowers a signature of their own. Five inches across is about the average size, with segments that are nearly always broad and neatly ruffled. The flower shape is gently rounded, rather than slavishly round, and the colors seem to run the gamut, but with fewer reds than pastels, though both Ed and Collier anticipate doing more with the darker colors in the future. They are both interested in ever more ruffles, surface texture resembling corduroy or seersucker, and, of course, plant habit. "I'm bringing along the best branching on the best branching," says Ed "and hoping that I can attach a good flower to it and put the whole ball of wax together."

Collier is relatively new to the daylily game. He used to live in a house trailer on the spot where the gazebo now stands and commute to his construction job across town. Then the dream of Corner Oaks began to take shape. "Daddy had said that he might do something with the corner property, and so we moved the trailer off, and he started the garden. I guess about five years went by, and he kept offering me the opportunity to come and work and live in the house on the corner. But I told him, 'Daddy, I just can't see myself growing flowers.'" However, as city traffic worsened and the daily commute became more of a battle, Collier had second thoughts, and three years ago he decided to give daylilies a whirl. It is a decision he appears not to regret.

Ed seems torn between pride in his son's participation and anxiety for Collier's financial future. "I never approached this thing from a business point of view before. But now that he is involved, we hustle. I begin to worry where I never even thought about profit before. Now it concerns me, and it's not for me, but for him. The bottom line is more meaningful than it used to be." Bottom line or no bottom line, it is love—not money—that motivates the Browns and makes a visit to Corner Oaks Garden a joy.

The Stamiles:
The Cutting Edge

A month after my return from Florida, I found myself at the Region Fifteen meeting in North Carolina, where Sarah took me gently but firmly in hand. "Pat Stamile is doing a workshop on converting diploids to tetraploids," she said. "You won't want to miss that. He has done some beautiful things—very impressive. He's coming out with some edgings by using a converted diploid, 'Siloam Virginia Henson', and it's fascinating to watch what comes from different areas of the country. I think Pat would be a good person for you to talk to." Four weeks later, I was at the Stamiles' Floyd Cove Nursery on Long Island.

Pat and his wife, Grace, are both hybridizers and, at this period in hemerocallis history, leaders in the field. When I set out on my daylily quest, their name was on everybody's "hit list." Very early on, Currier McEwen had said, "The Long Island Daylily Society [known by the acronym LIDS] has always been very active and is still going strong. Pat Stamile could tell you. He is a fine hybridizer and so is his wife, really magnificent. I think you ought to have them in your book, and somewhere a bit about the Long Island Daylily Society."

At the time of my visit, in addition to being deeply involved in the daylily world, the Stamiles were full-time teachers. Pat's field was general science; Grace taught gifted children at the elementary level, second through fifth grades. Their daughter Christine, a bright, bubbly seventeen-year-old, was entering her senior year—the most demanding in a high school student's career. Since then, the Stamiles' lives have changed. Pat has already left academe and Long Island for Sanford, Florida, where Grace will join him in the spring of 1992. In a five-and-a-half-acre glade of live oaks, they plan to devote themselves exclusively to daylilies. Meanwhile, Christine has gone off to college in upstate New York. But in the summer of 1990, the family was still together, and I spent the day with them.

It was a beautiful day but hot, and Grace had been laid low a few days earlier with an infection. Having never met her but knowing of her recent indisposition, I wasn't at all sure that the young woman with a mane of tawny hair who was vigorously prying apart a huge clump of daylilies was Grace. I found her in their Display Garden, where she was attacking her chore with the zest and energy of someone in the most robust good health. After spending time in her company, I realized that she does everything with verve and good cheer.

When she had completed her task, we drove over to the field where Christine and another youthful helper were waiting on a steady stream of walk-in customers. "It's a lot of work," Grace admitted with an untroubled smile. "But we're fortunate in getting summer help. We advertise for a local college boy or girl to give us a hand with the selling. The field gets very hot, so we try not to keep people waiting too long. Despite the nice breezes at the top of the slope, when you get down here where we have the nursery, it's a real heat trap—we call it 'Death Valley.'"

Christine took time out from work to answer my questions about her interests. "Science and math are just not my subjects," she announced blithely. "I've got a science teacher for a dad, a science teacher for an uncle, and it just goes in one ear and out the other! I think it really skipped a generation; I'm interested in music, the arts, and languages. And my parents met because they were both failing French!" Apparently Grace and Pat found themselves in the same crash course in French on the way to fulfilling the language requirement for their master's degrees.

Christine has strayed from the family pattern in other ways as well. She is as dark-haired as her mother is blonde, and she admits to not being particularly athletic, while her parents are. They both love outdoor activities and before the daylilies took up so much of his time, Pat was a jogger and a golfer. Grace mentioned a few of their other nondaylily activities. "We are both nature lovers and great fans of all the different birds and wildlife; we grew an organic garden for a long time. And we've always been interested in protecting the environment, preserving the groundwaters on Long Island, and getting involved in those kinds of groups."

When you hear the Stamiles' daylily story, keep in mind the spectrum of their other interests and obligations. Although selling daylilies helped to support the Stamiles' habit, it was of secondary importance to their breeding program. The division of the three-quarter-acre field reflected their point of view: About a fifth was nursery; the remaining four fifths was devoted to their own hybrids. Before the move to Florida, Pat used to don warm work clothes in April and begin lining out his three thousand seedlings, which were raised either under lights or in the little eleven-by-twelve-foot greenhouse attached to the Stamiles' house. Grace would plant out her four thousand miniature seedlings later in the spring.

She explained that she didn't plant her seedlings until May "because in April, Christine and I are doing all the shipping. We've gotten to be pretty big now, so Pat has to help us on Sunday to pack them. On Saturday we spend from dawn to dark digging. ..." Christine giggled and added with wry good humor, "My friends love that! At seventeen, packing daylilies on weekends is not my favorite thing!"

But it took all three Stamiles to do the job. And Christine knew it. "My mom couldn't do the spring shipping on Saturday without me," she said. "There's no way she could get it done because there's such a short period of time in which we can ship, so she really needs me." I remarked that it put her in the position of a farmer's child whose contribution is essential. This prompted more bubbly laughter and the remark, "I know what you mean. It's like, 'You've *got* to milk that cow!'" Nor was the daylily work confined to weekends. In the evening during the school week, Pat, Grace, and Christine made out tags, wrote shipping labels, and entered the orders in the UPS book.

In the South, life should be a bit easier, but out on Long Island, the Stamiles' spring schedule was grueling. At the time of my visit, Grace described a typical weekend. "We come out here on Saturday and just methodically go up and down the rows. We'll start digging and fill twenty, thirty, forty buckets full of plants. Then, when we get home, we let them soak overnight. On Sunday when we get up, we set up a makeshift shipping department in our garage. We pull the cars out, and Patrick puts four-by-eight-foot sheets of plywood on tables for us. Christine and I line out the daylilies alphabetically and start pulling the orders. Sometimes on a Sunday late in the afternoon when we're harried, all of a sudden we'll pull an order for, say 'Added Dimensions'. ..." Christine and Grace grinned and announced in unison, "and there's *no* 'Added Dimensions'!" One of the Stamiles would rush over to the field and quickly dig another fan of 'Added Dimensions'. On Monday morning from sixty-five to one hundred orders used to be picked up by the UPS truck.

If you think all this labor has taken anything away from Grace Stamile's pleasure in daylilies, you are entirely wrong. Her excitement is contagious. One of the lines on which the Stamiles are continuing to work is an eyed series using Mrs. Pauline Henry's neat, handsome 'Siloam Virginia Henson', which Patrick converted from a diploid to a tetraploid. By now the name, 'Siloam Virginia Henson', must have a familiar ring. The "tet" version is a hot item at the moment. An absolutely outstanding parent, this pink tetraploid with a ruby red eye zone has given the Stamiles and other breeders so many new beauties that they are hard put to select the best.

"With the 'Virginia Henson' kids," says Grace, her attractive husky voice rising in excitement, "we selected so many that we started wondering whether we were losing our objectivity. But there really were so many good ones. That's just a dynamite parent, and the breadth of what 'Siloam Virginia Henson' is going to do for the tetraploid world has not even been imagined! More than half the 'tet' hybridizers in the country are still crossing it. They've just gotten it, and some are blooming their first seedlings this year. And some will be blooming their first seedlings next year. They're blooming 'Virginia Henson' kids from California to Minnesota to Long Island south to Miami and west to Texas.

"I'm just running through my mind all the people who are working with it. I mean really key people. Van Sellers is using it in North Carolina. Trudy Petree is using it in Georgia; Jeff and Elizabeth Salter are using it in Florida—Jeff on big 'tets' for the eye patterns and Elizabeth on small 'tets', like I am. Both Patrick and I are using it. And on and on."

The idea of all these new seedlings, whether they are hers or Pat's or those of other hybridizers, thrills her because of the range of possibilities they present. Wherever tetraploid breeders are using the "tet" conversion of 'Siloam Virginia Henson', new and startling permutations are occurring in patterns and petal edges.

"They're all getting something different! Van Sellers is using 'Virginia Henson' with Brother Charles Reckamp's things, which have bubbly edges with hooks and nooks and crannies in the ruffles. Patrick didn't care about edges, he just wanted the wide, flat, rolled-back flowers with eyes. Interestingly enough, as a diploid 'Siloam Virginia Henson' didn't show contrasting picotee edgings. But every 'tet' seedling does. So in doubling the chromosomes, the color seems to have intensified and settled into the edging. Seedlings may have purple or red or even yellow edges, but they all have them. Don't you just love it? Doesn't this keep you excited—to do this?" Her voice ascended the scale another note or two. "'Plum Candy' and 'Strawberry Candy'—from the same seed pod! One is peach with purple picotee and a plum eye, the other one pink with a red eye and red picotee—sister seedlings! Very, very exciting."

In case you should think that Grace is the only member of the family who is caught up in the excitement of hybridizing, listen to her husband. I asked him about the foundation of his breeding program: "We all build on what turns out to be a breakthrough for a particular hybridizer. I've borrowed from Munson and from Peck, from James Marsh and from Elsie Spalding, and from Pauline Henry—people whose work I've admired very much and that has the characteristics I look for in a daylily. I've been pretty eclectic. You never know who is going to have the next breakthrough—who will have the next step or even where it will lead. I was thrilled to get 'Admiral's Braid' with the lovely gold edge—I consider that a little bit of a breakthrough because I've never seen anything like it in my seedling fields. Where this will lead, I have no idea. It could lead to all kinds of wondrous things or it could just be a dead end. But at least you have a starting point for a great adventure."

For the Stamiles, the great adventure will have a change of venue. I learned from Grace, who is still holding the fort on Long Island, that thousands of daylilies have already left by truck for Florida. "Digging the first pot was absolutely scary," she said in a recent phone conversation. "But somehow it all got done. I potted the last yesterday, would you believe?"

Insofar as it is possible to make such a generalization, Grace and Pat Stamile are typical daylily people. They both have a quality of psychic vitality that I have observed in all daylily people, regardless of age, sex, or background. This quality of spiritual and emotional vigor must often replace in the frail or elderly daylily person the physical energy and stamina enjoyed by younger colleagues like Pat and Grace. Another trait I have found universal among daylily people is a kind of intelligence that may have nothing to do with formal education. It has more to do with alertness, keenness of observation, and common sense. And finally, standard equipment for all daylily people includes an appetite and capacity for pleasure, a child's curiosity, an elder's patience, and a cockeyed optimist's conviction that tomorrow will be a better day.

Daylily People

Dan Tau
and Brieana

have heard the American Hemerocallis Society described as a microcosm, a community regarded as a miniature of the real world. Only a confirmed cynic could hold this view. To be sure, there are skeletons in the daylily closet. I have come across tales of overweening vanity and greed, lapses of integrity. One member remarked that there were people in the flower world who could cut throats "as easily as a butcher cuts meat." But in the real world, the injured would be the first to name names. In the daylily world, the victims are silent and members of the Society close ranks to conceal the misdemeanors of their own.

The Society is a small town, and its people are small-town folks. On the whole, they keep each other honest, help each other in a crisis, and for the rest of the time wrangle and complain like anybody else. There are feuds, factions, and clan loyalties. But there is also friendship, tolerance, and generosity. The old are respected; the young have their say. If simple goodness is corny, then daylily people are corny.

Let me tell you about a multigenerational friendship. I met Jeanne Rowles through the good offices of Sarah Sikes. The two women are close friends, though twenty years apart in age. All evidence to the contrary, Jeanne must be forty. "Sarah was our first 'famous' daylily person," she recounted in a letter. "Larry and I were taken with her immediately. Lar sat with her on the bus and bombarded her with questions. The following year she was a guest speaker for our local group, and we renewed our friendship. As you realize, she's a gem!" The friendship prospered through yearly meetings at daylily events, and when Jeanne's grandmother died, a plant of Sarah's cultivar 'Someone Special' arrived to serve the daylily's ancient purpose—solace in grief. According to a manuscript allegedly edited by Confucius himself, daylilies traditionally brought comfort to the suffering: "May the daylily behind the tree / Save me from my misery...."

Another of the Rowleses' close friends is Dan Tau, known to younger daylily people not as "Uncle Dan," but simply as "Uncle." On the occasion of his most recent birthday, Jeanne made pecan rolls and invited him to breakfast. "We *do* have fun," she wrote afterward. "And I'm proud to say that one of my closest friends is an eighty-four-year-old 'Gentleman Farmer'." She was, of course, referring to Dan by the name of a Sikes cultivar—one which Sarah had wanted to name for her husband. (Hugh Bach Sikes declined that honor, and instead Sarah named it 'Gentleman Farmer', his CB radio call name.)

May/December friendships like Jeanne and Larry's with Dan are common among daylily people. The cumulative knowledge of a long life devoted to *Hemerocallis* is prized by younger daylily people, while the satisfaction of sharing that knowledge amply repays the venerable giver. It has often struck me that only in horticulture and in the arts are the divisive barriers of age so effectively shattered.

Nell, Dan's real niece, with whom he lives, was responsible for the introduction which has so enriched all their lives. Nell and Jeanne taught in the same school. "Jeanne loved gardening in the small space at her condominium," Dan relates. "So my niece gave her some daylilies. That was the beginning. Then, a few years later, the Rowleses built a house in the country twenty-five miles south of my home in Washington. Larry, raised in the mountains near Clearfield, Pennsylvania, loved hunting and the out-of-doors, but not gardening. Anyway, when they moved, Nell and I loaded up my station wagon with "hems" and other perennials for Jeanne. I wonder how Larry felt preparing beds for so many plants! It got done, still with not much enthusiasm on his part. But the next year showed spectacular results."

I have seen photographs of the garden the Rowleses have created around their handsome contemporary brick and timber home. Raised beds in the same building materials tie the garden to the house and to the site and offer perfect growing conditions for the daylilies and other perennials introduced into their garden by mentor Dan Tau. An interesting variety of trees and shrubs — evergreen and deciduous — give structure to the landscape and provide a green background for the color-filled flower beds. This beautiful garden will be one of the treats in store for Society members attending the 1993 National Convention in Pittsburgh.

Jeanne claims that after meeting Dan and seeing his daylilies, Larry, too, gave himself up to *Hemerocallis*. "We became very close to Uncle after that. He would call to tell us about a beauty that was in bloom, and we'd drive the fifty-mile round trip to see if we agreed. When Brieana was born, Uncle and Nell gave us minis and flowers with appropriate names — 'Baby Betsy', 'Siloam Tom Thumb', 'Siloam Baby Talk', and 'Siloam Toddler' — to start a bed for her. Then, when she was two or three, he named a daylily for her. What an honor! She still feels special having such a distinctive flower named for her!" And she *is* special.

I met Brieana at the 1990 National Convention. A fourth grader with brown silk bangs and shoulder-length hair framing a face as fresh as any flower. Dan has a unique relationship with Brieana because when Jeanne was pregnant, he was on call to drive her to the hospital if Larry was away in Pittsburgh. "I knew the route perfectly," says Dan, "but no emergency runs were required, so Brieana Mae was safely delivered for all of us to love."

At the time of the Convention, I asked Jeanne what aspect of the daylily world had meant the most to her. She promised to think about my question, and finally a letter came. She wrote:

My favorite thing is waking each day to see what beauty will be visiting us for that single day. I feel close to God when I walk in our garden. Usually, I'm alone, since Lar leaves around 7:30 A.M. As we break bloom in the evening, everything is fresh the next morning. Sometimes, it's like a fairyland with the dew glistening in the sun.

I also enjoy the people who are bitten by the daylily bug. I have met so many dear people. I do *not*, however, enjoy people who HAVE to buy the very newest and the best and refuse to grow older varieties. Nor do I care for those who are out for blood—blue blood or blue ribbons. But growing daylilies is a great family hobby, and I hope that Brieana continues to be interested. Yes ... the daylily has been good to me.

The daylily has been good to me, too. I still do not know whether or not I am truly a daylily person. I know I am not a collector. It would be impossible for me to dispose of half my garden each season in order to make room for the newest cultivars. Nor could I give up my other perennials. I know I am not cut out to be a hybridizer. Hybridizing fascinates without attracting me. But if I am not a daylily person, why has yet another area of lawn been excavated for a new daylily bed? And why in the middle of dividing Siberian irises last fall did I suddenly find myself wondering what I could get rid of in order to have 'Someone Special'? I have no answers for these questions. But this much I do know: In a world without daylilies and daylily people, I would not wish to live.

Getting Started
with Daylilies

If you are not already growing daylilies, it is to be hoped that the enthusiasm of the hybridizers and growers represented in this book will have rubbed off on you. That being the case, you will want to join the American Hemerocallis Society at once and send for a copy of *Daylilies: The Beginners' Handbook* ($6 postpaid). However, you may not have the patience to wait until the *Handbook* arrives. The following tips on planting, maintaining, and propagating your new daylily acquisitions are for eager beavers who want to get started right away.

First, a few words on the nature of daylilies. Although they are members of the lily family, Lilaceae, they differ in a number of significant respects from true lilies (which belong to the genus *Lilium* and grow from bulbs). Belonging to the genus *Hemerocallis*, daylilies are herbaceous perennials whose leaves and scapes arise from a mass of fleshy roots. Some roots are thonglike while others are equipped with thickened segments for the storage of water. Both types occur on the same plant and form a dense mass. To increase a favorite cultivar, these roots can be pried and wiggled apart and the new plants (divisions) spread around your own garden or given to friends.

The point at which daylily roots meet the base of the leaves is called the crown, which is, in fact, a modified stem. Imagine the stem of a leafy shrub. At the base of each leaf, you have a node or point of attachment. Pull the leaf off, and you will find the bud that develops into next year's stem. Spaces along the stem between leaf nodes are called internodes. And in the daylily crown, all these structures are present in a very compact form. Nodes, internodes, and axillary buds are compressed like the folds of an accordion. On close inspection of a mature daylily fan, you can actually see thin rings encircling the stem where the leaves and roots meet. These are the leaf scars. And above each scar is an axillary bud, which can develop into a new crown.

The reason all this should concern the daylily buff is that new plants develop from the axillary buds. That is how daylilies increase in size and form clumps. As more and more new crowns develop above the old ones, the younger plants are raised above the soil level in a mound and placed at a disadvantage in the competition for moisture and nourishment. When this happens, it is time to divide the clump. Robust cultivars increase at a great old rate and have to be divided quite frequently—as often as every four or five years—while other cultivars increase so slowly that they almost never require division.

Because daylilies are long-lived perennials, it pays to find them a suitable site and to provide the very best soil you can. The soil nature provides is seldom ideal for growing garden plants. Where I garden in southwestern Connecticut, the soil is thin, rocky, and deficient in humus—that lovely dark brown substance resulting from the decay of organic matter. Humus improves the texture of the soil and increases its capacity to retain moisture without becoming waterlogged. Homemade compost, peat moss, rotted hay, leaves, and wood chips are all valuable sources of organic enrichment for your garden soil. The addition of one or more of these amendments lightens and improves drainage in heavy clay soil and increases water retention in sandy soils.

As daylilies require at least six hours of sun a day to flower abundantly, the position of your flower bed is important. Grown in the shade, these stalwart perennials will grimly hang on to life but their performance will be disappointing. Daylilies are sun worshipers, and except in the deep South, the more sun they receive, the better—provided they have adequate water, especially during the blooming season. However, full sun in the Northeast is one thing; in Florida, it is quite another matter. In the subtropics, daylilies enjoy the dappled shade of tall, deep rooted trees such as pines.

By happy accident, my own perennial border is ideally suited to daylilies. The east-facing slope receives sun all morning and well into the afternoon, and the incline is enough to provide good drainage. In waterlogged soil, all the available air spaces between soil particles are filled with standing water, and the roots literally suffocate. My slope carries off excess water while the lavish addition of compost and peat moss solves that familiar gardening conundrum, the need for well-drained but moisture-retentive soil. The slightly acidic soil of Connecticut with a pH range of 6.5 to 7.0 is ideal for daylilies.

With their thick, fleshy roots, daylilies are well equipped to survive drought. However, they perform their glorious best only when they have adequate water. In the Northeast, an inch a week is plenty. But plenty of water for heavy soil in Connecticut would be hopelessly inadequate where the soil is sandy and the temperature hot. In Gainesville, Florida, Bill Munson irrigates as often as every other day, providing three inches of water or more a week. As he remarked, "Florida is so sandy, you can have a four-inch rainfall one day and plant the next."

Potted daylilies bought at garden centers can be planted at almost any time. However, the selection is often very limited. When there are well over thirty-three thousand cultivars in existence and approximately fifteen thousand in commerce, it seems a pity to make your selection from a mere handful. The alternative is to order by mail, preferably from a nursery specializing in daylilies (see the list of sources at the end of this book). Although bare-rooted daylilies can safely be planted in most sections of the country from spring through fall, a good rule of thumb is to avoid planting during periods of high heat and humidity. In the North, fall planting is not recommended, either. If cold weather closes in before the plants have formed anchoring roots, they may be heaved out of the ground with the first prolonged freeze.

The problem in selecting daylilies from mail-order catalogs is the embarrassment of riches which faces a prospective buyer. With regard to color, let your imagination soar with the vivid—if sometimes inaccurate—descriptions. Most daylily colors are appealing, anyway. Choose sizes and heights that fit in with your garden scheme—anything goes. But be advised that there are three classifications of daylily foliage: deciduous (or dormant), evergreen, and semi-evergreen. These are based on the response of the plant's leaves to the changing seasons and do not necessarily denote hardiness. At least some varieties in all three classes can be grown in cold climates. However, those described as dormant are considered the best choice for northern gardens, while evergreens—which are the most tender—do the best in the far South.

Most of the daylilies I grow are of the dormant variety. In the fall after repeated hard freezes, all the leaves die down, and I remove them to reduce the chances of harboring pests and diseases during the winter. My experience with evergreens is limited. But Gregory Piotrowski of the New York Botanical Garden offers the following observations about the behavior of evergreens at the Botanical Garden (Zone 6). "'Nubs' of foliage may remain green above the ground near the crown, all else usually turns brown. However, evergreens are quick to grow during warm spells in late winter." While evergreens with dormant blood in their veins often do very well in the North, a beginner might want to play it safe and choose the foliage type best suited to the climate. Incidentally, semi-evergreens seem to do well in most parts of the country.

Winter Mulch

In the Northeast, a winter mulch is beneficial to daylilies regardless of their foliage type. The purpose of a winter mulch is to keep the temperature of all the plant parts, and of the surrounding soil, as consistent as possible. If you have a sunny day followed by a night of 10°F, the fluctuation in temperature can damage living plant tissues. By shading the soil area with thick layers of loosely packed leaves, evergreen branches, or pine needles (anywhere from six inches to eight or more inches), you prevent the soil from being warmed up by the sun, and subsequently exposed to extreme cold.

There are two schools of thought about the best time to apply a winter mulch. One that early application—in October—postpones dormancy and therefore gives the plants more time to develop. The other school withholds the mulch until just before the first hard freeze on the theory that new shoots will be damaged if plants from a warmer climate continue growing.

If you are ordering daylilies by mail for the first time, you may panic at the sight of the new arrivals. As a moist medium like sphagnum moss might encourage rot, your daylilies will be shipped in a dry packing material. In addition, the foliage will have been cut back to eight to ten inches. But don't be alarmed by their appearance. The cruelty to which the foliage has been subjected is intended to conserve water by reducing the surface area of the leaves. With a modicum of care, the plants will soon recover. The moderately priced cultivars—which are a beginner's best bet—have usually been around for a number of years and have withstood the test of time. They are strong, resilient plants that have earned their keep in gardens from coast to coast.

Let us say that you have just received a representative collection of old favorites like the lusty, lovely dark red 'Ed Murray'; knock-your-socks-off orange 'Rocket City', with darker-eyed zone; pale yellow 'Renee'; light pink 'Lullaby Baby'; and orchid pink 'Siloam Bo Peep', with a purple eye to go with the small but vigorous purple 'Little Grapette.' These cultivars would be good choices for the Northeast and indeed for much of the country. At this point, your plants may not look like much—after all, they have been in transit for a couple of days—but if you soak their roots in cool water for anywhere from an hour to overnight, they will perk up.

Now, assuming that you have found a sunny spot on your property, prepared the bed to a depth of one foot, and added generous amounts of organic matter to the soil, you are ready to plant your new acquisitions. Set the plants in holes eighteen to twenty-four inches apart. The planting may seem sparse at first, but well-spaced daylilies grow better and require dividing less often than crowded ones. The planting holes should be large enough to accommodate the roots with room to spare. Some authorities suggest making a raised cone of earth in the middle of the hole, placing the plant on top, and spreading the roots out on either side. The crown should be level with the surface of the soil or slightly below. Fill soil around the roots and tamp down the soil firmly. Water well and keep the soil evenly moist until the plants are established and new leaves are beginning to appear. After that, a good soaking once a week will be enough, unless it is very hot and dry.

Once your daylilies are properly planted, an organic mulch should be spread over the bed to a depth of two or three inches. The purpose of a spring or summer mulch is threefold. In the first place, a layer of shredded leaves, pine needles, buckwheat hulls, citrus pulp, or whatever is locally available will eventually rot, adding nutriments to your soil and constantly improving its texture. Second, mulching conserves moisture and maintains an even soil temperature, which greatly benefits the plants. And by eliminating light from the soil, the mulch also benefits the gar-dener—it discourages weed germination. In every way, mulch is marvelous, but leave a little unmulched space around the crown of the plant. You don't want to discourage new growth or encourage rot.

If your new daylilies were planted in the spring and were a reasonable size when you received them, you can look forward to flowers that summer. However, the plants will not achieve their full beauty and stature for another year or two, depending on where you live. In the South, daylilies develop and increase much more rapidly than they do in the North. But wherever you live, you are bound to be thrilled with your first crop of blos-soms. And in all probability, you will succumb that very first season to the daylily addiction. One recent victim urges growers to print a warning in their catalogs. "It might read, 'Warning: Falling in love with daylilies may be dangerous to your savings account, your mortgage payments, and your wardrobe, which may get dated before you know it.'"

With your affliction in full spate, you will soon want more daylilies. As your original plants grow into husky clumps, you will probably want to divide them to make room for new arrivals. Daylilies can be divided at almost any time of year, but it is just as well to avoid the heat of summer, and in the North, it should not be left too late in the season. A division is entitled to the same treatment as a new, bare-rooted plant—which for all intents and purposes it is. Division couldn't be simpler. Dig up the clump, wash the earth off the roots, and cut back the foliage to about eight inches. Cutting back the foliage makes your task easier and reduces water loss through the pores of the leaves. Now wiggle, shake, and pull apart the fans. Unless you want to get as many single plants as possible from a clump, the divisions can have as many or as few fans as you like. Replant the division as if it were a new arrival in your garden and give the rest away.

For the harried or slovenly gardener who has let a daylily clump become gigantic, there is still hope. I speak from experience. If the mass of roots confronting you when you have washed off the dirt is an impenetrable tangle, take a heavy knife with a serrated blade and hack away. This drastic action causes considerable damage and severs roots, but there are so many in a large clump that it doesn't matter. Clean up the remaining clumps or single fans, trim broken roots, and treat as you would any other division.

Maintenance of a daylily planting is no more and no less taxing than maintenance of any other relatively carefree perennial planting. Compared to fussy plants like delphiniums, daylilies are a breeze. But *no* perennial planting is maintenance free. Indeed, what gardener worth his or her salt would want a garden in which there was nothing to do? For daylilies, watering and mulching are important. Fertilizing also has its advocates, but rigorous soil preparation and the addition of large quantities of organic matter go a long way toward keeping daylilies and other perennials happy. Many daylily growers recommend the spring application of a 5-10-5 commercial fertilizer and a fall application of a low-nitrogen fertilizer. The best way to find out what your soil needs is to send samples to your local county agricultural agent or to the state Agricultural Experiment Station. You will receive instructions for taking soil samples and, when the study has been made, a computer printout with an analysis of your soil.

Daily removal of the spent daylily flowers is an activity that most growers enjoy—unless the sheer volume makes so-called "dead-heading" onerous. In any case, if you miss a day or two, it is of no consequence. The important thing is to prevent seed production, which saps the plant's energy. After flowering, the outside leaves of most cultivars begin to look tired. These can be removed to improve the looks of the plant. In the fall, a new flush of leaves will arise, and your daylilies will remain respectable until the end of the season. Lucky Southerners can enjoy the mounds of graceful foliage all winter. But in the North, many growers—myself among them—cut the leaves down to the ground. Another school of thought maintains that the dead leaves act as a natural winter mulch.

The subject of daylily pests is complicated by several factors. Although I grow a great many daylily cultivars, the majority are hardy souls not too many generations removed from the species. Mine from the forties, fifties, and sixties seem very trouble free. Moreover, they are mixed in with other easy-to-grow perennials, and I have never really had a severe insect or disease problem. That is not to say that the foliage is always pristine or that every flower is perfect, but I have never felt the need to spray the daylilies. The American Hemerocallis Society *Handbook* has this to say about spraying: "If you have never sprayed and have had little damage, *do NOT begin* a program of spraying. Continue to remove the unsightly blooms."

Daylilies are subject to certain pests. A specific genus of bright green aphid feeds on the leaves and sucks the plant juices from both the new foliage and from the flower buds. Damage—

in the form of yellow leaves and distorted flower buds—is usually done in the spring. Aphids can be seen often at the base of the leaves and on either side of the midribs. The spider mite, another sucking insect but almost invisible to the naked eye, leaves a fine web on the affected plants. Yellow or dying foliage often heralds the presence of this pest. Spider mites are at their worst during hot, dry summers. Thrips are small gray-black insects that damage daylily buds by squeezing in between the closed segments and rubbing their legs and bodies against the plant's delicate tissues. The irritation causes the petals to bleed and wounds disfigure the buds, inhibiting proper opening. Alas, slugs also like daylilies and make ugly holes in the leaves.

"Spring sickness," in which the inner leaves of vigorously growing daylilies suddenly rot and turn to mush, is a disease I have had no experience with, although it is purported to be more common in the North. Authorities believe that the rot sets in when daylilies in the first flush of spring growth are subjected to freezing temperatures. Not much else is known about this condition, but it is currently the subject of research at the University of Vermont, according to Lewis and Nancy Hill, coauthors of an excellent book about growing daylilies (See the "Sources of Information About Daylilies" section of this book). A bacterial disease commonly called "crown rot" is another potential hazard. High temperatures, high humidity, and waterlogged soil favor its development. More prevalent in the South, it is another daylily affliction with which I am unfamiliar.

Lest you feel discouraged by the bad news, the good news is that daylilies have less than their fair share of ailments. Every perennial is prey to plagues and pests. Deal with your daylily problems according to necessity and your conscience. If you do have to resort to spraying, always read the label of fungicides and insecticides with care. And remember that if your garden doesn't harbor one pest, it will certainly harbor another. That's gardening!

Glossary

Anther. The structure at the tip of the stamen, containing pollen.

Asexual reproduction. Propagation by division or similar vegetative means, rather than by seed, which is sexual reproduction.

Backcross. In hybridizing, the cross-pollination of a daylily to one or another of its parents.

Band. A pattern of a different but darker color confined to the inner flower segments (the petals) just above the throat of the flower.

Bicolor. A blossom displaying two different colors in the flower segments, the petals being of a darker hue than the sepals. In a reverse bicolor, the sepals are darker than the petals.

Bitone. A flower which combines two different shades of a single color, such as deep pink and pale pink. In a bitone, the petals are more intensely colored than the sepals. In a reverse bitone, the sepals are of the deeper shade.

Blend. An entire blossom in which two colors, such as cream and pink, intermingle.

Bordered, edged, tipped. The base petal color is highlighted by a rim or tip of either a contrasting color or else the same color in a darker or lighter shade.

Bract. A modified leaf on the scape just beneath a node or a flower bed.

Bud building. A phenomenon in which a daylily continues to form buds at the apex of the scape after the flowers have begun opening. While so-called "bud builders" provide a long season of bloom, they also exhibit many scars on their elongated scapes.

Chimera. A plant made up of two genetically distinct tissues. In daylilies, a plant which possesses both diploid and polyploid tissues, usually as a result of incomplete tetraploid conversion.

Chromosome. One of a given number of minute rodlike bodies located in the cell nucleus and responsible for the transmission of hereditary traits. In diploid daylilies, the number of chromosomes in each cell is twenty-two. Triploids have thirty-three and tetraploids have forty-four.

Clone. (See *Cultivar*) A plant that has been reproduced by asexual means and consequently is identical to its parent.

Colchicine. A poisonous alkaloid derived from the autumn crocus (*Colchicum autumnale*) and used to induce polyploidy.

Cross-pollination, cross. The pollination of one plant with another. Pollen from the anthers of one plant is placed on the receptive stigma of another plant. Soon a pollen tube develops and travels down the style to the ovary containing the ovules or egg cells. After the pollen tube ejects the sperm cells and one unites with an egg cell, fertilization takes place.

Crown. The part of a plant where the roots and stem meet.

Cultivar. A term used to replace "cultivated variety," cultivar refers to a garden plant as distinct from a wild species. Daylily cultivars originally derive from a single specimen and are propagated asexually to preserve the plant's distinguishing characteristics.

Cytology. The branch of biology which deals with cells.

Diploid. A plant having the basic number of chromosomes. In daylilies, each cell has the basic complement of twenty-two, except the sex cells (the sperm and the egg), each of which has eleven. Upon fertilization, the number is restored to twenty-two.

Diurnal. Belonging to the daytime. A daylily flower which opens in the morning and remains open during the day.

Division. The separation into smaller increments or individual fans of a daylily plant that has formed a clump.

Dominant. The prevailing characteristics which appear in the first generation of a hybrid to the exclusion of the so-called "recessive" characteristics, which are submerged but may reappear in later generations.

Dormant. A classification of daylilies which lose their leaves in the fall, remain inactive during the winter, and resume growth with the return of warm weather. The old leaves having died back completely, new leaves appear in the spring.

Double. A daylily with more than six floral segments. There may be as few as one or two additional segments or as many as eighteen. The effect can be full and fluffy or tailored with one set inside another in a configuration similar to the hose-in-hose blossoms of some azaleas.

Dwarf. A term used in referring to the stature of a daylily, not to the flower size. Daylilies with scapes under fourteen inches are classified as dwarf, but the flowers may be miniature, small, or even large.

Evergreen. A classification of daylilies which retain their green leaves during the winter. In the north, the leaves of evergreens are damaged by freezing and do partially turn brown. Hardy evergreens recover; tender ones do not. For this reason, evergreens are generally regarded as less hardy than dormants and semi-evergreens (See *Semi-evergreen*). In warm climates, evergreens continue growing all year.

Eye zone, eye, or halo. An eye zone describes a darker pattern at the center of the flower appearing on all the floral segments. A halo is similar in design but the pattern is less intensely colored, while a band is a darker shade that appears on the petals only.

Fan or ramet. An individual plant composed of the paired leaves characteristic of the daylily, the crown (the compressed underground stem), and the roots.

Fertile. Able to produce viable seeds, pollen, or both. A daylily that is described as "fertile both ways" means that it can develop viable seed from the pollen of another daylily and, in addition, successfully pollinate a different plant.

Filament. The slender, threadlike stalk of the stamen which bears the anther at its tip.

Fulvous. Dull reddish yellow or brownish yellow; tawny.

Gene. One of the units of DNA on the chromosome responsible for the transmission of hereditary traits.

Genus. A group containing closely related species, ranking lower than the family in the classification of plants.

Haploid. The reduced number of chromosomes found in sperm and egg cells. Each sexual reproductive cell contains half the number of chromosomes found in the cells which make up the body of the plant.

Hybrid. The product of cross-pollinating two plants that are genetically distinct.

Introduced. To be introduced, a daylily has to be priced and offered for sale in a dated, printed, or otherwise mechanically duplicated list or catalog.

Large-flowered daylily. The official American Hemerocallis Society designation for a daylily with flowers four and a half inches in diameter or more.

Meiosis. A process of nuclear cell division in which the number of chromosomes are reduced to half in the development of a reproductive cell.

Midrib. The vein running lengthwise through the center of a leaf or flower segment.

Miniature. The official American Hemerocallis Society designation for a daylily with flowers less than three inches in diameter.

Mitosis. Nuclear cell division in which the chromosomes divide and separate, forming two new cells with identical nuclei.

Mulch. Often an organic material such as shredded leaves, wood chips, buckwheat hulls, or pine needles spread on the surface of the soil to retain moisture and retard weed germination.

Nocturnal. A daylily that opens in the evening, remains open during the night, and closes sometime during the following day.

Node. The point on a stem where leaves and roots may emerge.

Outcross. In hybridizing, the practice of crossing cultivars of different genetic lineage.

Ovary. (See *Pistil*) The swollen part of the pistil which contains the ovules. After fertilization, the ovules grow into seeds, while the ovary develops into what is commonly referred to as the seed pod.

Overlay. Also described as a wash or dusting, the terms may be used to describe texture, as in "a velvety overlay," or may refer to a thin layer of color superimposed on another.

Ovule. The seed-to-be located within the ovary.

Perianth. Daylily flowers are made up of six tepals (three outer segments, or sepals, and three inner segments, or petals). The unit including all six segments is the perianth.

Pistil. The female reproductive organ consisting of the ovary at its base where the seeds develop; the tubular style; and at the tip of the style, the stigma which accepts the pollen.

Pollen. Dustlike grains which carry the sperm cells. (See *Stamen*)

Polychrome. A flower in which several colors are combined and intermingled.

Polyploid. A plant having three or more sets of chromosomes in each cell. In the daylily, triploids have thirty-three chromosomes (three sets of eleven) and tetraploids have forty-four (four sets of eleven) in each cell.

Proliferation. A leafy shoot developing from a node on a scape. Proliferations can be rooted in a moist growing medium and treated like cuttings. The new plant will be identical to its parent.

Ramet. (See *Fan*)

Reblooming, remontant. The habit of producing more than one set of scapes during the growing season. Continuous bloom can be had from cultivars which produce new scapes before or shortly after the previous ones have finished blooming. Rebloom and continuous bloom are relatively rare in the Northeast. (Exceptions: 'Stella De Oro', 'Bitsy', and a few others.) In warm climates rebloom and continuous bloom are more common.

Recessive. (See *Dominant*)

Registration. The procedure set up in accordance with the International Code of Nomenclature for Cultivated Plants whereby the description of a cultivar along with the name of its originator (and introducer if introduced) are submitted for approval to the Registrar of the American Hemerocallis Society. Upon acceptance, a named cultivar is considered registered. Only one clone may be registered under a given name.

Remontant. (See *Rebloom*)

Reverse bicolor. (See *Bicolor*)

Rhizome. A modified stem, distinguishable from a root by the presence of nodes. In the species *Hemerocallis fulva* and its near relations, including *H. fulva* var. *rosea*, these rhizomes may stray as far as three feet from the parent clump or fan, sending up a new fan at the far end. This undesirable trait has been eradicated from modern cultivars. In today's daylilies, these underground stems are either very short or nonexistent.

Roots. Daylilies have two kinds of roots. Some are thonglike, while others are plump and fleshy. Both types may appear on the same plant.

Scape. The stalk which bears the flowers. Leafless at the lower end and branched above, the scape can display bracts at each node in the upper portion.

Seed. The fertilized, ripened ovules which can germinate and produce a new plant.

Seedling. A term applied to an unnamed and unintroduced plant grown from seed.

Self. A flower in which all six perianth segments are the same color. The throat, however, may be yellow, gold, orange, or green. In a complete self, the throat, pistil, and stamens all match the perianth segments.

Selfing, to self. Placing the pollen of one flower on the stigma of the same flower, or on another flower of the same cultivar or species.

Semi-evergreen. A daylily whose leaves only partially die back in the fall. In the north, the leaves of a semi-evergreen behave like those of a dormant daylily. They die back to the ground. However, in the South, they behave more like those of an evergreen.

Sepals. (See *Perianth*) The outer three segments which, before opening, form the outside of the bud.

Small-flowered daylily. The official American Hemerocallis Society designation for a daylily with flowers at least three inches but less than four and a half inches in diameter.

Species. In the singular, one individual having characteristics which distinguish it from other species in the same genus. In the plural, a group of closely allied individuals, all belonging to the same genus, that share one or more distinguishing characteristics.

Spider. A daylily with long, thin segments having a length-to-width ratio as high as five-to-one. Most modern spiders, however, are more likely to have a length-to-width ratio of four-to-one, which is acceptable according to the official American Hemerocallis Society rule adopted in 1989.

Stamen. The male reproductive organ which consists of a threadlike filament attached to the petal and bearing at its tip the pollen-filled anther.

Sterile. Incapable of reproduction. Some daylilies are entirely sterile. Some are "pod sterile" and can fertilize another daylily but cannot set seed themselves. Others are "pollen sterile" and cannot produce viable pollen. Yet others are "self sterile" and cannot fertilize themselves.

Style. The tubular structure connecting the stigma and the ovary of the pistil.

Taxonomy. The science of classification of plants and animals according to relationships. In this orderly system the botanical categories now in common use are, beginning with the highest grouping: division, class, order, family, genus, species, and subspecies or variety.

Tepal. A segment of a flower in which the sepals and petals are markedly similar.

Tetraploid. A plant with four sets of chromosomes in each cell, except the pollen and egg cells, each of which have half that number.

Triploid. A plant with three sets of chromosomes.

Variegated. Green foliage with markings in some color other than green.

Variety. A term still in use instead of "cultivar." The proper use, however, is in reference to a botanical subdivision of a species, as in *H. fulva* var. *rosea.* This plant was considered by Dr. A. B. Stout to be sufficiently similar to *H. fulva* to be included in this species but different enough to warrant a varietal designation.

Sources of Information
About Daylilies

The American Hemerocallis Society

Address inquiries about membership to:

Elly Launius, Executive Secretary

1454 Rebel Drive

Jackson, MS 39211

In addition to *Daylilies: The Beginners' Handbook,* the Society offers small booklets on special subjects such as daylily culture, hybridizing, using daylilies in the landscape, and more scientific subjects like tissue culture and genetics.

Books

Daylilies, by A. B. Stout. Originally printed by Macmillan in 1934. Reprinted by Sagapress, Inc., in 1986 and distributed by R. and P. Kraus, Route 100, Millwood, NY 10546.

A history of the daylily up to 1933 with clear, accurate descriptions of all the known species and descriptions of over 170 early cultivars developed by pioneer breeders, including the author. Taken together, these provide the serious student of the genus *Hemerocallis* with insight into the development of the modern flower. Black and white photographs of the ancestors of our present cultivars are enlightening. The beautiful color plates have been reproduced from original watercolors by Eleanor Clarke and Mary Eaton.

Daylily Encyclopedia, edited by Steve Webber, 1988, distributed by Webber Gardens, 9180 Main Street, Damascus, MD 20872.

A most useful paperback, with articles ranging from an excellent exploration of the many shapes and forms available in daylilies to one on the up-and-coming miniatures. The heart of the book, however, is a list of "One Thousand Grand Daylilies," which is particularly valuable because it represents a "culmination of Webber Gardens' business of gathering popular, historically interesting, and genetically useful daylilies to market, to hybridize, and to enjoy." Descriptions of the flowers listed are more accurate and more complete than most.

Hemerocallis: The Daylily, by R. W. Munson, Jr., Timber Press, 1989.

A gorgeous book! Every daylily fan will want this sumptuously produced book filled with wonderful color reproductions of individual cultivars and of daylily gardens. But Munson's book is more than a coffee-table picture book. It begins with a thoughtful essay about the direction in which modern hybridizers are going. The author cautions his colleagues not to sacrifice the health of the plant for the beauty of the flower. Another service this book provides is a visual history of the daylily, from species to modern cultivar. Stout's descriptions of thirteen species from *Daylilies* are included, with color reproductions of these wild forebears of today's daylilies. In addition, descriptions of the species discovered or described after the publication of Stout's book expand our historical perspective. Descriptions of the post-Stout species have been reprinted from an in-depth article by Dr. Shiu-Ying Hu, originally appearing in *The American Horticultural Magazine* (The Journal of the American Horticultural Society, Inc.) in 1968.

Daylilies: The Perfect Perennial, 1991, by Lewis and Nancy Hill, A Garden Way Publishing Book, Storey Communications, Inc., Schoolhouse Road, Pownal, VT 05261.

Get this handsome, reasonably priced softcover book immediately. The Hills have been growing daylilies in Vermont since the late forties, and they know what they are talking about. Fortunately, they talk articulately about everything you need to know to grow daylilies successfully, from choosing them to using them. There is even a plan for a mixed border of daylilies and other perennials. The cultural information is superb. You really couldn't go wrong. And with the Hills at your side, you might want to start hybridizing. There is more. Darrel Apps has contributed mouthwatering color photographs of cultivars and gardens, and the drawings by Robin D. Brinkman are fine.

Sources for Daylilies

Adamgrove
Route 1, Box 246
California, MO 65018

Alpine Valley Gardens
2627 Calistoga Road
Santa Rosa, CA 95404

Ater Daylilies
3803 Greystone Drive
Austin, TX 78731

Balash Gardens
26595 H Drive North
Albion, MI 49224

John Benz
12195 Sixth Avenue
Cincinnati, OH 45249

Big Tree Daylily Garden
777 General Hutchinson Parkway
Longwood, FL 32750

Bloomingfields Farm
Lee Bristol Nursery
P.O. Box J5
Gaylordsville, CT 06755-0005

Blossom Valley Gardens
15011 Oak Creek Road
El Cajon, CA 92021-2328

Ed Brown
Corner Oaks Garden
6139 Blanding Boulevard
Jacksonville, FL 32244

Busse Gardens
Route 2, Box 238
Cokato, MN 55321

Cordon Bleu Farms
P.O. Box 2033
San Marcos, CA 92069

Crintonic Garden
Curt Hanson
County Line Road
Gates Mills, OH 44040

Crochet Daylily Garden
P.O. Box 425
Prairieville, LA 70769

Daylily World
P.O. Box 1612
Sanford, FL 32771

Helen Deering
2847 64th Street
Byron Center, MI 49315

Albert C. Faggard
3840 LeBleu St.
Beaumont, TX 77707

Floyd Cove Nursery
Pat & Grace Stamile
725 Longwood-Markham Road
Sanford, FL 32771

Four Winds Garden
P.O. Box 141
South Harpswell, ME 04079

Guidry's Daylily Garden
1005 E. Vermilion Street
Abbeville, LA 70510

Hem'd Inn
Lucille Warner
534 Aqua Drive
Dallas, TX 75218

Hermitage
John & Dorothy Lambert
Route 2
Raleigh, NC 27610

Herrington Daylily Garden
Route 1, 204 Winfield Road
Dublin, GA 31021

Howard J. Hite
370 Gallogly Road
Pontiac, MI 48055

The Hobby Garden
Lee Gates
38164 Monticello Drive
Prairieville, LA 70769

Iron Gate Gardens
Route 3, Box 250
Kings Mountain, NC 28086

E. R. Joiner Gardens
33 Romney Place, Wymberly
Savannah, GA 31406

Klehm Nursery
Route 5, Box 197
South Barrington, IL 60010

Lady Bug Beautiful Gardens
857 Leopard Trail
Winter Springs, FL 32708

Lake Norman Gardens
580 Island Forest Drive
Davidson, NC 28036

Larkdale Farms
Dave Talbott
4058 Highway 17 South
Green Cove Springs, FL 32043

Louisiana Nursery
Route 7, Box 43
Opelousas, LA 70570

Meadowlake Gardens
Route 4, Box 709
Walterboro, SC 29488

Mercers Garden
6215 Maude Street
Fayetteville, NC 28306

Bryant K. Millikan
6610 Sunny Lane
Indianapolis, IN 46220

Moldovan's Gardens
38830 Detroit Road
Avon, OH 44011

Oakes Daylilies
Route 3, Box 3
Corryton, TN 37721

Olallie Daylily Gardens
Marlboro Branch Road
South Newfane, VT 05351

Oxford Gardens
3022 Oxford Drive
Durham, NC 27707

Petree Gardens
Trudy Petree
4447 Cain Circle
Tucker, GA 30084

Powell Nursery
Route 2, Box 86
Princeton, NC 27569

Renaissance Gardens
1047 Baron Road
Weddington, NC 28173

Rollingwood Gardens
P.O. Box 1044
Eustis, FL 32727

Roycroft Nursery
Belle Isle Road
Route 6, Box 70
Georgetown, SC 29440-9217

Saxton Gardens
1 First Street
Saratoga Springs, NY 12866

Seawright Gardens
134 Indian Hill
Carlisle, MA 01741

Soules Garden
5809 Rahake Road
Indianapolis, IN 46217

Spring Creek Daylily Garden
25150 Gosling
Spring, TX 77389

Springlake Ranch Gardens
Route 2, Box 360
De Queen, AR 71832

Tranquil Lake Nursery
45 River Street
Rehoboth, MA 02769

Andre Viette Farm & Nursery
Route 1, Box 16
Fishersville, VA 22939

Wayside Gardens
1 Garden Lane
Hodges, SC 29695-0001

Gilbert H. Wild and Son, Inc.
1112 Joplin Street
Sarcoxie, MO 64862

Wimberlyway Gardens
7024 NW 18th Avenue
Gainesville, FL 32605-3237

Windmill Gardens
P.O. Box 351
Luverne, AL 36049

Woodside Garden
824 Williams Lane
Chadds Ford, PA 19317

Index